Oracle Press

Oracle CRM
On Demand
Deployment Guide

Jeff Saenger, Tim Koehler, and
Louis J. Peters, Jr.

New York   Chicago   San Francisco
Lisbon   London   Madrid   Mexico City   Milan
New Delhi   San Juan   Seoul   Singapore   Sydney   Toronto

The **McGraw·Hill** Companies

Cataloging-in-Publication Data is on file with the Library of Congress

McGraw-Hill books are available at special quantity discounts to use as premiums and sales promotions, or for use in corporate training programs. To contact a representative, please e-mail us at bulksales@mcgraw-hill.com.

Oracle CRM On Demand Deployment Guide

1 2 3 4 5 6 7 8 9 0   DOC DOC   1 0 9 8 7 6 5 4 3 2 1 0

ISBN   978-0-07-171763-2
MHID   0-07-171763-3

Sponsoring Editor Lisa McClain	**Copy Editor** LeeAnn Pickrell	**Illustration** Glyph International
Editorial Supervisor Patty Mon	**Proofreader** Susie Elkind	**Art Director, Cover** Jeff Weeks
Project Editor LeeAnn Pickrell	**Indexer** James Minkin	**Cover Designer** Pattie Lee
Acquisitions Coordinator Meghan Riley	**Production Supervisor** Jean Bodeaux	
Technical Editor Robert Davidson	**Composition** Glyph International	

About the Authors

Jeff Saenger is Vice President of Advanced Product Services for Oracle CRM On Demand. He has held numerous management roles with CRM On Demand since its launch in 2003. Jeff has spent the majority of his career helping organizations automate their front- and back-office systems. His teams have deployed enterprise software applications to over half a million business users across desktop, web, and cloud computing technologies. Jeff has been involved with Software-as-a-Service for over a decade, where he has helped to revolutionize the way enterprise software is sold, set up, and supported.

Jeff and his family live in the San Francisco Bay Area.

Tim Koehler is a Director of Quality of Service for Oracle CRM On Demand. Since joining the CRM On Demand team in 2006, he has implemented a variety of initiatives designed to promote efficient implementation, user adoption, and the business impact of CRM On Demand. Over his 25-year career, Tim has studied the organizational factors that influence sales and service performance while consulting with companies across a variety of industries. His passion is in helping companies implement the process changes and management reinforcement necessary to ensure business impact is achieved from CRM technology initiatives. Prior to joining Siebel/Oracle in 2000, he was a principal at MOHR Development Inc., a leading sales and management consultancy.

Tim lives in the Boston area with his wife. He has three grown children.

Louis J. Peters, Jr., has been fortunate to have spent his entire career (to date) in the software industry. Working at multiple start-ups, Louis cut his teeth in software programming and web site development. After earning an MBA from Xavier University in Cincinnati, Ohio, he heeded the call of the "dot com" boom and headed west to San Francisco. There, he transitioned to consulting and went on to manage numerous enterprise software deployments, eventually running a mid-size consulting organization.

In 2002, Louis joined a small company called UpShot in Mountain View, California. There he met Jeff Saenger, and the two began a long collaboration in devising innovative strategies to deliver consulting services effectively within the Software-as-a-Service model. UpShot was acquired by Siebel, which, in turn, was acquired by Oracle. As Director of Professional Services for CRM On Demand, Louis pioneered the development of standards and tools for SaaS CRM deployment—tools used in implementations at over 400 companies for thousands of users. Currently, he is a Principal Product Manager, providing advanced support and guidance to Oracle's largest CRM On Demand customers and partners.

When not working, Louis spends time with his wife, son, and daughter, enjoys running and skiing, and is an active leader in the Boy Scouts of America.

About the Technical Editor

Robert Davidson has spent his career exclusively in IT, moving through sales, operations, consulting, and product management. Robert started as a contractor for IBM, supporting technical deals involving the IBM PC/RT and RISC System 6000. He leveraged this hardware experience in consulting, moving to a small IBM partner and then on to Andersen Consulting, acting as a systems architect for large implementations and developing channel relationships with emerging technology providers. Robert spent a few years working in the channels side of IT, leveraging his systems architecture experience with both hardware and software companies, eventually landing at Siebel Systems in 2000. Being with Siebel/Oracle for 10 years means a lot of moving around.

Starting first with the Siebel CRM products on the pre-sales side as Channels Technical Support and later as a technology specialist for Workforce Management, Robert later moved over to CRM On Demand Consulting, leveraging his systems experience to better define business requirements for the customer. This combined focus has served CRM On Demand customers well, as Robert drives the implementations to completion, never losing sight of business needs and the value to be delivered within the capabilities of the framework.

Robert is also a motorcycle rider and sailor. He rides competitively in motorcycle drill formation and obstacle competitions, but sailing is purely for relaxation—unless he's on a catamaran. Then the race is on!

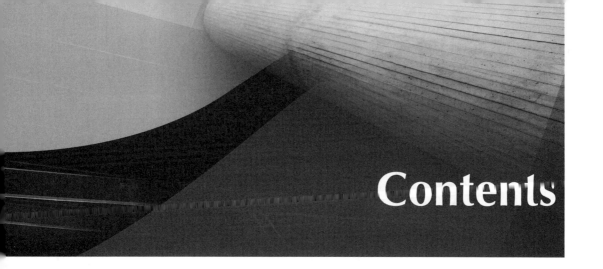

Contents

ACKNOWLEDGMENTS xi
INTRODUCTION xiii

1 What You Should Know About Software-as-a-Service **1**
What Companies Like Most About SaaS 2
What Companies Wish They Had Known About SaaS 4
The True Benefit of SaaS: Freedom to Focus on the Business 5
Shared Responsibilities and Obligations 6
    Application Hosting 6
    Design and Configuration 6
    Software Upgrades 7
    Ongoing Support and Maintenance 7
Summary 7

2 Overview of Oracle CRM On Demand **9**
The CRM On Demand Application 10
The CRM On Demand Architecture and Service Model 14
Configuration Options 17
CRM On Demand Extensions 18
Summary 20

3 Getting the Most from Your Oracle CRM On Demand Service **23**
Self-Service Through a Single Point-of-Access 24
Navigating to Support Resources 24
CRM On Demand Training 26
    Recommended Training Courses 27
Using the Knowledge Base 31
    Implementation Templates and Tools 31
    Web Services Resource Library 32
    Online Help 33

Customer Support 33
   Mission and Model 33
Forums: Leveraging the Experts 36
Oracle Notifications and Communication 37
   Planned and Unplanned Events 37
   E-mail Communication 38
   Registration to Receive E-mail Notification ... 38
Testing: What Are the Options? 38
   Typical Testing Objectives 39
   Choosing the Best Environments for Testing ... 39
Summary 41

4   Planning Your Oracle CRM On Demand Implementation **43**
Setting the Course for Program Success 45
   Engage Business Leaders 45
   How to Establish a Business Context for
      Your CRM On Demand Program 46
   Sample Business Objectives 53
   Using Business Objectives to Guide Project Management 53
Success Factors in CRM On Demand Implementation Planning 55
   Plan for Ongoing Improvement 56
   Improve Processes 57
   Allocate Time for Design 57
   Choose an Effective "Rollout" Strategy 57
Roles, Responsibilities, and Resource Requirements 59
   Business Roles 60
   Technical Roles 61
End-User and Management Adoption 63
   Assessing the Scope of Your Adoption Program 64
   Human Factors Behind Adoption 66
   Developing a User Adoption Plan 66
   Influencing User Adoption 69
Summary 69

5   Designing Oracle CRM On Demand **71**
Designing the Object Model 73
   Baseline Objects 74
   Modifying the Object Model 82
   Best Practices for Object Model Design 83
   Customizing Business Processes via
      the Object Model and Workflow 85

Designing the Business Process 85
    Campaign Management Process 85
    Sales Process 87
    Service Request Management Process 94
    Business Process Design Basics 96
Designing Data Access and Security ...... , , , ,   , , , , , , , , 97
    Functional Aspects of Roles 97
    Analytics Access 99
    Best Practices for Designing Access and Security 100
Designing for Analytics 101
    Reports vs. Analytics 101
    Understand Baseline Analytics and Assumptions 102
    Considerations When Designing for Analytics ...., ... 102
Summary , ... 103

6 Sample Oracle CRM On Demand Designs **105**
Horizontal Solutions: Business to Business (B2B)
    Equipment and Service Sales 106
        B2B Sales Process Flow 107
        CRM On Demand Design for B2B Sales 111
Horizontal Solutions: Consumer Support Services 115
        Support Services Process Flow 116
        CRM On Demand Design for Support Services 118
Vertical Solutions: Retail Banking Sales and Service 122
        CRM On Demand Design for Retail Banking Sales and Service 124
Vertical Solutions: Pharmaceutical Sales Call Tracking 127
        Pharmaceutical Sales Call Tracking Process Flow 128
        CRM On Demand Design for Pharmaceutical Sales Call Tracking ... 130
Specialty Solutions: Delivering Relief to Families in an Emergency 133
        Emergency Relief Issue Tracking Process Flow 134
        CRM On Demand Design for Emergency Relief 135
Specialty Solutions: Account Planning 137
        CRM On Demand Design for Account Planning 138
Summary 140

7 Best Practices for Configuring CRM On Demand **141**
Field Configuration 142
        Cascading Picklists 144
        General Field Configuration Considerations 145
        Field Management 147

Page Layouts 148
    Web Applets 150
    Dynamic Layouts 151
Custom Objects 153
    Advanced Custom Objects 155
    Considerations for Custom Objects 156
Data Access and Security 157
    Access Controls 157
Workflow Management 161
    Considerations for Workflow Management 161
Summary 162

8   Integration in Oracle CRM On Demand **163**
User Interface Integration 164
    Web Tabs 164
    Web Linking 165
    RSS Feeds 166
    Web Application Integration 166
    HTML Extensions 166
    External Portal Integration 168
    Considerations for User Interface Integration 170
Data Integration 170
    Web-based Data Import 170
    Oracle Data Loader 171
    Data Export 171
    Considerations for Data Integration 172
Web Services 172
    Web Services Architecture 173
    Common Uses for Web Services 173
    Web Services Best Practices 175
Summary 178

9   Ongoing Maintenance and Administration **179**
Monitoring User Adoption 180
    Monitoring User Adoption by Monitoring Data Quality 180
Identifying and Addressing Performance-related Issues 182
    CRM On Demand Performance Characteristics 183
    Troubleshooting CRM On Demand Performance Issues 184
Preparing for Patches and Upgrades 188
    Production Pod Maintenance 188
    Stage Pod Maintenance 189
    Upgrades 190

Deploying New Features and Customizations 192
   Deploying Standard Features 193
   Deploying Advanced Customizations 193
   Deploying Custom Reports 194
Summary 194

A   **Advanced Configuration with CRM On Demand** **197**
Creating Relationships 198
   Creating One-to-Many Relationships 198
   Creating Many-to-Many Relationships 199
   Creating One-to-One Relationships 199
   Creating Many-to-Many Relationships
     Using Advanced Custom Objects 201
Embedded Analytics 203
Advanced Field Management 208
   Default Values on a Service Request 208
   Derived Default Value 208
   Opportunity Field Validation 209
   Lead Field Validation 209
Workflow Rules 210
   Opportunity Field Update 210
   Service Request E-mail Notification 211
   Cross-Object Workflow 211
   Integration Event 212

Index **213**

Jeff would like to dedicate this book to Ted and Gayle Saenger.
Thank you, Mom and Dad.

Tim would like to acknowledge the love and support of his family—
Laura, Ryan, Courtney, and Jackson.

Louis would like to dedicate this book to Heather, Nathaniel,
Heidi, and Max for their encouragement and inspiration.

Acknowledgments

ll books are acts of creation. An author begins with nothing more than a spark of an idea, which becomes the first (poorly written) sentences on a blank sheet of paper, until finally, the idea is fully developed and the words fill page upon page.

All books are also feats of project coordination and teamwork. It takes a lot of people to make an idea into an ISBN. For our project, we were very lucky to have such talented people on our team. Thanks to Lisa McClain at McGraw Hill, who recognized a market opportunity for Software-as-a-Service application guides and worked her magic to get our manuscript proposal approved. We were fortunate to have Robert Davidson as our technical editor. His attention to detail was much appreciated, as were his many rewrites and suggested content additions. He has the makings of a budding author, and we hope to see him take up his pen some day soon.

Thank you to our friends on the CRM On Demand product team: Chris Haven, Binh Le, Bobby Dey, Piers Evans, and Sean Duffy—for sharing your expertise and answering our questions. Thanks to our Oracle colleagues, Xan Garlick and Mary Wade, for contributing to the development of the business transformation methods in this guide. Special thanks to those who offered design and other suggestions for the book—William Yu, Mike De Hennin, Joel Downie, Jackie Hoover, Bob Bray, Nigel Hodges, Kathy Kirk, and Drew Shanklin. Thanks to LeeAnn Pickrell and Meghan Riley at McGraw Hill for their advice and edits. And finally, many thanks to our families, friends, and colleagues for helping us along the way. We are grateful.

Introduction

I n less than a decade, the online delivery of software has transformed the business software landscape. The concept of online delivery is simple: A software company develops an application, hosts the software on its own servers, and makes it available to companies over the Internet. Companies sign up to use the application and pay for it on a subscription basis. No longer burdened with the time and expense necessary to maintain the software in-house, these companies are now free to focus on improving business processes and driving greater productivity and efficiency—the very reason they purchased the software in the first place.

From this simple concept, a whole new industry was born. Online delivery, also known as *cloud computing* or *Software as a Service* ("SaaS" for short) has grown to become one of the fastest growing segments in the world of enterprise software. Oracle Corporation has been at the forefront of the SaaS wave, with a suite of enterprise and productivity applications that have received customer and critical acclaim. The most successful of Oracle's SaaS applications has been CRM On Demand.

Since its launch in 2003, Oracle CRM On Demand has grown to become one of the fastest growing product lines in the Oracle applications family. The tremendous success of CRM On Demand has spawned a new generation of Oracle SaaS offerings, ranging from innovative web applets such as Sales Library, Sales Prospector, and CRM Gadgets, to enterprise-class applications such as PeopleSoft Talent Management and Siebel Deal Management. Oracle SaaS applications provide anytime, anywhere access directly from a web browser. Some applications also offer access from Blackberry and iPhone mobile devices. There is even an Oracle application that runs in Microsoft Outlook.

Oracle CRM On Demand is a suite of sales, marketing, and service applications that help companies better connect with their customers. Thousands of organizations around the world use CRM On Demand to capture customer information and coordinate customer interactions across their sales, service, and marketing organizations. In essence, this is the core value proposition of *customer relationship management,* or "CRM" for short.

Organizations use CRM On Demand in many different ways to support a variety of business functions. Many companies are new to CRM technology and use CRM On Demand to consolidate their customer information so every employee at the company works with a single, shared view of the customer. Other companies are further down the CRM technology path and have integrated CRM On Demand into their global supply chain in order to respond quickly to customer requests and to anticipate customer needs. Regardless of where they start, CRM On Demand provides a flexible platform to start simply and quickly add capabilities as you need them.

We, the authors of this book, were part of the original team formed to exclusively support the new CRM On Demand offering. Over the years, we've worked with a myriad of companies around the world to design CRM On Demand to meet their unique business objectives. Over time, we've developed a good sense for what does and does not work when it comes to deploying a CRM application in a SaaS delivery model.

Every time we begin work with a new customer, they ask, "All those customers who have deployed CRM On Demand before us—what lessons can we learn from them? What can we gather from their success? How do we avoid their mistakes? How do we get the most from the CRM On Demand service?" In this book, we will tell you what we tell them.

About This Book

The *Oracle CRM On Demand Deployment Guide* shares best practices, winning designs, and hard-won lessons collected from hundreds of CRM On Demand projects. These lessons have been developed from years of experience working with many different customers spanning multiple industries. Based upon these experiences, we've compiled what we've learned—how to plan and execute a successful project, how to design and configure the application so it meets your needs today and grows with you tomorrow, how to take advantage not only of the software, but also of all the services that come with your Software-as-a-Service subscription as well. Most of these lessons have not been documented—until now.

Chapter 1 begins with a brief introduction to Software-as-a-Service and how the customer/vendor relationship is different in the SaaS model compared to the traditional licensed software model. We explain how the SaaS model creates shared responsibilities and obligations between you and Oracle, and what this means for your CRM deployment. Chapter 2 provides an overview of CRM On Demand, details of the application features and underlying architecture, and a discussion of how you can customize and extend these features within the bounds of the SaaS model. Chapter 3 wraps up the introductory section with an overview of the CRM On Demand support model and how to get the most from the training, support, and collaboration resources that are included with every company's subscription.

Now that you have an understanding of how the CRM On Demand service works, we move on to the implementation. Chapter 4 focuses on planning your CRM On Demand deployment. Here, we share common strategies for delivering projects that lead to high user adoption and rapid business impact. Next, Chapter 5 details the configuration tools and techniques you will use to design your CRM On Demand solution. Chapter 6 is the heart of the book. It contains example CRM On Demand designs we've created for a range of industries and business processes. These designs are based on what we've learned working with many customers over the years to meet common types of needs. Chapter 7 describes the best practices for configuring CRM On Demand to promote usability, performance, ease of maintenance, and seamless upgrades.

Data integration is a critical step for companies who want to leverage CRM On Demand across the organization. So we've dedicated Chapter 8 to the key architecture and design considerations for building fast and reliable integrations to back-office systems, cloud applications, and custom applets. Chapter 9 finishes with tips for managing CRM On Demand in a "business as usual" production mode. In addition to day-to-day administration, there are maintenance and upgrade events to anticipate, a centralized support model to leverage, and new requirements from demanding business users to address. We offer guidance on what to expect during the upgrade process and how to rollout new capabilities to your organization so CRM On Demand continually delivers business value. Finally, we've filled the Appendix with detailed examples and sample code for configuring Custom Objects, writing complex workflow routines, embedding Analytics reports into homepages, and scripting business and validation rules.

How to Use This Book

This book is for the CRM project team—the business and technical experts charged with designing, deploying, and maintaining CRM On Demand within their company. On the following pages, you will find valuable insights for designing CRM On Demand and working with Oracle's SaaS development and support model. The book follows the subscription life cycle and highlights the key considerations and critical decisions you will make as you progress through initial deployment and beyond. Our goal is to help make your deployment successful by sharing the information and insight gained from the many successful deployments that came before you. Use the book as a guide to understanding what decisions need to be made, and refer back to it whenever you want to know how other customers tackled a particular requirement or deployment challenge. We look forward to sharing our hard-won lessons with you.

So, let's get started.

CHAPTER
1

What You Should
Know About
Software-as-a-Service

W elcome to the CRM On Demand community. It is a thriving community, made up of thousands of companies from dozens of industries. These companies employ hundreds of thousands of sales, marketing, and service people located in more than a hundred countries around the world. Each of these employees signs in to CRM On Demand from their browser or mobile device to interact with an application that has been uniquely configured for their business and that converses with them in the language of their choice. And, each company, like yours, expects CRM On Demand to help their people do a better job of connecting with their customers.

If you are like most companies who subscribe to the CRM On Demand service, this is your first foray into the world of Software-as-a-Service or SaaS-based software applications. At first glance, this world may not look much different from what you've dealt with in the traditional buy-and-install licensed software world. After all, an application is an application regardless of who hosts the software, right?

As it turns out, Software-as-a-Service is very different than what you're used to with licensed software, although much of this world will be familiar to you—after all, you are deploying application "software" that performs a set of functions to meet a business need. It is the "service" aspect of Software-as-a-Service that differs. As it turns out, who hosts the software matters quite a bit. When you subscribe to CRM On Demand, you are, in essence, transferring responsibility for hosting the application to Oracle. Once you make this shift, you create shared responsibilities and obligations between yourself and Oracle that will transform the way you manage your CRM On Demand deployment. We'll discuss these "service" implications in the following sections.

What Companies Like Most About SaaS

Customers choose to subscribe to SaaS-based applications like CRM On Demand for many reasons. Whenever we begin working with a new CRM On Demand customer, we try to find out what they liked most about the benefits of Software-as-Service that made them sign up. The following are the most common answers we hear:

- *I don't have to worry about the technology any more. That's Oracle's problem now.* We hear this most often from our customers, particularly from those who come from the business side of the organization. Customers are practically giddy over the fact that they are no longer responsible for managing the technical infrastructure. Installation, scaling, maintenance, security, upgrades—these tasks typically eat up the lion's share of time, cost, and agony for an enterprise software deployment, and project teams are very happy to be done with it.

■ *CRM On Demand is so easy to administer; I no longer have to rely on someone else to maintain the application.* As a rule, SaaS-based applications are easy to set up and administer. This is a direct benefit of the vendor-hosted model. The SaaS vendor has a vested interest in making its customers as self-sufficient as possible; self-sufficiency leads to higher customer satisfaction and lower vendor support costs. To do this, the vendor has to design the application and provide tools that make it easy for customers to manage the applications themselves. In the case of CRM On Demand, Oracle provides a comprehensive set of administrative tools that require minimal training in order for a business user to become proficient in the setup and maintenance of the application. What has resulted is a profound shift in responsibilities from the IT group to the business group. Whereas in the past the IT organization (or a third-party consultant) was the only one capable of administering the application, now the business operations team has the tools and the expertise needed to manage the application.

■ *I can deploy CRM On Demand globally at the push of a button.* As a cloud computing application, CRM On Demand is available anywhere, anytime, from the Internet through your browser or mobile device. This feature has far-reaching implications for the way you deploy the application. No longer do you need an army of consultants traveling from site to site installing the software and training your users. With SaaS applications and remote communication technologies, a small project team can simultaneously deploy CRM On Demand to every user around the globe with a few keystrokes. With the technical hurdles of deployment removed, you are now free to deploy as fast as you want and iteratively deploy new capabilities as often as you need.

■ *The upgrade process gives me timely access to the features in the latest release of CRM On Demand.* A key benefit for SaaS customers is the periodic release of new functionality, which is also a direct benefit of the SaaS model. In order to minimize support costs, Oracle hosts one version of CRM On Demand for all customers. Each subscribing company will configure the application to meet it unique needs, but the underlying code that everyone uses is the same. With traditional license applications, a vendor has to support multiple versions of its software, which drains resources from building new features. Customers as well must weigh the functional advantages of a new license software release against the substantial effort and cost for them to upgrade. Not so with SaaS applications. CRM On Demand typically releases two or more new versions of its software every year. And, because Oracle hosts the software, customers automatically upgrade to the new release, while maintaining the flexibility to deploy new features at their discretion.

What Companies Wish They Had Known About SaaS

Along with the benefits, customers also tell us what surprised them about the new SaaS model. The following are some examples of what we hear:

- *I didn't appreciate how structured the operational support model actually is.* Each CRM On Demand subscription comes with a service-level agreement that details the operational expectations for service uptime and performance. The service levels are appropriately high, and in order for Oracle to maintain these levels, they must have a disciplined approach to managing the operations infrastructure. Consistency is the name of the game. To do this, Oracle maintains a maniacal focus on execution to published processes—production maintenance windows, staging use policies, upgrades calendars—without exception. A company will find itself in an unfortunate situation if it turns out it has a conflict with these policies.

- *I didn't realize that the needs of the community sometimes outweigh mine.* How do you run a successful SaaS service for thousands of companies? You do so by focusing on doing the greatest good for the greatest number of companies. In general, this approach works well for everyone; if there is a software bug or performance issue that affects multiple companies or threatens the overall health of the environment, Oracle will give it immediate attention. If, on the other hand, you have a need that conflicts with the needs of the overall service, you may find that your needs do not take precedence. Say, for example, you want Oracle to delay maintenance because the schedule conflicts with your business calendar. Your request will most likely be politely refused. Why? Because the potential negative impact to the larger community would far outweigh the benefit that you, a single company, would receive.

- *I didn't fully comprehend the self-service nature of the model.* Another characteristic of SaaS applications is the inherent self-service nature of the offering. With CRM On Demand, you can literally order a trial subscription, configure the application, and be ready to go live before speaking with a salesperson. Customers often under-appreciate that the CRM On Demand subscription includes the administrative tools, training, and knowledge library for them to build up their own expertise and self-sufficiency. The implication of this self-service focus, however, is that if you find yourself in need of assistance, you must take the initiative to reach out and get the help you need.

The True Benefit of SaaS:
Freedom to Focus on the Business

In the end, most companies agree that surprises are to be expected when adopting a new software delivery model. Once they adjust their expectations to fit within the boundaries of the model, they find the service delivers on its promise of consistency, reliability, and continuous innovation.

In the end, we believe this price is a small one to pay in order to realize the true benefit of the SaaS model—the freedom it allows you to focus your time and energy on improving your business. As we all know, CRM technology initiatives must be aligned with corresponding people and process improvements in order to achieve the anticipated business results. With traditional license software projects, these improvements inevitably get lost in the shuffle as technology inexorably consumes the attention of the project team. Will the software install cleanly? How will the application perform in our technology infrastructure? Is it compatible with our legacy systems? How do we keep from customizing the application to the point where we can't upgrade to future software releases? Once the focus shifts to the technology, you lose sight of the original business objectives and downplay the non-technology factors that impact the value of a new system. The end result is usually a disaster—an overly customized application grafted to poorly designed business processes that invariably fails to deliver the promised improvements.

With the shift in hosting responsibility, most of the technology issues (for you, at least) are minimized in the SaaS model. So how should you focus your time and energy? We recommend you do three things:

- Ensure your business leaders agree on the specific results they want to get from your CRM initiative and the improvements to business processes and user behaviors that will be needed achieve these results.

- Choose the set of features, configuration options, and product extensions that best meet your requirements, and take them live as quickly as possible. Don't focus on perfection; make sure the features are minimally sufficient to meet your business needs and no more. If a particular feature doesn't quite meet your needs, or will require significant configuration or extensions to work, consider deferring the item to a later date.

- Take advantage of the fact that you can deploy at the push of a button. Beyond the initial deployment, ensure CRM On Demand evolves to meet the changing dynamics of your business by introducing improvements on a periodic basis. Build a team to administer the application so you can roll out new features rapidly as your requirements change. Use these periodic releases to improve your existing configuration as well as to take advantage of new capabilities that Oracle delivers in their software updates.

By first setting a business context to your initiative, and then agreeing to match your needs to what is available from the service, you've defined a working project scope that greatly simplifies application design, configuration, and launch. Then, by following a continuous release process, you take the pressure off having to get everything right the first time and establish an ongoing program that ensures constant value added for the organization.

Shared Responsibilities and Obligations

With freedom comes responsibility and, with the move to SaaS, comes a new set of shared obligations between you and Oracle, your SaaS provider. These obligations fall into four categories.

Application Hosting

As the SaaS provider, Oracle takes primary responsibility for the hosting of CRM On Demand. This responsibility includes maintaining the hosting software and hardware infrastructure and ensuring the service meets the contracted uptime and performance levels. To do this, Oracle keeps to a rigorous process, which is documented in great detail in the terms of use and operations policies. Understanding the policies under which Oracle manages the service is your responsibility, as is aligning your activity to work within those policies. At a minimum, you need to know the maintenance schedule for your production environment and understand the use policies and availability for any of the non-production environments you may use for development and testing activities. The key is to avoid unnecessary interruptions to your work caused by schedule conflicts that should have been anticipated.

Design and Configuration

The primary responsibility falls to you. Oracle has provided you with intuitive tools to configure and administer the application. In order to take advantage of these tools, you need to ensure you build the right expertise within your team. At a minimum, your designated CRM On Demand administrators should take the appropriate product training; we've provided suggestions on the proper learning paths in Chapter 3. If you plan, like most companies, to have your business teams take ownership for application administration, then you will also need to develop their expertise around traditional IT skills such as project management and application lifecycle development. If you don't have this type of expertise in-house, you should consider contracting or hiring CRM On Demand experts to get you started.

Software Upgrades

CRM On Demand maintains a steady cadence of new functionality releases, typically two to three per year. The upgrades are intended to be seamless for users. On Friday night, you log out of the old release, and on Monday morning, you sign in to the new release, and your application and data look exactly as you left it. New features are turned off until you choose to enable them, so you don't have to worry about dealing with a bunch of exposed new features every time CRM On Demand rolls out a new release. You are, however, expected to conduct some basic validation testing ahead of each upgrade to ensure your configurations and integrations work as expected with the new release. As such, you need to anticipate and plan for these activities, and, when Oracle announces your upgrade schedule, be prepared to work within the scheduled timeframes.

Ongoing Support and Maintenance

This responsibility is shared between you and Oracle. As the application host, Oracle is responsible for the overall health and maintenance of the infrastructure. They will ensure the hardware and software is up-to-date, properly tuned, and properly scaled to meet user demand. As the owner of the application configuration, your responsibility is to monitor user adoption and to troubleshoot configuration issues that arise over time. Chapter 9 discusses the typical items you will need to address. If you need assistance, there are plenty of resources at your disposal, just note that most are self-service in nature, and you must take the initiative to find the help you need.

Summary

Software-as-a-Service is a business model that is here to stay. It offers tremendous advantages over traditional license software: no installation is required, it's easier to administer, and it's faster to deploy. Companies no longer have to worry about the technology—installing, customizing, upgrading, and maintaining the software—and instead are free to focus on improving how they interact with their customers. After all, that was the reason for purchasing a CRM system in the first place.

With the benefits of SaaS come new obligations as well. Most of the responsibilities fall to the vendor; they host the software and have to deal with the problems that come with any complex infrastructure. You have obligations as well, however, to know the terms of service, the plan for upgrades, and maintenance schedules. You also must take ownership to develop your product and deployment expertise. Do these well, and you can take advantage of all that the SaaS model has to offer.

CHAPTER
2

Overview of Oracle CRM On Demand

n order to make the best design choices for your CRM On Demand deployment, you must first understand what the product can do and how you can design and extend the application to meet your specific requirements. This chapter will introduce you to the functional features available "out of the box" within CRM On Demand and how you can extend these features via configuration and customization. We'll also discuss the underlying computing environment, as this, too, will impact the deployment choices you make. As you will find, CRM On Demand is an extremely powerful and flexible application; however, as with all hosted applications, you need to be familiar with what CRM On Demand can do—and by extension—what it cannot do. In the following pages, we will explore CRM On Demand's features and functions in greater detail to help you appreciate its overall capabilities.

The CRM On Demand Application

CRM On Demand consists of a suite of applications that are delivered in a SaaS model and sold as a single subscription fee. The application suite delivers core sales, marketing, and service functionality that enable typical front-office business processes (see Figure 2-1). The core application traces its heritage back to the Siebel Enterprise CRM product suite, and although it still shares a good bit of the original data model and business logic from its on-premise predecessor, the entire user interface and administrative setup have been modified to support a multi-tenant SaaS model. The core application is tightly integrated to a data warehouse and reporting engine based on the Oracle Business Intelligence (formerly Enquire/Siebel Analytics) platform. The data warehouse capabilities are quite extensive; you have access to consolidated life-to-date historical data and key metrics for each of the major functions.

CRM On Demand comes prebuilt with an extensive set of configurations that revolve around a particular business process. Each business process, such as Opportunity Management, comes with preconfigured roles that define the screens, data, and functional responsibilities for a typical end-user, line manager, and executive. Many organizations find the out-of-the-box configurations a close fit and need only make small changes to meet their particular needs. Those organizations that require more specialized configurations will generally use the out-of-the-box configuration as a starting template.

The core CRM On Demand application consists of seven main feature sets:

- Campaign Management supports the creation of marketing campaigns and the tracking of the campaign details from inception to completion. Campaigns consist of recipients (e.g., Contacts), which are created by analyzing the CRM On Demand Account and Contact information to segment your target audience. As marketing communications are sent to a recipient, CRM On Demand tracks receipt and response information.

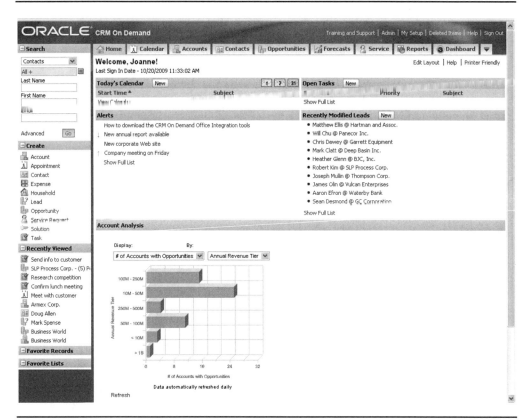

FIGURE 2-1. *CRM On Demand combines sales, marketing, and service automation with an embedded data warehouse.*

Campaign responses convert to Leads that feed into the CRM On Demand Lead and Opportunity Management feature sets, which allow you to track a campaign's effectiveness throughout the sales cycle.

■ Lead Management supports the registration of sales prospects and guides the prospect through a qualification process that ultimately results in a sales opportunity or a rejection. CRM On Demand utilizes a two-tiered Lead process, which manages the Lead disposition process separately from the Opportunity sales process. This feature allows organizations to have a separate lead-generation team who focuses on identifying and cultivating leads and, once qualified, hands them off to a sales representative to work the opportunity. Because the Lead is stored separately in CRM On Demand, you can build a lifecycle program around the Lead, attach activities and assessments, and report on key metrics for the Lead and associated marketing campaign (aging, conversion rates, and so on). Once converted to a Sales Opportunity, the Lead remains associated with the resulting Account, Contact, and Opportunity, which allows for a closed-loop reporting view into marketing return on investment.

- Account Management supports the tracking of organizational details needed for business-to-business transactions. Accounts are the main organizational object within CRM On Demand and can be set up to provide as much granularity as needed: single site, independent multiple sites, or an *n*-level parent/child hierarchical view of a consolidated organizational entity. Along with the Customer Profile, CRM On Demand tracks asset inventory, order history, call notes, and activity history against a particular account.

- Contact Management supports the tracking of key individuals, their relationships with other individuals, and their roles within organizations. In the business-to-business model, CRM On Demand tracks Contacts and their relationships to particular accounts. In the business-to-consumer model, Contacts are tracked individually or grouped in family units known as *households.* Within an Opportunity, CRM On Demand tracks the related Contacts and their role in the sales process (such as the buyer, stakeholder, consultant, and so on). Along with the Contact Profile, CRM On Demand tracks call notes and activity history against the particular Contact.

- Opportunity Management supports sales opportunities and related information. Opportunities can be tracked at a summary or detail level. Different deal types can follow separate sales processes, with their own business rules for tracking information, sales stages, and required activities (for example, new orders versus renewals). Products can consist of durable goods or services. Deal amounts can be tracked at a summary level or product level. Deals can be structured as one-time events, according to a fixed schedule, or played out as an annuity. In addition to the opportunity details, CRM On Demand tracks the related partners, competitors, activity history, and audit history for the Opportunity. A unique innovation to CRM On Demand Opportunity Management is the Sales Process Coach, which automates key activities, enforces data entry for required fields, and delivers context-based help and documentation for each stage of the sales cycle.

- Sales Forecast consists of the submission and roll-up of probable opportunities committed to close during a particular time period. The CRM On Demand auto forecast process is a formal process where Opportunities are flagged for submission according to a predefined schedule. CRM On Demand takes a snapshot of the Forecast (opportunity, product, revenue, and splits) and rolls up the Opportunity totals and any manager overrides through the sales territory hierarchy. The snapshots are then stored for historical trending analysis.

■ Service Request Management supports help desk service request tracking. Service requests can be tracked against Accounts or Contacts and their purchased Assets. Detailed information can be captured via scripted questions known as *assessments*. Work-flow rules route service requests based on attributes such as location, product, or agent skills, and can escalate service requests that do not meet time-based service levels. CRM On Demand comes with a solutions database to expedite service request resolution. Along with the service request details, CRM On Demand tracks the affected asset, call history, and audit history.

The reporting and analytics capabilities within CRM On Demand are powerful and extensive. Within the application, there are three types of reporting:

■ **Lists**   Embedded within each of the homepages is a basic list report capability for sorting data. You can provide basic filter comparisons for querying the data and choosing what data fields to be returned. These lists are nothing more than table-based reports, designed to help users manage their daily workload. They are not intended for reporting against large sets of data; that is a job for the following report tools.

■ **Real-time reports**   Also known as Answers On Demand, this is a full-featured reporting engine that allows you to build interactive charts, pivot tables, and reports, using up-to-the-minute data from the transactional database. Real-time reports are intended to report against larger sets of consolidated data, such as daily or weekly summaries up to the company level.

■ **Historical Analytics**   CRM On Demand takes daily snapshots of your data and stores this information in the data warehouse. The real value of the data warehouse is in the prebuilt metrics that are captured along with the daily snapshot. CRM On Demand compiles key measurements for each of the major processes, such as sales cycle duration, win rates, top performers, and service request aging. These measurements allow you to develop comparative reports that reflect data trends based on the values captured over time. Historical analytics are designed to be used for complex reporting against consolidated data over monthly, quarterly, and yearly timeframes.

The power of CRM On Demand Analytics lies in its ability to embed reporting data directly into the application. These reports can be viewed in the stand-alone traditional manner, or embedded within homepages, dashboards, or detail pages to provide the user with insightful information as he or she navigates the application. For example, you can add a current quarter pipeline summary report to the sales manager's homepage, or update the sales representative's detail page to show the service request history for his or her accounts.

Most subscribing companies use the CRM On Demand Standard Edition, which is the general-purpose business-to-business version of the CRM On Demand suite. In addition to the Standard Edition, there are five Industry Solution Editions that tailor the interface, data, and workflow to the specialized terminology and process flow of a particular industry. The Industry Solutions consist of two business-to-business models, two consumer models, and a hybrid business-and-consumer model:

■ The Hi-Tech Edition extends the Standard Edition's direct to business model with indirect partner channel management. The Hi-Tech Edition builds upon the account and marketing campaign functionality to provide these features. In addition to the Standard Edition's features, this edition of CRM On Demand tracks partner details and related marketing-development-fund budgets and funding requests. The Analytics data warehouse has been extended to report on Return On Investment (ROI) metrics for marketing development funds against related marketing campaigns and partner-sourced opportunities.

■ The Wealth Management/Insurance Editions are the consumer versions of CRM On Demand. The Wealth Management edition extends the contact management functionality in the Standard Edition, and introduces additional objects to support household relationships, financial accounts tracking, and long-term financial planning functions. The Analytics data warehouse has been extended to support financial account and portfolio performance summaries, household net-worth analysis, and consolidated client reporting.

■ The Life Sciences Edition extends the Standard Edition to support pharmaceutical sales teams that call on both individuals and institutions. The Contact Management functionality has been extended to support physician tracking, call planning and reporting, medical education event planning, and samples management. The Account Management functionality has been extended to support institutional tracking and key account planning.

■ The Automotive Edition extends the Standard Edition with fleet and warranty management for captive or independent dealer franchises. The Automotive Edition extends both the Account and Contact Management functions, so dealers can track fleet and retail customers' vehicle warranty, service information, and service history.

The CRM On Demand Architecture and Service Model

Now, let's discuss the overall architecture of the CRM On Demand service.

CRM On Demand offers three separate subscriptions: Multi-Tenant, Single-Tenant, and @Customer. The Multi-Tenant subscription is a shared model where multiple companies reside on a single computing environment within Oracle's data center. By utilizing this shared environment, multi-tenant customers receive the lowest per-seat subscription fees of all the deployment options. The Single-Tenant model is a dedicated model where a single company occupies its own environment within Oracle's data center and pays a premium fee in exchange for a more personalized service. The @Customer model is the high end offering, where a company hosts CRM On Demand behind its firewall on dedicated hardware within the company's own data center, and Oracle provides remote software support.

Regardless of the subscription type you choose, CRM On Demand utilizes the same underlying Multi-Tenant-enabled architecture for every computing environment. Figure 2-2 shows how the architecture works. Within a single physical environment of CRM On Demand, every company (or tenant) shares a common code base and infrastructure. Individual *company instances* are made up of virtual partitions within this physical environment. These virtual partitions store the metadata that defines each company's look, feel, and flow—business rules, objects and fields used, and layouts and reports. Each company instance begins with an exact copy of CRM On Demand, but a company can turn on or off the features it wants and configure the look, feel, and flow it needs. A Multi-Tenant environment can support a virtually unlimited number of company instances, each running its own configured version of the application.

Individual CRM On Demand physical environments are referred to as *pods.* In addition to the Production pod, CRM On Demand offers two other environments for use as part of your subscription. The Stage pod contains a quarterly snapshot copy of the production configuration and data, which Oracle uses for technical support troubleshooting and to test software patches and upgrades. This is an Oracle-owned environment and is subject to restrictions, but when not in use, many customers use the Stage pod as their development environment. The Customer Test Environment pod is a company-controlled environment that is essentially a separate production instance of CRM On Demand dedicated to your development, testing, and training needs. The Customer Test Environment is a stand-alone environment that requires a separate setup as there are no automated copies from production. CRM On Demand allows for an ability to promote certain configuration settings between the Production pod and the Staging and Customer Test Environment pods.

Pods undergo routine maintenance on specific time zones. The standard maintenance window is Friday evening 21:00 hours local time for the U.S. Central (GMT –6), UK (GMT), or Hong Kong (GMT +8) time zones. Maintenance generally occurs on a monthly schedule, with exceptions for critical software patches and upgrades. During the maintenance window, the CRM On Demand application cannot be accessed.

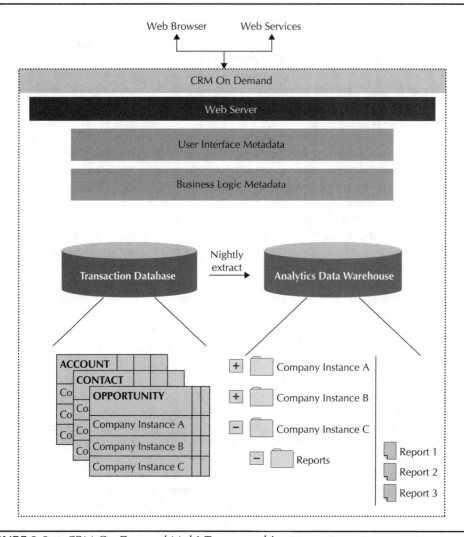

FIGURE 2-2. *CRM On Demand Multi-Tenant architecture*

The CRM On Demand provisioning and installation process is much different than traditional software purchases. Upon your order, CRM On Demand provisions a new company instance on a particular Production pod, based upon the type of subscription (Single- or Multi Tenant), the number of licenses purchased, the primary business language employed, the financial calendar, and the default local time zone. Your company instance consists of a standard copy of CRM On Demand, configured for your language, time zone, and financial calendar, provisioned on a regional pod whose maintenance best matches your default local time zone. At this point, you have unrestricted access to your company instance and are free to commence with your implementation.

Configuration Options

If the out-of-the-box processes don't quite meet your needs, CRM On Demand offers a robust set of configuration features that allow you to extend the look, feel, and flow of the application. A number of options are available to you:

■ Fields may be renamed, added to, or removed from each object to better represent your business needs. Each of the application objects (Account, Contact, Opportunity, and so on) contains a predefined set of Custom Fields that you enable as you need them. Custom Fields come in multiple data types (text, currency, pick-list), and there are a fixed number of total fields available to choose for each object.

■ Screen Layouts may be configured to show or hide any of the available objects and fields for a particular business process. You can also set up layouts to dynamically change what fields show up, depending on the type of data being viewed or a particular stage in your business process. For example, you can set up the Opportunity Screen Layout to dynamically display different revenue fields, depending on whether the opportunity is a product or service deal.

■ Roles and Access Profiles may be set up to control the features, layouts, and ability to manipulate data for different segments of users. For example, you may want to set up an Access Role for your salesperson that grants access to all fields for an Account, but defines a more limited Access Role for your customer-support agent that hides the sales-specific fields that are not relevant to the support job role.

■ Data visibility may be implemented to secure data access at the individual, team, and organization levels based upon the security needs of your company. For example, a direct sales organization may want to restrict an Account's viewing and editing rights to only the responsible salesperson and his or her direct managers, whereas an overlay sales organization may want a team of people to view and edit Account data. Or, you may want to grant Account access to a group of users across an entire geographic area or line of business. Among the group, team, and book of business access models, there are few limits to the number and type of organizational structures you can model.

- Workflow may be defined to support your customized business processes. You can define validation rules for managing how users enter information and create specialized rules that automatically trigger record updates, e-mail notifications, or kickoff customized integration processes.

- Advanced configuration options allow you to create your own mini-applications within CRM On Demand. Custom tabs and web applets allow you to create your own mash-ups with external applications. Custom objects allow you to extend the underlying data model and create your own object types and relationships. All of these configuration changes can be made within the application and are available within the administrator setup screens.

CRM On Demand Extensions

CRM On Demand also offers an extensive set of prebuilt extensions to the service. These are SaaS and/or mobile applications that are sold under a separate subscription and offer out-of-the-box plug-and-play integration to CRM On Demand. The extensions fall into two categories:

- CRM On Demand sales productivity extensions delivered by Oracle

- Partner solutions delivered via the CRM On Demand certified partner program

CRM On Demand offers six productivity extensions: Email Marketing, Deal Management, Partner Relationship Management, Call Center On Demand, Mobile Sales Assistant, and Sales on the Go. Email Marketing adds outbound e-mail campaign and response tracking to the standard CRM On Demand campaign management function. Email Marketing supports campaign creation, contact segmentation, personalized HTML/text e-mail creation, outbound e-mail execution, delivery and response tracking, and reports on key campaign metrics via CRM On Demand analytics. Deal Management extends the standard CRM On Demand opportunity pricing features. Deal Management is an Analytics application that compares an opportunity's deal structure to the margins and historical price points of similar opportunities and offers price recommendations based on financial rules set by the company.

Partner Relationship Management adds indirect channel management to CRM On Demand. Partner Relationship Management supports lead and opportunity sharing, marketing development fund requests, special pricing authorizations, and reporting on channel performance and marketing campaign effectiveness. Contact Center On Demand is a call center application that adds hosted inbound call center capabilities to CRM On Demand. Contact Center On Demand supports Automated

Call Distribution routing, telephony integration with CRM On Demand Service Requests, and integration with CRM On Demand Analytics for tracking call metrics such as speed to answer, call resolution, and wait times. Mobile Sales Assistant adds mobile access to CRM On Demand data via the iPhone and Blackberry. Mobile Sales Assistant supports "store and forward" synchronization to CRM On Demand appointments, contacts, accounts, opportunities, and forecasts; tight integration to mapping and social networking sites to find driving directions and check up on clients; and Bluetooth integration for wireless data sharing with other mobile devices. Sales on the Go is a tablet PC-based application that integrates with the CRM On Demand Life Sciences Edition and provides mobile support for pharmaceutical sales call activities such as call scheduling, personalized presentation content, and signature tracking for samples inventory management.

CRM On Demand partner solutions are third-party SaaS applications that provide complementary functionality integrated with the application. The partners sell these applications separately under their own terms and subscription fees. Oracle maintains a small group of trusted partners, known as the *Inner Circle,* whose applications have been certified to work tightly with CRM On Demand. Examples of these solutions include a multichannel marketing management solution, data cleansing and de-duplication services, a product configuration and quoting solution, Google integration services, enterprise application integration services, and sales compensation. A summary of the key features and select partner extensions is presented in Table 2-1.

Business Process	Key Features	Industry Solution Extensions	Oracle Productivity Extensions	Partner Extensions
Lead Management	Campaign tracking Two-tier distribution Lead scoring Embedded Analytics	Medical events	Email Marketing	Marketing automation Google integration
Account Management	Company profile Hierarchies Asset/order history Activity/call history Embedded Analytics	Partner Profile Dealer Profile Institution Profile Account planning	Partner Relationship Management	Data cleansing Data quality
Contact Management	Contact Profile Activity/call history Embedded Analytics	Households Portfolios Policies Physicians	Mobile Sales Assistant	Data cleansing Data quality

TABLE 2-1.   *CRM On Demand Features, Industry Solutions, and Product Extensions*

Business Process	Key Features	Industry Solution Extensions	Oracle Productivity Extensions	Partner Extensions
Campaign Management	Campaign profile Campaign ROI tracking Embedded Analytics	Marketing fund management	Email Marketing On Demand Segmentation wizard	Extended e-mail marketing
Opportunity Management	Multiple sales stages Product, service, and annuity tracking Sales Process Coach Partners/competitors Activity/call history Embedded Analytics	Industry-specific fields and sales stages	Deal Management	Sales Methodology compliance Complex product configuration Sales incentives
Sales Forecast	Automatic rollup Manager overrides Deal splits Historical snapshots Embedded Analytics Multiple Forecast types	Industry-specific Forecast rollups	Partner Forecasts	Extended forecasting
Service Requests	Service Profile Automated routing Escalations Solutions Knowledge base Embedded Analytics	Vehicle warranty Insurance claims	Contact Center	Customer portal Service workflow and communication

TABLE 2-1. *CRM On Demand Features, Industry Solutions, and Product Extensions (continued)*

Summary

In summary, the CRM On Demand is an extremely sophisticated application and infrastructure that provides a wealth of functionality out of the box and a breadth of options for extending the base functionality through configuration and product extensions. In this chapter, we've provided a high-level overview of the service and a general description of how each of the major CRM On Demand business processes function. In the following chapters, we will go into greater detail about how you can mix and match functionality, configurations, and product extensions to meet your specific business objectives.

As you go about determining what mix of features, configurations, and product extensions are right for your company, keep the following points in mind:

- Take the time necessary to understand the application. CRM On Demand is a complex application, and you need to get into the details in order to understand its capabilities. For those with prior Siebel or Enquiro experience, do not assume your enterprise product knowledge transfers directly to CRM On Demand. These applications may share a common past, but they both have evolved to become very different products from one another.

- If you find a functionality gap with a particular business process, look across the application for alternatives and extensions before discarding the feature. Start first with the industry solutions; oftentimes, there are feature extensions that you can repurpose to your needs. Then look to customization options. Finally, look for partner extensions that meet your particular needs.

- Be sure to understand the maintenance and service components of the SaaS service. Take time to understand service-level agreements, use policies for the nonproduction environments, and pod maintenance calendars, as these, too, will affect your design and deployment decisions.

Let's move on to getting the most from the CRM On Demand service.

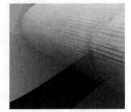

CHAPTER
3

Getting the Most from Your Oracle CRM On Demand Service

n the last two chapters, we described the key features of CRM On Demand and how the underlying SaaS infrastructure simplifies deployment and speeds your ability to deliver business value to your organization. In this chapter, we turn to the knowledge and skills you will need to become really effective in your implementation and ongoing management of CRM On Demand. The good news is that Oracle has developed a variety of resources specifically for CRM On Demand that will help you acquire the knowledge and awareness you'll need to configure, deploy, upgrade, and maintain your company instance over the term of your subscription. The key is to know what resources are provided, why a resource would be useful, and where to access what you need.

This chapter will acquaint you with the resources and tools that you should draw on during the implementation process and after launch as issues arise. In each section, we will highlight

- The resources available and where to find them

- When and how to use a specific resource or tool

Self-Service Through a Single Point-of-Access

By design, all the supporting information and tools are organized and made available to you through the CRM On Demand application. You have self-service access to training courses, technical documentation, implementation tools, system notifications, and the ability to submit service requests. The objective is to have a single point-of-access and common source of information that you can "pull" from when logged into the service.

Navigating to Support Resources

Let's begin with a high-level view of the specific links on the CRM On Demand user interface that provide access to resources you will be using in the implementation process and beyond. Note that these links will bring you to the resources referenced later in this chapter.

After you log in to the CRM On Demand service, you'll find a series of links at the top and bottom of the home page layout; we refer to these as *global* links because they are found on every page regardless of where you navigate in the application. See Figure 3-1a and b.

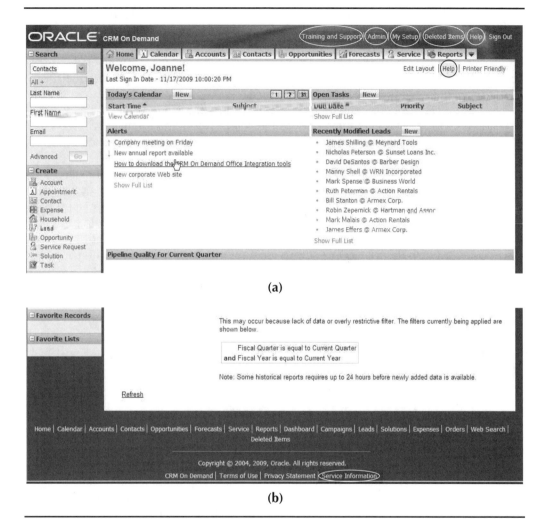

FIGURE 3-1.   *CRM On Demand Key Support Links*

The first link at the top, *Training and Support,* will take you to the CRM On Demand Training and Support Center. The Training and Support Center provides a central point-of-access for most of your support needs, including training courses, implementation tools, technical documentation, user forums, system notifications, and maintenance calendars.

Moving left to right, the next link is *Admin*. This link will take you to the Administration homepage with detailed information, tools, and templates that the project team will need to set up the system according to your requirements.

Next to Admin is the *My Setup* link to your Personal homepage. The Personal homepage has preference settings for individual users who want to personalize their experience within your unique company instance.

Next is the *Deleted Items* link. Any deleted records will be found here and may be restored up to 30 days after they have been deleted. This administrative tool is useful to highlight for *all* users. There are additional details governing this function that you will want to understand in greater detail, however.

You'll note that the user interface has two links to online help. The *Help* link at the top next to Deleted Items is a global link to all the content areas included in the general help library. You'll note an index and search function are available. A Help link can also be found on the upper-right corner of every page layout; this Help link is context-sensitive, meaning it will navigate to the information in the knowledge base most relevant to the user's current location and problems in the application.

Finally, note the *Service Information* link at the very bottom of the user interface. This link will provide useful operational information specifically related to your company's instance in Oracle's hosting environment. You'll find the software version numbers for your company instance, information about service availability, and scheduled maintenance events for your stage and production environments.

Now that you understand where to find these resources, let's discuss the capabilities that are most critical to your initial implementation.

CRM On Demand Training

Among all the factors that influence program success, the competence of your implementation team is among the most critical. Before you begin the implementation project, your implementation team must have adequate knowledge of CRM On Demand functionality, understand how to configure the application, and be able to complete the variety of tasks necessary to set up the system. Implementation teams who jump right into the configuration process without first educating themselves about the application's features and functions will likely experience delay and frustration before the project is finished. A common root cause of usability and system performance problems is poor design. Poor application design is a common result when the implementation team does not develop adequate product knowledge nor follow "best practices" for configuring core functions. Effective training alone will not assure the success of an inexperienced team. We strongly encourage implementation teams who are new to CRM On Demand to enlist experts with prior experience with the nuances of CRM On Demand configuration and what it takes to tailor a CRM application to meet the needs of front-office end-users.

To help your team build the necessary technical competence, Oracle has developed a broad library of training courses specifically for CRM On Demand that will help prepare your implementation team to be effective in their assigned roles. By completing the live and recorded courses, your team will deepen their functional knowledge of the application, as well as learn how to configure the environment to your business requirements. The training curriculum offered for CRM On Demand is accessed through two delivery channels:

- Technical courses delivered live online by instructors through Oracle University (for a fee)

- Prerecorded, task-based webinars available through the Training and Support Center (for free)

You will find brief descriptions of the course offerings and where to source them in the sections that follow. We will start by providing recommendations on the most useful courses to complete in the timeline of a typical project.

Recommended Training Courses

Since no single course can provide you with everything you need to know, and trying to take all the available courses before starting your project would be counterproductive, we recommend a series of courses in Table 3-1 for implementation teams with limited CRM On Demand experience. The courses in the *Core* track will develop a comprehensive understanding of the end-to-end system setup activities and are appropriate for any person who will support multiple stages of your implementation project, or post-launch administration. *Administration Essentials* is the most important of these courses. In terms of timing, it is important to complete the courses in the Core track before beginning your project. The courses in the *Data Import* and *Report Development* tracks can be taken after the project commences, but ideally will be completed before the project requirements and schedule have been fixed. Doing this ensures that you and your team have the knowledge necessary to complete the initial implementation project in an efficient way. In Chapter 4, we will describe the recommended project team roles when you have a multiperson implementation team and can assign people to concentrate on specific project tasks. In the event you can delegate the work effort among a team by assigning functional concentrations, you will note specific learning tracks for Data Import and Report Development.

In each row of Table 3-1, you will find the track designation, course title, brief objective, delivery format, and course duration. The courses are listed in the sequence we recommend they be completed.

Track	Course Title	Objective	Format	Duration
Core	Using Oracle CRM On Demand	System Overview	Recorded webinar	< 30 minutes
Core	Administration Essentials	Teaches about all aspects of system setup and administration	Live, online ILT	24 hours 4+ days
Core	What's New in Release 15	Overview of new features	Recorded webinar	< 30 minutes
Core	What's New in Release 16	Overview of new features	Recorded webinar	< 30 minutes
Core	Understanding Data Access & Visibility Control	Overview of how data is structured and exposed based on configuration rules	Recorded webinar	< 30 minutes
Core	Flexible Data Sharing Using Books-of-Business	Teaches how to configure Books-of-Business to company requirements	Recorded webinar	< 30 minutes
Core	Managing Groups	Teaches how to use groups to control data access and the visibility of company requirements	Recorded webinar	< 30 minutes
Data Import	Data Import Workshop	Teaches each step of the data import process	Live, online ILT	2 days
Data Import	Importing Your Data (Parts 1 & 2)	Teaches specific details on the import and validation process	Recorded webinar	Part 1: < 30 minutes Part 2: < 30 minutes
Report Development	Advanced Analytics Workshop	Teaches foundation skills necessary for using analytics and report development tools	Live, online ILT	2 days
Report Development	Build Your Own Reports: 1	Teaches how to control visibility to report data	Recorded webinar	< 30 minutes
Report Development	Build Your Own Reports: 2	Teaches how to create List Reports	Recorded webinar	< 30 minutes
Report Development	Build Your Own Reports: 3	Teaches how to format Custom Reports	Recorded webinar	< 30 minutes

TABLE 3-1. *Recommended Courses*

Track	Course Title	Objective	Format	Duration
Report Development	Build Your Own Reports: 4	Teaches how to create charts for reports	Recorded webinar	< 30 minutes
Report Development	Build Your Own Reports: 5	Teaches how to create pivot tables for reports	Recorded webinar	< 30 minutes
Report Development	Build Your Own Reports: 6	Teaches how to control access to reports	Recorded webinar	< 30 minutes

TABLE 3-1.   *Recommended Courses (continued)*

Live Courses

Three CRM On Demand courses are offered online through Oracle University:

- ■ **Administration Essentials**   A comprehensive workshop that teaches the fundamental concepts and tasks for configuring and maintaining the application. Under a facilitator's guidance, participants complete hands-on exercises that reflect the primary setup activities in a typical implementation project.

- ■ **Data Import Workshop**   A deep-dive workshop to guide the collection and cleansing of a source data, the steps in the import process, troubleshooting, and best practices to avoid common errors.

- ■ **Advanced Analytics Workshop**   A deep-dive workshop on the business intelligence functionality that teaches the end-to-end steps for building analytics dashboards and reports. Participants learn best practices for building complex reports that are easy to use and perform effectively.

Experienced instructors teach each of these courses in a live virtual format. The courses include participant guides, and all exercises are completed in a dedicated CRM On Demand production environment. They range from two to four days in length, and there is a tuition fee. You can enroll in these classes through Oracle University or by following the links to Live Training via the Training and Support Center. As indicated in the training recommendations in Table 3-1, these courses provide the foundation knowledge necessary to prepare you for your CRM On Demand implementation.

Recorded "Task-Based" Webinars

There is a library of more than 40 pre-recorded, task-based courses available online through the Training and Support Center. The course titles address a range of topics that provide practical guidance on the execution of a specific task in the configuration, administration, or use of the application. Some of the titles were developed to assist administrators with more complex, multistep processes associated with a specific functional capability in the application. Others teach end-users how to execute end-to-end business processes. And there are a few that explain specific application features. These courses are available to any users at any time through the Training and Support Center, and most are under 30 minutes in length, making it simple and easy to develop your knowledge on a selected topic when a question arises or you need to execute a given task. You can access the titles by topic area or job role, so you can find the appropriate topic quickly.

In addition to the web courses recommended for implementation teams who are preparing to launch CRM On Demand for the first time, there are additional courses we recommend you consider taking to promote a deeper understanding of the service.

The first set is appropriate once you have initial experience working with the application:

- Consulting Best Practices for Application Configuration

- Consulting Best Practices for Data Import

- Consulting Best Practices for Setting Access & Visibility

As the titles imply, these webinars highlight the tactical lessons learned from Oracle consultants based on their implementation experiences, and they provide practical guidance to help you avoid common pitfalls that result in poor usability and performance. If your project has challenging requirements, the information offered in these courses will be helpful to you.

The second category of recommended courses is produced in support of every major release of CRM On Demand. There is a general overview called, "What's New in Release (current #)" that will highlight the new functionality associated with the release. The "What's New" course will acquaint you with the benefits and general purpose of all the new features in a given release. To understand the new features in greater technical detail, a series of Transfer-of-Information (TOI) courses are developed for each major release cycle. These courses will describe and demonstrate the typical use case for a given feature and, when necessary, how it should be configured. If you are planning to deploy a new feature, the TOIs will provide just-in-time guidance to help you integrate the new capability in your production system.

Using the Knowledge Base

Even after completing the appropriate training, you will still have questions in the day-to-day administration and use of CRM On Demand. Oracle has developed an extensive knowledge base with practical information organized to respond to the needs of different stakeholders during the program lifecycle. This knowledge base should be your "go-to" resource anytime a question or obstacle arises. The content available takes many forms, including white papers, guides, samples, tools, and templates. They explain how to use different features, outline best practices, support system setup and administration tasks, and explain technical reference material. But consistent with the self-service design, you need to know where to go to find what you need.

In this section, we will highlight the three locations in CRM On Demand where you can access information and documentation in support of the implementation process:

- Implementation Templates and Tools in the CRM On Demand Knowledge Center on My Oracle Support

- Web Services Resource Library in the Training and Support Center

- Administering CRM On Demand section of online Help

We suggest you, and the other implementation team members, become familiar with the range of resources available in these locations so you can quickly access the right information when a need arises.

Implementation Templates and Tools

The resources found in the Implementation Templates and Tools section contain documents that will be especially useful to your implementation team during the initial system setup. You can download these documents via the Training and Support Center by following the Knowledge and Training links, which take you to the Oracle CRM On Demand Knowledge Center in My Oracle Support. The documentation found here includes proven tools that have been developed by CRM On Demand experts for use on their implementations. The documentation is organized in six sections corresponding to the consulting phases in a typical implementation project schedule (see Table 3-2). The Administrators Rollout Guide found in the Project Organization section provides an overview of the steps in a standard implementation and explains when and how to use the other documents included in this knowledge base. Using these templates and supporting information will help you to organize

Topic	Document Name
Project Organization	Administrator Rollout Guide
Access Management	About Analytics Visibility
	User, Group and Role Set-up Template
Application Layout & Customization	Field Set-up Template
	Page and Related Information Layout Template
	Homepage Layout Template
	Search Layout Template
	Sales Methodology Template
	Assessment Set-up Template
Assignment Rules	Record Assignment Template
Data Import	Before You Import Your Data
	Data Preparation and Clean-up Guide
	Address Mapping Template
	Import Errors and Warning Messages
Validation	Validation Checklist

TABLE 3-2. *Implementation Project Documentation*

planning, discovery, design, configuration, and validation tasks. The materials point out best practices and potential risk areas. We recommend that your project manager review this library of tools when planning your implementation, and incorporate them into the appropriate project stage.

Web Services Resource Library

If the scope of your requirements includes customization, the Web Service Resource Library contains practical guidance for building custom integrations to CRM On Demand using web services. The link is located on the Navigation Bar on the left side of the Training and Support Center homepage. You'll find development guides, reference documentation, and sample code to help your developers with the baseline information needed to begin the development process. We recommend you start with the *Web Services Guidelines and Best Practices* presentation found in the *Documentation* section. This presentation will explain the general guidelines and best practices for building custom integrations to CRM On Demand using web services.

Online Help

Online Help, which is accessed through the CRM On Demand interface, should be the first place to check for answers when you have a question about how to execute a task or when you are seeking information about an individual feature or function in the application. You'll note that in addition to the Help link at the top of the user interface, there is a context-sensitive Help link on every page in the user interface. This link takes you to Help content related to your page location in the system.

During the course of the implementation project, when there is time pressure to complete every task, the Help documentation can be a very effective source of real-time support for the detailed questions that arise. When you launch Help from the Admin Homepage, the Help documentation will open to an extensive section titled, *Administering Oracle CRM On Demand*. This documentation provides a great deal of information to support the execution of each administrative task, including step-instructions, examples, and reference to any hard limits. By invoking the context-sensitive Help link from any Administration subsection, you will find instructions and reference material to support the specific Administrative task that you are executing. For example, from Import and Export Tools under Data Management you'll note record limits by object for each data import cycle and a series of steps for preparing data for import.

Customer Support

During the course of your subscription, there will be times when you want to contact Oracle about a problem with the service, a question that you cannot resolve on your own, or to request a product improvement. To provide assistance at those times, the Oracle Support team provides 24×7 access to every licensed subscriber, bundled within the CRM On Demand service. In this section, we will give you a brief orientation to the mission of the Oracle Support team, the approach they take toward issue resolution, and the expectations you should have in your interactions with them.

Mission and Model

The Oracle Support team follows a traditional "break/fix" support model, reacting to formal requests submitted online or by phone from users. They triage each inbound request, gathering additional details from the "owner," to understand the issues involved and the impact on the company's business operations. Once created, a Service Request (SR) is then categorized by type and assigned a severity level for follow-up action. (Note the information you should supply when submitting a request and how requests are prioritized in the sections that follow.) Oracle Support will solve issues immediately whenever possible. When additional expertise is necessary to resolve a problem, the Support Specialist will work with the appropriate engineering, operations, and product management teams who "work" behind the scenes to investigate, identify solutions, and develop an appropriate response. Throughout the cycle, Oracle Support is your single point-of-contact for communicating updates and resolving your request. If you are unsure who to direct questions to regarding CRM On Demand, a call to Oracle Support is the best and quickest way to point you in the right direction, but recognize that they will not be able to respond to every type of request.

Activating Additional Capabilities

While the base application code is common to all customers, new accounts are provisioned with certain attributes based on the your specialized requirements (i.e., industry versions). At your request, the Oracle Support team will modify certain attributes and some other variables for your account to expand the capabilities of the service. The following list reflects the requests you can make:

- Expose one or more of the vertical objects associated with Industry editions.

- Activate work flow functionality.

- Activate advanced field management.

- Expose up to 15 dynamic custom objects.

- Activate web services APIs.

- Change company profile parameters (i.e., default timeout, single sign-on).

Critical Information When Submitting a Service Request

The preferred method to submit a Service Request is online via the Service Request link on the Training and Support Center homepage. You may also contact Oracle Support by phone when the request is urgent or has a level of complexity that is difficult to convey in writing. However you submit a service request, to expedite follow-up action, you should provide the following information:

- State the problem clearly, with all known supporting facts.

- List steps to reproduce the problem and describe expected application behavior.

■ Describe the business impact of the problem to establish priority.

■ If applicable, include a screenshot.

Prioritizing Response by Request Type

Although you are free to submit any type of question or problem, the primary mission of Oracle Support is to resolve technical problems that inhibit the performance of the system in production. Their highest priority is to respond to reported application problems that have a negative impact on your business operations. You should promptly report any perceived feature/function defects, degraded system performance, and system outages as soon as they occur so the support team can begin to investigate the problem.

In the course of configuring your instance during the setup process, you may encounter unexpected behavior from the application and believe that you have encountered a functional defect or bug. You may also discover you are unable to configure the application to meet a particular requirement and want to get help from Oracle to understand how a feature works or a recommended "workaround." Be advised that in any situation where you are trying to understand how a functional characteristic of the application performs, the ability of Oracle Support to provide assistance will be more limited—they do not have on-staff consulting expertise. When you submit a Service Request, particularly when you believe there is a product defect, Oracle Support will only be able to confirm that the functional behavior of the application is normal. They may also suggest training or documentation in the knowledge base so you can better understand how the feature/function in question works. In the event you require a capability not yet available, they can provide guidance to help you submit an Enhancement Request to product marketing that will formally document the desired feature for consideration in future releases.

Finally, there are two general areas that fall outside the boundaries of the assistance Oracle Support will be able to provide. The first is any request that relates to setup, design, or configuration of the application. Oracle Support does not provide consulting advice, and you will likely be referred to Oracle Consulting Services for billable assistance. The second is any request that involves integration with CRM On Demand. Oracle Support is not able to diagnose problems with or review custom Web Services integrations, and they will deflect any request in that area. In the next section, we will highlight the User Forums for CRM On Demand. These are terrific sources of expertise for implementation and customization questions that you should consider.

Forums: Leveraging the Experts

When you can't find technical "how-to" information from one of the self-service sources in the knowledge base, another option is to tap into the global community of CRM On Demand experts. Oracle established a group of forums to promote information sharing among the global community of professionals working with CRM On Demand. The CRM On Demand Forums are interactive message boards where you can post questions, share information, learn tips, and join in discussions with other CRM On Demand administrators, implementation consultants, and product experts. There are three forums hosted by the Oracle Technology Network (OTN) that are organized around a specific functional theme:

- Oracle CRM On Demand Administration Forum for issues related to setting up and configuring the base application

- Oracle CRM On Demand Analytics and Reports Forum for issues related to developing and using the business intelligence capabilities in the product

- Oracle CRM On Demand Integration Development Forum for issues related to the extension of core capabilities through integrations developed via web services

Posting a specific "how-to" question on the appropriate forum is an easy way to gather information and recommendations quickly from a diverse base of experienced CRM On Demand experts. You can also search the discussion threads from previous postings by keyword to research the topic of interest. A review of the discussion threads is a terrific way to discover the lessons learned from actual customer implementations on a range of topics, and they can often help you solve a problem or answer a question quickly.

While the site is moderated by Oracle, the information found in the discussion threads is not officially endorsed by Oracle, even when provided by an Oracle employee. However, the forums are the only source of consulting expertise or advice that you can tap for free. The Integration Forum is especially useful since CRM On Demand does not provide formal support or documentation for developing web service extensions to the service.

You need to register to participate in the forums, but the process is quick and easy. The discussion threads are accessible in a read-only format to all subscribers. We suggest that you explore each of the forums to get a sense of the value they can provide. You will find a link labeled Access Forums on the homepage of the Training and Support Center.

Oracle Notifications and Communication

One of the big advantages of CRM On Demand is the peace of mind it brings in knowing that Oracle is responsible for availability of the system 24×7. An extensive team of people is working continuously to ensure the service is available, reliable, and performs well. They are also conscious of their responsibility to communicate with you about major events and make operational status available via the self-service channels to help you manage your CRM On Demand programs effectively.

Planned and Unplanned Events

In the course of fulfilling their operational responsibilities, the CRM On Demand operations team monitors service performance, responding to reported outages or performance issues and conducting maintenance. As with any IT system, resources are allocated to support the maintenance schedule as well as respond to any unforeseen issues that impact the availability or performance of the service.

Planned Events

Common planned events include upgrades, patches, stage refreshes, and other maintenance necessary for the health of the hosting environment and overall application performance. These events could include issues related to required security and operating system patches, network maintenance, and hardware replacement. It is useful to remember that the planned maintenance, although inconvenient at times, will improve your overall satisfaction and reduce unplanned outages. You should factor the maintenance schedule for your instance into the management of your program. Oracle posts notice of scheduled maintenance events; just click the Service Information link found on the CRM On Demand homepage. You can also find a maintenance schedule posted under System Notifications on the Training and Support Center homepage.

Unplanned Events

Whenever your ability to use the service is interrupted due to degradation in the application performance, or a system outage occurs outside scheduled maintenance period, CRM On Demand posts the current system status for all impacted customers under System Notifications on the Training and Support Center homepage. The notifications will describe the problem, which hosting environment is impacted, the actions underway to restore the service, and an estimated time to restore the service to production.

E-mail Communication

There are two types of e-mail messages CRM On Demand subscribers can receive:

- **CRM On Demand Announcements**   Provide information about major new releases or significant performance issues impacting a large number of customers. These e-mails are distributed to all primary contacts and users with Always Send Critical Alerts selected in the User Detail screen.

- **CRM On Demand Support Alerts**   Provide timely notification of system status to all affected accounts related to maintenance events, system outages, or degraded functional performance. You can subscribe to e-mail pushes of this information by contacting Oracle Support and asking to be added the distribution list for system alerts.

Registration to Receive E-mail Notification

When a new CRM On Demand instance is provisioned, a primary contact for the company account will be designated based on the information provided in the order documents. Oracle distributes critical communications to the primary contact and to any other users who have been designated to receive communications. Changing the primary contact, or adding other users to the distribution list for your account, is a self-service task performed by your current primary contact. It is critical that the primary contact designation is updated (as necessary) while your account is active to ensure you continue to receive important information from Oracle. You should follow the instructions here to update the primary contact or add additional users to the distribution list for important communications.

- To update the primary contact, click Admin | Company Administration | Company Profile | Edit | Update Primary Contact in Company Key Information.

- To update user contact preferences, click Admin | User Management & Access Controls | User Management. Then drill down to User Detail | Edit, and check or uncheck Always Send Critical Alerts in Contact Preferences.

Testing: What Are the Options?

One of the benefits of CRM On Demand is that Oracle completes rigorous quality assurance and testing so the base environment is "production ready" when you log in for the first time. Before any patch or upgrade of the software is released to customers, Oracle tests and debugs the software and tunes the infrastructure. You can be confident, therefore, as you begin the setup process that you have a stable environment that has met Oracle's testing standards required to meet the service-level obligations in the license agreement. We recognize that testing methodologies and standards for "in-house" IT systems vary from company to company and believe it is important for you to consider how your typical protocols should apply in the SaaS model, where many of the obligations are assumed by Oracle.

We do recommend you take steps to verify that usability and performance expectations have been met after your configuration work is complete and before deploying your configured instance to end-users. Conventional User Acceptance Testing protocols are typically sufficient. In this section, we will explain the options you have for conducting testing activities and the advantages and limitations of one environment over another.

Typical Testing Objectives

Before considering which environment or combination of environments you may want to use for testing purposes, consider your objectives. Implementation teams typically require environments for

- Validating that the configuration meets business requirements, object layouts are correct, automated workflows function, and a typical user can execute basic processes

- Verifying that imported data is exposed correctly in the configured object model, custom reports and dashboards expose data accurately, and system performance is acceptable with anticipated data loads

- Conducting web services testing for any integrations or application extensions to your configuration

- Conducting acceptance tests or end-user training

- Enabling ongoing development and testing after the initial production launch

Choosing the Best Environments for Testing

As we discussed in Chapter 2, when your "company instance" is provisioned, you will have access to two environments: Production and Staging. There is a third environment, called the Customer Test Environment (CTE), which is available on request from Oracle Support. Each of the environments has different characteristics that influence their utility for testing purposes. Remember that all of the environments are subject to the policies and restrictions detailed in your user agreement. In the next section, we'll discuss the general benefits and limitations associated with each environment.

Production Environment

The Production environment is appropriate for testing purposes if your requirements are relatively simple, and you don't expect extensive ongoing changes after deploying the application to your users. If you are conducting "one-time" tests before the initial launch, you can easily validate the configuration and data loads in the Production environment, as each phase of your configuration is completed. You can also set up a fictional company test instance on your Production environment, with an identical configuration and dummy data, in order to conduct testing cycles in parallel with your development work or for training purposes. Note that any user license set up in this test instance counts against your subscription. Another advantage is that a configuration tested in the Production environment, with a representative data load, will reflect the actual performance your users will experience.

Staging Environment

As a mirror image of your Production environment, the Staging environment is very effective for testing your configuration and integration work in an environment that contains a (quarterly) snapshot of your production data. The biggest downside to using Staging for testing purposes is the lack of control that you have over the environment. Oracle uses the Staging environment for periodic maintenance, for testing patches and upgrades before they are promoted to your Production environment, and, intermittently, for troubleshooting when a performance problem is encountered. As a result, you should never use your Staging environment for ongoing training or business demonstrations. Your time window for testing activities should be relatively brief and your schedule flexible.

Note that any configuration work done in the Staging Environment will be erased with every quarterly refresh of the Production Environment data. The environment is refreshed as part of a maintenance activity. It is important that any configuration work done in the Staging Environment be well documented and that the work migrated to Production well in advance of the refresh.

Customer Test Environment

The Customer Test Environment is a stand-alone environment that is under your control to use for development, testing, and training purposes. The Customer Test Environment instance is provisioned on a standard, Multi-Tenant production environment that reflects the current release of the application, and it is provided at no extra cost to the you. In addition to standard testing activities, it provides a terrific "sandbox" for ongoing configuration and testing of new functionality, as well as for conducting user training. The environment is not refreshed so you have complete control over the configuration, data, and any integration, without intrusion by Oracle.

The limitation of the CTE from a testing perspective is that you are responsible for configuring your instance and managing data consistent with your production build. You should also compare the scheduled maintenance windows between your test and production environments, as they will likely be different, and your team will need to take this into account when planning their work. Finally, only a limited number of user licenses are available, so you need to plan ahead if you are using the Customer Test Environment for activities that require many users to log in to the service, such as acceptance testing or training.

Summary

This chapter provides an effective orientation to the range of resources included in your CRM On Demand subscription. Now that you know how the self-service model works, you should be prepared to take advantage of these resources as different needs arise throughout your subscription life cycle. As the functionality grows with each new release, Oracle expands the supporting resources to improve your customer experience and the value you receive from the offering. We recommend you take time to educate yourself about the different capabilities referenced in this chapter and integrate them in your CRM On Demand planning.

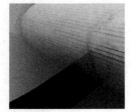

CHAPTER
4

Planning Your Oracle CRM On Demand Implementation

uring the process of selecting CRM On Demand, you probably began to think about the effort that would be necessary to implement the application successfully. What kind expertise would be required? What would the demands be on your organization? How could you estimate the costs and timeframes? And what would be the most important things you could do to increase the probability of adoption? With many questions to answer and decisions to make in a short period of time, planning the launch of your CRM On Demand program can be daunting.

History tells us that technology projects in the front office, particularly in sales organizations, are often challenging to manage with unpredictable results. Although the potential business benefits of automation may be clear, it's always been harder to design an application that will accommodate the variance in sales or service practices, be embraced by the user community, and deliver the expected results. The "people" and "process" factors associated with the use of a CRM application have proven time and again to have a big influence on any actual performance improvement achieved. Yet the time and effort to install the technical infrastructure and customize the application typically consume a disproportionate share of the focus and resources. And when projects become too technology focused, it is easy to lose sight of the original business objectives in the urgency to get a solution into production.

Because the CRM On Demand delivery model eliminates much of the technical complexity for you, many of the challenges and pitfalls associated with deploying traditional on-premise deployments can be avoided—if you leverage the advantages of the SaaS delivery platform and focus your time and energy in the right areas. Despite the variety of customer requirements and the ways that different industry sectors make use of CRM On Demand, the most successful implementations share some common characteristics:

- They start with clear business objectives.

- They have defined processes that support the desired results.

- They build application configurations that leverage the inherent functionality.

- They reflect an urgency to get the solution in the hands of business users as quickly as possible.

These "success factors" are interrelated, and specific decisions need to be made in the planning phase to ensure that each of these factors are addressed in your project plan.

In this chapter, we'll show you how to incorporate these "success factors" into your deployment. We'll also offer best practices for tactical project planning to help you develop a project plan, staff your implementation team, and choose the right rollout strategy for your deployment.

Setting the Course for Program Success

Every company that implements CRM On Demand has a business rationale behind their selection decision. However, many customers fail to translate the initial business case into specific objectives to guide the implementation project, and the system design can become disconnected from the desired results. In the absence of a clear usage model for the new system that supports the broader business goal, user adoption and ROI usually suffer. For example, a company may plan to consolidate customer account and sales opportunity data from multiple legacy systems in CRM On Demand, but not think through how the single new system will be used going forward to improve on current performance. The most successful implementations are lead by people that have clarity about the business results they are trying to achieve with CRM On Demand. They also have an awareness that people need to be guided by processes, enabled by the application, in order to achieve results.

But getting organizational consensus about the desired outcomes BEFORE you start the implementation work can be difficult. With the selection process behind you, and the clock running to deploy the service, pausing to engage business leaders in a conversation to confirm the program objectives and success criteria can be challenging. The good news is that if you establish a clear business context for your program upfront, the rest of your project work should be relatively easy.

Engage Business Leaders

It begins with engaging the business sponsor and key stakeholders. You want the business leaders who will ultimately need to drive adoption to participate actively in defining the business drivers for your CRM On Demand implementation. Although you could probably draft a list of business objectives from your knowledge of the selection process, you'll have missed an opportunity to generate the broader sponsorship for the deployment and "buy-in" among the business leaders that will make a big difference down the road. Ideally, you should work with the executive sponsor to nominate managers and other stakeholders from the business community to form a program steering team. This team should shape the business context for your program and make decisions about the implementation strategy. The time commitment for a typical CRM On Demand steering team should be limited to a couple of working sessions in the planning phase and periodic status meetings until the launch date. We will discuss more about these activities in the sections ahead.

Why is it important to form a steering team to establish the business focus and goals for your CRM On Demand program?

- To be realistic and credible, the business context—objectives and success measures—have to be generated and endorsed by the line management team.

- You'll be more successful if the influential business leaders guide the changes in practices, processes, and expectations that are necessary to achieve the results you are seeking.

■ You'll generate "buy-in" for the CRM On Demand program and transfer "ownership" for driving performance improvement to the leaders who will ultimately drive adoption of the new CRM OnDemand system.

■ Business leaders have insight about the effectiveness of current processes and practices and can nominate subject-matter experts in the organization to assist the project team.

■ A group process will force consensus and be more effective in making key decisions in a short period of time.

Once formed, one or more members of this team should also be available to participate in project status meetings prior to launch. To maintain your implementation timeline and the results focus of the initiative, business leaders should be actively involved in program governance to help make decisions on escalated issues and remove blockers.

How to Establish a Business Context for Your CRM On Demand Program

In this section, we outline an approach to help you define the components of business context that are useful in guiding your implementation.

Figure 4-1 depicts a sequence of activities for establishing a business context in the planning process for your CRM On Demand implementation. By following this approach, the solution you launch will be anchored to specific business outcomes selected by your company's leaders. You should aim to complete the planning activities in this process before you fix the project schedule and deployment timetable. We're going to drill into the steps and provide some examples so you understand the intent and outputs of this approach.

Step 1: Understand the Vision

The process of establishing a business context to your objectives begins by understanding how business leaders view the CRM On Demand initiative and

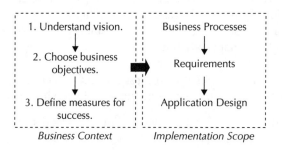

FIGURE 4-1. *CRM On Demand Planning process*

the value they expect to get in return. We call this *vision,* but it is just a simple way to characterize the forward-looking view you want people to have before an initiative begins. Understanding what leaders are thinking as you begin setting objectives is important, because it gives you a starting place for shaping consensus. As you might expect, a leader's expectations can range from being very specific to very high level. What aspects of sales or service execution are keeping your leaders awake at night? How are competitive dynamics in your marketplace changing the way you acquire new customers? What financial pressures are impacting the marketing, sales, and service functions in your business?

When opening a discussion about the "vision" for your CRM On Demand deployment, it is not unusual to find leaders who haven't thought about what they expect from the initiative nor how job expectations should change to drive improvement. Ideally, your business leaders will be aware of the organizational changes that will be needed to complement the technology deployment underway. But if it turns out they view the CRM On Demand implementation as just a technology deployment, you'll want an opportunity to convince them that the way people use CRM On Demand and the underlying processes enabled by the application are critical factors in driving improvements in marketing, sales, or service performance.

For example, when the implementation of CRM On Demand is positioned as simply a replacement of the current system for cost reasons, leaders may expect the new system will mimic the functionality of the legacy system. However, simply replicating what you are doing now can be a mistake and missed opportunity. You'll want to take advantage of the migration effort to improve on current practices and take advantage of CRM On Demand functionality to improve the efficiency and effectiveness of current processes wherever possible.

Sometimes leaders understand the functional capabilities of CRM On Demand, but have not thought through how they expect their employees to use the application in order for the business to benefit. For example, they may talk about how great it will be when CRM On Demand gives them a 360-degree view of a customer's products and services, but they may not have thought through how sales or service people will specifically use that capability to drive revenue or customer satisfaction. When program success is defined only as providing a functional capability, user expectations are likely to be vague and the business benefit will be hard to reach.

Ideally, leaders will view the implementation of CRM On Demand as an opportunity to bring best practices into the organization. For example, many companies use their CRM On Demand deployment as a way to establish a common sales process across the organization with the stated objective of improving pipeline visibility and close rates.

The key questions you should pose for your leaders are

■ How do we want the service to help improve business performance?

■ What changes in work process and job expectations are needed to complement the system to get the results we are looking for?

■ What are realistic criteria for measuring the success of the initial launch?

The point is to understand what your leaders are thinking about CRM On Demand before asking them to choose business objectives. Since the goal is to build consensus around what you are trying to accomplish and how success will be measured, it is helpful to know how different leaders view CRM On Demand and how uniform this perception is among the key players. Don't be surprised if there are differences of opinion about the business context—that's why you put together a steering committee. Acknowledge the differences, and get the team working to define common business objectives.

A couple of final notes on program "vision" and how to leverage it throughout the CRM On Demand lifecycle. As you complete key milestones during the initial implementation, you'll want to check back to make sure the design and configuration of the service continues to be aligned with the initial vision. Also recognize that the "vision" guiding your program should evolve and expand over time as the needs of your business evolve and your use of CRM On Demand becomes more sophisticated. Healthy programs will continue to improve CRM On Demand in order to meet the dynamic changes in their business.

Step 2: Choose Your Business Objectives

With a baseline understanding of how different leaders view the program, you can begin working as a team to define concrete business objectives for the program. *Business objectives* describe what CRM On Demand should enable your company to do better, faster, or cheaper when it is launched. Your company will likely have more than one business objective for the program, which is appropriate. But with a limited amount of time and budget, not all the business objectives may be achievable during the first deployment. It's better to deliver a usable system that satisfies one or two priority business needs with the core features of the product and get it in the hands of the users quickly, than to try and address all the business expectations in the initial launch. We recommend creating a charter document for the CRM On Demand program to record your business objectives and the design requirements for each release cycle. It is helpful to have a written record if you have to defer a business objective to a later release and to maintain a history of the evolution of your unique instance. The discipline of establishing business objectives should continue for each release cycle.

Business objectives may be expressed in a variety of ways. The most typical categories are

■ To improve the bottom line in sales or service performance

■ To enable a standard process or methodology across the company

■ To establish a system of record and single repository for customer, client, or constituent data

■ To gain insight into performance by reporting trends for select metrics

■ To automate an operational task that improves user productivity

Ultimately, you are investing in the service to improve some aspect of organizational performance. The use of technology alone typically has an indirect impact on sales, service, or marketing performance, so it's logical to also define objectives in terms of the process, or behavioral changes, that will be needed to drive improvement. What is important is that your selected business objectives describe how your company expects CRM On Demand to impact results. Your job is to make sure the selected business objectives are expressed with sufficient detail to assess them objectively after launch.

The framework shown in Figure 4-2 will help you to translate the business leaders' vision of desired business outcomes into specific business objectives and success measures. Defining your objectives through the lens of this framework will not only set the goals for your implementation, but also make it much easier to define requirements for setting up and configuring the application. We'll review the model and provide some examples.

■ *Use system.* At the bottom is system use. While using an application will not improve performance by itself, some organizations need to first think about consolidating customer information into a single system. In every case, the application is a necessary foundation for overall improvement. The typical example is to establish a single system of record for all Leads, Opportunities, or Service Requests. Another example is to consolidate customer data in CRM On Demand to get a 360-degree view of each customer's relationship and transactional history.

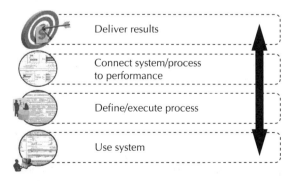

FIGURE 4-2. *Framework for developing business objectives*

■ *Install/execute a process.* The second level speaks to the fact that you need standardized, common business processes that are enabled by the application to drive improvement. Examples of process-related objectives are having a standard Opportunity Management process, Pipeline Management process, SR Escalation process, or Lead Management process.

■ *Connect system/process to performance.* The third level refers to the importance of reporting on the key performance indicators that reveal insights into job performance. These inform management decisions and coaching activities and ultimately tell you how well you are executing the processes and activities that will improve performance. Examples include trend analysis of opportunity close rates, change in average deal size, or aging of service requests.

■ *Deliver results.* The category at the top of the framework captures the sales, service, or marketing performance metrics that should improve with the adoption of CRM On Demand and the processes that are enabled by the system configuration. Examples of results are to improve average deal revenue ($), decrease sales costs, and decrease service request handling time.

Let's take a look at an example from a sales implementation that reflects how vision translates into business objectives and success measures.

The business leaders in Company Q selected CRM On Demand as part of an initiative to install a uniform sales process across the company. They believed that the variance in sales practices and reporting was impacting their overall sales effectiveness and contributing to an increase in their sales costs. Their vision was to invest in CRM On Demand and establish a single sales process across the company to improve top-line sales revenue and improve the efficiency of the sales process at the same time. After meeting to define business objectives, as shown in Figure 4-3, they decided the following:

■ To "deliver results," they want to increase gross sales revenue and decrease the cost of sales. They also want to increase products sold per account and retain a greater percentage of their more profitable customers every year.

■ To "connect system to performance," they want to set up the analytic capabilities in CRM On Demand to report on all sales opportunity revenue in the pipeline, with trend reporting on opportunity close rates, revenue per opportunity, and products per opportunity.

■ To "define and execute processes," they want to develop a comprehensive lead-to-order sales process that will be enforced in CRM On Demand. For the initial deployment, they decide to focus on improving and deploying a uniform Opportunity Management process across the company.

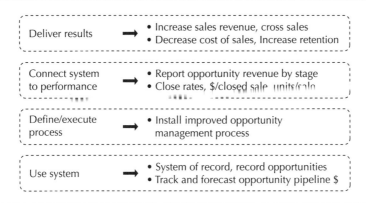

FIGURE 4-3.   *Examples of business objectives*

- To "use system," they agree to make CRM On Demand the system of record for managing all sales opportunities, including the forecasting of revenue and close probability. They also wanted to capture the sales activities related to each opportunity.

As you can see in this example, the customer's original vision to increase sales revenue from the CRM On Demand implementation was broken down into the business objectives that need to be accomplished in order to achieve the desired outcome. Anchored by this broader vision, business leaders and the implementation project team will have a clearer picture of the specific objectives guiding the initial release and can manage the project to achieve those outcomes.

Step 3: Define Success Measures

After the implementation team has identified business objectives, you will have a clearer picture of the application functions, processes, and usage expectations that will form the scope of your initial implementation. But how should you measure the success of the initial deployment? And what improvement should you expect?

Success measures identify the improvement in the performance metrics that will be tracked to assess how effective the solution is when adopted by users. An improvement goal is often set to reinforce the expectation of business benefits from the initiative. Ideally, you should select success measures from the data that can be reported directly from the CRM On Demand application. In most cases, the core processes can be configured in the application to generate the metrics that provide the desired performance insight.

We've found it useful to have business leaders help to select success measures after the business objectives have been identified and the system design has been validated against those objectives. You need to define your success measures, a goal for improvement, and identify a means of reporting them by the go-live date. In most cases, there will not be a starting benchmark of performance against which you can measure improvement. In those cases, capturing performance data in the first few months post-launch is important in order to establish a credible benchmark or starting point for assessment.

Success measures provide

- Focused business targets for users and managers to guide adoption

- An objective means of measuring the effectiveness of the implementation

- Insight into the performance of individuals and teams to target post-launch support where it is needed

Let's look at an example of success measures, illustrated in Figure 4-4, for a customer implementing CRM On Demand for lead management. From a business results perspective, this company wants to improve the efficiency of their lead

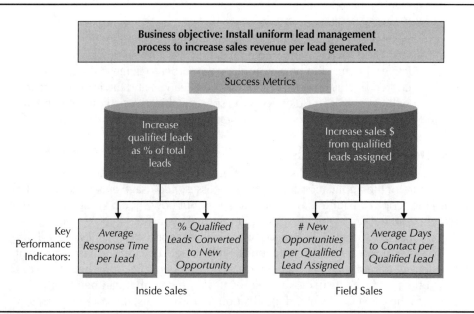

FIGURE 4-4. *Success measures, lead management example*

generation activity and generate more sales revenue. Their business objective for the initial deployment is to implement a new lead management process, enabled by CRM On Demand, to improve the efficiency and effectiveness of their salespeople companywide. They decide to define separate success measures for the inside salespeople and field salespeople based on their respective responsibilities in the lead management process. For the inside sales team, they focus on improving lead qualification, and for the field sales team, on the conversion of qualified leads.

The new lead management process is designed to promote more efficient lead assignment and more thorough lead qualification. For the inside team, the company establishes a specific goal for increasing the percentage of qualified leads, using the Analytics in CRM On Demand to measure *lead response* (elapsed time between receipt of lead and initial contact with potential customer) and *qualified lead conversion rate* (percentage of qualified leads that are converted to sales opportunities). For the field sales team assigned the qualified leads, the company sets improvement goals to generate: more sales revenue from the lead pool, a greater number of opportunities generated from qualified leads, and decrease the average number of days leads age (create date until first contact).

You should define these sorts of success measures in advance of deployment to have objective criteria for assessing the effectiveness of the initiative after "go-live."

Sample Business Objectives

Selecting business objectives for your CRM On Demand initiative will improve your implementation effectiveness in two ways. First, by defining business targets, the user community will be clearer about the overall purpose of the application and what the expectations will be for each user role—provided this information is formally communicated. Second, the chosen objectives will assist the project team in developing a scope of functional requirements for configuring and customizing the application.

As you begin to choose business objectives for your initial implementation, thinking about what you are trying to achieve from a functional perspective can be helpful. Table 4-1 provides examples of business objectives broken down for several typical functional uses of CRM On Demand.

Using Business Objectives
to Guide Project Management

Setting realistic business objectives should be the first step in your implementation project. Doing so will help to define the scope of the application design and allow you to make informed decisions about which product features, configurations, and extensions to deploy in your initial implementation. If you use the framework we

	Lead Management	Opportunity Management	Service Request Management
Expected results	■ Increase number of qualified leads. ■ Reduce lead "spoilage."	■ Increase sales revenue. ■ Decrease sales cost. ■ Expand relationships.	■ Decrease service support costs. ■ Improve customer retention/ satisfaction. ■ Increase use of self-service tools.
Performance insights	■ Lead conversion and close rates. ■ Campaign effectiveness. ■ Performance coaching.	■ Forecast accuracy. ■ Close probability. ■ Sales stage conversion. ■ Performance coaching.	■ Open Service Request (SR) volume, aging trends, % closed on first contact. ■ Average time to resolution (Aging). ■ Deflection/ resolution rates (% closed on first contact).
Processes	■ Implement uniform lead management process. ■ Implement lead scoring. ■ Automate lead assignment. ■ Improve lead qualification.	■ Implement uniform opportunity management methodology. ■ Implement uniform forecasting methodology. ■ Implement customer segmentation for offers, pricing, service level support. ■ Implement Opportunity profiling tool to capture specific data.	■ Implement uniform SR capture and management. ■ Automate escalation process.
System use	■ Create system of record for all lead management activities. ■ Monitor and track lead lifecycle.	■ Create system of record for all opportunities. ■ Create system of record for all sales activities (planned and executed). ■ Record forecast values.	■ Create system of record for capturing and resolving service requests. ■ Monitor and track volume and resolution times. ■ Monitor and track SR lifecycle.

TABLE 4-1. *Business Objectives by Functional Category*

described previously, then determining your business objectives will give you a clearer picture of the

- Business processes to be enabled

- Data to be captured and maintained in the system

- Performance Insights to be derived from Analytics

- Actions to be taken by users to improve performance

A few clear business objectives will help constrain the project scope, so you can generate more accurate estimates of the deployment effort necessary to configure and customize the application, and increase the probability that you can maintain your project schedule and "go live" date.

Once the project is underway, business objectives can help you to manage the project by

- Simplifying the task of gathering requirements by targeting the relevant business functions

- Providing the business context to test the validity of your application design

- Giving you reference points to assess risk and validate progress at each project milestone

From an enablement perspective, clear business objectives and success measures will help your leaders prepare the user community for adopting the new system. They provide you with a specific rationale that explains why the system is being implemented, what the expected benefits will be, and how job expectations will change. We will discuss these issues in greater detail later in "End-User and Management Adoption."

Next, we will highlight implementation planning tips and tactics unique to CRM On Demand that will help you to launch on time and deliver an application that will be adopted and meet the expectations of your business users.

Success Factors in CRM On Demand Implementation Planning

Every new release of CRM On Demand expands the range of processes and requirements that the application can support. But that flexibility comes with a cost. Developing an effective implementation plan for CRM On Demand will require that you balance competing pressures to address an ever-expanding range of business expectations and to launch the service as quickly as possible. Finding the balance between these competing forces is critical to program success. Voltaire's quote that "the perfect is the enemy of the good" is an appropriate admonition for CRM On Demand implementations.

By deploying a workable solution that addresses priority business needs quickly, you may have to defer more complex requirements. But if you can deliver a usable solution that addresses the key requirements with core features of the product, and get it in the hands of users and managers quickly, the business community's reinforcement and acceptance will outweigh the impact of deferring some functional capability.

Plan for Ongoing Improvement

The CRM On Demand delivery platform makes it easy to deploy changes and modifications quickly. In addition, you should expect Oracle to deliver an expanding feature set and administration tools in major and minor new releases every year. By structuring your program to deploy new functions in periodic release cycles (quarterly is appropriate), you'll deliver incremental value as you align the service to the most pressing business priorities. This approach also enables you to take advantage of the new capabilities Oracle is making in CRM On Demand with each upgrade.

The phased approach works best if you are able to limit the scope of features and functions that are deployed to the user community in any given release cycle. As we've discussed, the capabilities that you add should be based on validated business priorities and a favorable cost/benefit assessment. From a project management perspective, smaller, more frequent releases of new functionality will limit your design, configuration, and testing costs. From a business adoption perspective, it encourages user "buy-in" because the changes are more incremental, the learning curve is shorter, and any resistance to change is lessened.

For the initial deployment, you should follow the recommendations we provided to develop targeted business priorities for the program. As we discussed, your business leaders are likely to have a number of priorities. But for the initial launch, we suggest you limit the scope of CRM On Demand capabilities deployed. Select priorities that can be easily configured within the standard feature set and performance capabilities of the current release of CRM On Demand. Going forward, you can address deferred priorities in subsequent releases to your user community employing the same prioritization approach. For example, if you have extensive customization requirements, but the capability provided by an extension is not business critical, you should consider introducing the service to users first and then customize it in a subsequent release. By delivering incremental value through smaller, predictable release cycles, you will build a robust application that is adopted more effectively by your business organization and take advantage of the investments that Oracle is making in the service.

Improve Processes

Customers who spend time to consolidate and optimize business processes before they enable them in CRM On Demand typically deliver the greatest business value. Real performance improvements—as measured by timesavings, cost reductions, or sales/service effectiveness—will depend on the adoption of common business processes you have woven into the application. If your sales, service, and marketing processes vary by geography or line of business (or are undefined in current practice), you should spend time to design common processes that will support the business improvements that you seek. Well-designed sales and services processes are necessary to gain insight into performance. The Analytics capabilities in CRM On Demand, particularly historical reporting, will rely on process-generated data.

So as you begin to focus on a specific business objective, consider any process improvement effort that needs to be included in your project schedule. Key questions to ask are

■ What processes will be enabled by the system?

■ Are those processes currently documented?

■ Are they standardized across the user base and commonly practiced?

■ Do they need to change to drive the business improvement you are targeting?

You'll want to have standardized processes in place that have been approved by business experts before you finalize business requirements. So include any process design and documentation efforts in your project schedule.

Allocate Time for Design

Before jumping into configuration, allocate time to develop an overall design that thoroughly defines the business process, data model, and functional requirements of your release. Developing a design first will validate that all requirements in the scope of the release can be supported by the product's capabilities, as well as expose requirements that might be difficult to achieve through standard configurations. If customizations are necessary, the design process will help you understand how the extension will interact with CRM On Demand. The design exercise will produce a more comprehensive rendering of the application that you can use to gather feedback from business stakeholders before you begin configuration.

Choose an Effective "Rollout" Strategy

Because CRM On Demand can be deployed very quickly, you have quite a bit of flexibility in choosing a rollout strategy that will promote program adoption. In general, you want to choose a rollout strategy that will support the business objectives you are trying to achieve, along with a plan for introducing the new application to your user community. If the new system requires significant change, then you'll limit risk by introducing the application to a small number of users in a controlled environment first, with adequate time to optimize the solution based on their feedback, before moving to the next group. If there is a compelling market event driving implementation, then you may need to launch to a broader audience more rapidly, but you may want to provide more field support resources immediately after launch to resolve performance or adoption issues quickly. When a segment of the user base (either by geographic region or job function) relies on a common business process and customer data to perform their work, plan the deployment so as to minimize disruption in normal business operations. Although there are variations, there are basically three approaches to consider:

- **Companywide by business unit**   Launching to all users in a particular business function or job role and then moving to the next unit or job function

- **All users by region**   Launching to all business users in a defined geographic region regardless of function or role and then moving to the next region

- **Big bang**   Launching the system to all targeted users on a single "go-live" date

Any of these options should be preceded by a "pilot" launch to a small population of users so you can gather feedback, make modifications, and validate that the service meets expectations before rollout to the broader business audience. Your training plan and resources may also constrain the speed of completing the deployment. When you are migrating from a legacy system to CRM On Demand, it may be necessary to schedule the rollout to preserve business continuity as you transition from the old system.

In Table 4-2, you'll find guidelines on the circumstances under which each rollout strategy is recommended.

Regardless of the rollout approach you choose, be sure to complete user validation and testing activities prior to launch. We cover the "how tos" in Chapter 3, in the section "Testing: What Are the Options." You will also find information on testing in Chapter 9 in the section, "Upgrades: Customer Validation Testing." The point here is to ensure that you have completed the configuration process, verified the application performs based on the requirements and design, and has been tuned for production data loads—before beginning your rollout to users in a live production environment. If you are planning a "proof-of-concept" or "pilot" phase in your rollout, be sure to add sufficient time following the completion of those activities, and prior to continuing your rollout, to gather feedback, make adjustments, and conduct a user acceptance test for any adjustments.

Rollout Strategy	Recommended For	Examples
Business unit	Unique business unit configurations/functionality Phased introduction of functionality	Each business unit has unique processes and requirements Phasing in new functional capabilities
Regional or country	Large, decentralized organizations with common processes Multi-country/language	National or global sales organization with uniform practices Deploy, train, and reinforce within operating geographic area and then move to next region
"Big bang"	Mission critical legacy system replacement	Impact of maintaining data in old/new systems

TABLE 4-2. *Guidelines for Selecting Rollout Strategy*

Roles, Responsibilities, and Resource Requirements

In this section, you'll find a brief description of the business and technical roles that we believe are necessary for successfully deploying and managing CRM On Demand. Where appropriate, we include the approximate time commitment for each role for a deployment of average complexity. As you would expect, resource demands are greatest in the initial implementation phase, whenever you deploy new functionality or when validating a major upgrade. If you anticipate using a phased release strategy, then you should consider staffing a team for the ongoing management of the program.

The resources needed for your deployment will depend on the complexity and volume of requirements you've set for your initial implementation. As a general rule, a technical resource with the proper training and experience can fill several roles in projects with a smaller requirements scope and less aggressive timetables. If possible, find a project manager with prior CRM On Demand implementation experience; he or she will be better able to validate the feasibility of your design, assess risks, and help guide you around the typical minefields. If you are unable to staff the implementation team with experienced resources, make sure everyone working on your implementation has completed the recommended training in Chapter 3. Even properly trained staff will need to "ramp-up," so cushion your project schedule if your team is implementing CRM On Demand for the first time. Some customers choose to outsource the system setup work to Oracle or an implementation partner with CRM On Demand experience.

Business Roles

We'll start with the roles that are needed for a successful program on the business side, both for initial implementation and ongoing program management: executive sponsor, business stakeholders, and CRM On Demand administrator.

Executive Sponsor

Executive sponsorship is very important in providing direction and leading the governance of the program. Especially in the initial implementation phase, you need someone with power on the business side of the organization to represent the program's importance, make the big decisions, secure resources, referee political agendas, and overcome roadblocks as issues arise. As discussed earlier in the chapter, the executive sponsor, along with the contributions of other leaders, will define the business objectives and success measures for the initiative and set expectations for adoption as the system is deployed. After launch, the sponsor should participate in the program governance process to ensure the application evolves to meet business needs over time. The executive sponsor should expect to spend at least a quarter of their time on the deployment.

Business Leaders and Stakeholders

Selected representatives of the frontline contributor (user) role and line-management role are needed to provide process and business knowledge input when working out business requirements. These representatives should have a deep understanding of current practices, but also embrace the "vision" of the new system and have knowledge of the target business objectives. These individuals will also validate the design and finished configuration of the application. Post launch, they will also participate in shaping decisions regarding new functionality if you use a phased release strategy. This requires a commitment of several days over the deployment timeline.

CRM On Demand Application Administrator

Over the course of your subscription, the CRM On Demand Administrator has the primary responsibility to maintain and update the system as information changes in your organization. The administrator will know your system design and configuration settings most intimately. He or she will be called on to make timely updates to

■ Global company settings and licensed users

■ Application setup data, lists of values, field and page layouts, and other parameters

■ Product catalogues and pricing tables

■ Data access, visibility, and assignment rules based on your organizational structure

■ Data preparation and execution of one-time data imports

In addition, the administrator will be responsible for the accuracy of sales forecasts, revenue reporting, and creating ad hoc reports and analyses. The ideal candidate will have a deep knowledge of company operations in the relevant functional areas. He or she will also need technical skills typical of a business analyst to maintain the application. Ideally, the administrator will be selected and available to "shadow" the initial implementation during the deployment phase and formally assume responsibility (full- or part-time depending on organizational demands) after deployment. In large organizations, one administrator should be assigned per business unit or geographic area. Selecting your administrator is the most important staffing decision you will make for the program.

Technical Roles

Next we'll move on to the roles that are needed on the technical side: project manager, business analyst, configuration specialist, data migration expert, organizational business analyst, integration specialist, reporting specialist, and training lead.

Project Manager

The project manager will be responsible for resource management, schedule maintenance, milestone review, and risk assessment for the duration of the implementation project. The project manager will also be responsible for providing weekly status updates to the executive sponsors within your program governance structure. He or she will be responsible for quickly escalating any obstacles that require the guidance of the executive sponsors. The ideal candidate will have both strong project management skills and credibility with the business side of your organization. It is also helpful if he or she has experience with SaaS-based project methodology. The role will be a single point-of-contact to manage project communications within your business and IT organization. He or she will act as liaison to the business organization for gathering information for the project team. A majority of the tough decisions will come from the business side; therefore, a project manager with an experienced business analyst's profile is best suited to manage project delivery. The project manager role is a full-time position during the course of the implementation.

Business Analyst

The business analyst will gather and document the business requirements and coordinate user input/feedback during configuration, prototyping, and validation testing. This role is generally part-time during the course of the deployment.

Configuration Specialist

The configuration specialist executes system setup based on defined business requirements. The candidate for this role should have strong technical knowledge of the CRM On Demand application and be capable of completing all configuration tasks, including process automation. This role is generally part-time during the course of the deployment.

Data Migration Expert

The data migration expert will ensure correct data mapping and data requirements are communicated for data import. He or she will be responsible for data sourcing and preparation prior to import and should be available at key points during the business requirements and data import phases. The data migration expert role is generally part-time during the course of the implementation.

Organizational Business Analyst

This resource will facilitate leaders to establish business priorities, define key performance indicators, and lead process optimization, change management, and adoption strategy. Consider a candidate with business consulting acumen if your initiative is broad-based, including changes to your go-to-market model, organizational structure, job roles, business processes, or practices. This role is generally part-time during the course of the implementation.

Integration Specialist

The Integration Specialist will design and develop customizations using web services. If you plan to develop a web services integration, you should work with an experienced web developer to determine your staffing needs.

Reporting Specialist

The reporting specialist should be knowledgeable in CRM On Demand business intelligence capabilities in order to design and develop custom reports. This role is part-time.

Training Lead

The training lead executes training strategy. The role will be responsible for delivery design, curriculum development, trainer certification, and distance learning/classroom delivery. This role is part-time.

End-User and Management Adoption

Anyone who has deployed software technology understands that getting business people to use a system is critical to achieving business results. We've talked about the importance of business objectives and success measures to guide the design and configuration of your application. The business context, as we call it, is also a key driver of adoption. All of the best tactics for adoption rely on the clarity with which you ask people to do things differently in their jobs and explain why. No matter how well you've designed your application, there are still proactive steps you need to take in order to prepare your user community for the change you are introducing. People in general are resistant to change, so your job will be to explain why you are introducing change, how it benefits them, and how you expect them to use the application in the context of their job.

If your CRM On Demand implementation is part of a broader company initiative, effective communication and training will explain how use of the application supports other organizational changes (e.g., to go-to-market strategy, sales reorganization, new sales methodology, or a new service delivery model). If your implementation of CRM On Demand is the only change you are making, your business people still need to know how to access and use the service to do their job effectively.

In the sections that follow, we will explain a recommended strategy to help plan for activating CRM On Demand in your company. Before we get into the assessment of your adoption challenge and the actions you can take to help your user community build the application into the way they perform their job, we want to highlight a few of the other "best practices" demonstrated by more successful CRM On Demand implementations.

- *Start small and add functionally frequently over time.* Consciously limit the scope of your initial deployment and manage your program to introduce new capabilities periodically over time. By doing so, you will increase your probability of delivering value more quickly and reduce the learning curve for primary users.

- *Test application design for usability.* Understand the common tasks performed by the primary users and configure the application to be as simple and intuitive as possible. The "three-click" rule championed by web interface experts suggests that if it takes more than three steps to source a record or complete a task, then the average user will become frustrated and avoid using the application. Take advantage of the application features that improve usability in your design process. To support more complex multistep tasks, consider using the Sales Coach functionality in CRM On Demand to provide real-time performance support.

■ *Make data quality a priority.* The accuracy, completeness, and integrity of the data managed in the application will significantly influence the perceived business value of the program. Limit the historical data you import to CRM On Demand to records that are critical to support your business objectives. Consider the three *Cs* of data quality: Is your data complete, current, and correct? Then make sure the data has been cleansed and de-duped before importing it into the system. Develop a conscious strategy for managing data quality after deployment. The credibility of real-time and historical reporting will depend on data quality.

■ *Get executives and managers to utilize Analytics and reporting capabilities.* In the requirements gathering phase of your project, be sure to identify the information that your managers and executives need on a daily, weekly, and monthly basis to run the business. Then develop reports and dashboards that expose the key insights. By making CRM On Demand the system of record for critical business information and enabling the management team to use its native business intelligence capabilities, you will accelerate the adoption of the system by all users.

■ *Describe application benefits from the user perspective.* Understand how use of the application will deliver value to your customers, company, and the primary users so you can clearly explain the benefits of adoption through your communication and training activities. Business value is typically achieved in one of three ways:

  ■ Automating a task to save time

  ■ Capturing and reporting business activity to better understand current performance

  ■ Providing access to customer data to guide planning and decision-making

Since business benefits are typically realized over time, and only when the application is being used by a majority of your target audience, set realistic expectations about the level of adoption necessary for achieving program benefits.

Assessing the Scope of Your Adoption Program

We've observed how these best practices, or the absence of them, influences the ease and speed of user adoption across a broad spectrum of companies using CRM On Demand. At the same time, your company's culture, the comfort in using technology among the primary user demographic, and the actual change in behavior that you are asking of employees in the primary job roles are the factors that should frame the steps you take to drive adoption. Among the questions you should ask to assess your adoption challenge are

- How will your current automated system(s) for customer management and CRM On Demand differ? Are you moving from a manual data management model or a comparable CRM application? The bigger the shift, the bigger the change communication and training effort needed to prepare users with necessary skills and knowledge to adopt CRM On Demand in their business role.

- How much process variance is there in the way people or groups do their jobs? Will the implementation require people to adopt a single method? Change is hard. User resistance will decline if the purpose and benefits of moving to a standardized process are communicated, and training for the new processes is done in the context of the application.

- How much will daily routines and tasks change after implementation? Will CRM On Demand consume more or less time for the average user? If the new system demands more time to meet organizational expectations, then there will have to be a justification and offsetting benefits. Here again, an effective communication strategy delivered prior to training through the line management hierarchy will explain to the user community not only why adoption of CRM On Demand is necessary in business terms but also what the expectations are for each user role. Communications need to be complemented by effective training to reduce the learning curve by teaching users how to execute routine tasks.

- Will users have discretion in the degree to which they use the new system? The more users have a choice, the more effort needs to go into communicating benefits and reinforcing use after launch. In general, communicate minimum expectations for each user role. Then you will want to monitor user adoption post-launch to identify where remedial training may be necessary.

- Will management consider CRM On Demand the system of record for critical business data and insist on a level of compliance? Management behavior can undermine the adoption of a new system very quickly; executives and managers should be accountable to lead communication and reinforcement activities.

■ Will managers and executives rely on reports and analytics in CRM On Demand to assess performance and make decisions? The best strategy to drive adoption is to use the native business intelligence capabilities to expose the information that managers and executives use to run the business and then train them to use CRM On Demand to access that information.

Human Factors Behind Adoption

With a deeper understanding of the factors behind user adoption, you are ready to build an overall plan that details what you'll do to prepare users. In our experience, effective adoption of CRM On Demand will hinge on three factors:

■ *The degree to which the target audience understands and "buys into" the reasons for implementing CRM On Demand.* The answer to the question of "why" implement CRM On Demand must be rational and credible to the business organization—especially first-line contributors and managers.

■ *The degree to which primary users are willing and able to execute the business processes enabled by the system.* If current methods or processes change when the new system is implemented, the new expectations must be clear, reasonable, and aligned toward achieving the overall business objectives for the program.

■ *The degree to which primary users find that CRM On Demand is accessible, easy to use, and performs acceptably when executing core processes and tasks.* Although there is no completely objective assessment of "usability" or "performance," a majority of the users should be able to access the information they need and complete routine tasks within a reasonable timeframe.

These factors are interrelated, and all three should be addressed when developing the adoption plan for your program. You should also think about challenges to adoption at each level of the organization—users, managers, and executives. The messages, training, and assistance needed may differ depending on user role. Next, we'll detail the deliverables reflected in each element of an effective adoption plan.

Developing a User Adoption Plan

An adoption plan is simply the combination of communication and training activities that you will deliver before, during, and after go-live. The purpose of the activities in an adoption plan is to transition your business community from its current state to a future one where CRM On Demand has been accepted into the fabric of your business culture, and people are using the system to achieve your stated business objectives.

The main elements of a user adoption strategy include the following:

- **Program Charter Document**   Describes the business objectives and success measures.

- **Change Communication Plan**   Describes the timeline of actions to take that will inform the user community and company of the rationale for the deployment of CRM On Demand along with group and individual expectations.

- **Training Plan**   Describes the activities that will teach the front-line, management, and executive users how to use the application.

- **Post Go-Live Support Plan**   Describes the field coaching activities and resources (people and information) to assist users after deployment.

Now we'll give you a brief description of each element and the activities that are typically included.

Program Charter Document

Earlier in this chapter, we provided the background on creating and developing business objectives. You'll want to reinforce those objectives consistently in the program communications and training courses, so having an "approved" document that describes the business objectives for your program and the rationale for selecting CRM On Demand makes sense. By documenting the business context endorsed by the business sponsors, you'll have a reference to distribute to stakeholders and project team members to guide the implementation. We refer to this as the *Program Charter Document.* Having an "approved" record of this information will be very useful in the program governance process, especially in managing project scope creep and in keeping the program focused on achieving business goals versus deploying technology.

The reference document may also include a breakdown of the processes that will be enabled by the system, the key performance metrics that will be reported, management insights that are expected from system use, and expectations for each user role. The document may be revised with additional detail as the project moves from the early phases through the requirements and design phases. This enables project staff to draft messages, presentations for communicating changes, and talking points for training courses from a common reference document.

Change Communication Plan

The user community, both contributors and managers, will be better prepared to accept CRM On Demand when it is launched if they understand "why" the system is being implemented and what the implications are for their job roles. The *Change*

Communications Plan describes the timetable of "events" when information will be delivered to the organization about the CRM On Demand initiative. The plan will include the messaging channel (i.e., e-mail, recorded presentation, live meeting), the messengers and target audience, and content details (i.e., business objectives, launch timetable, training plans). In general, the messengers should be figures of authority who have credibility within the business team. Some of the typical events in a Change Communication Plan include

- A program announcement from the executive sponsor to the entire organization describing program vision project goals and the timeline as the implementation project begins.

- Team meetings led by middle managers to orient users in advance of the CRM On Demand rollout; the purpose is to describe how CRM On Demand will change and improve the users' day-to-day work and the high-level expectations for using the system.

- Pretraining invitations for users; the purpose is to communicate training logistics and system go-live dates, clarify new work process responsibilities, and prepare legacy data for import.

Training Plan

An effective CRM On Demand *Training Plan* will include an end-user curriculum that is scenario-based ("day-in-the-life"), reflecting the expected tasks and processes for each end-user role. It will also detail the delivery modes (web, live session, self-paced learning) and the delivery schedule for coverage of the target audience. While line managers are encouraged to complete the end-user curriculum given to members of their team, the training plan should also include dedicated manager and executive training curriculum. Management training should focus on the use of analytic tools and any custom reports, on how to extract actionable information, as well as on how the system supports any management processes.

Post Go-Live Support Plan

The moment of truth for adoption of any new business application occurs back on the job, in the weeks following the initial "go-live." The most successful CRM On Demand programs provide a safety-net of resources to help users get past the initial barriers they experience when they first begin to use the service. Some of the tactics for support include

- Staffing "superusers" for 1:1 mentoring and assistance in the field

- Capturing how-to feedback from early adopters in the first waves to be shared via a program web site

- Publishing job aides that detail step actions for key processes

- Making program expertise available via an internal help desk with phone and e-mail access

You'll want to design your post-launch support to address the expected change in daily routines and business processes. The key is to help users get the guidance needed to complete a task when otherwise they might have abandoned the system. Field-based support early in the implementation process can be the most cost-effective investment toward achieving a high level of adoption.

Influencing User Adoption

When launching a new CRM system, no amount of extra effort to explain "why" or to train people in the "how-tos" will help them adopt an application that is not aligned with their business reality and designed to help them execute their job responsibilities more effectively. On the other hand, expecting business people to integrate the use of new processes and tools into their daily routines without clarifying expectations and showing them how is not realistic. A well-planned and executed series of communications will create the organizational mindset for change. Hands-on training to help people use an application's features and functions to execute their business processes will reduce the learning curve and accelerate the business improvements at the core of your mission.

Summary

Effective planning of your CRM On Demand implementation requires that you consider many of the factors associated with deploying any business application in your organization. Understanding the business requirements, following a proven project methodology, staffing adequate resources with the right expertise, preparing the user community, and having sufficient executive sponsorship are all important considerations. By taking advantage of the SaaS delivery platform, you can eliminate much of the technical effort and invest your time and resources in the areas that will have the greatest impact on your success. In this chapter, we focused on the things we have learned from prior CRM On Demand implementations, and highlighted the choices and investments made by the more successful customers during their implementations.

As you approach your implementation, keep the following points in mind:

- Taking the time to establish a business context with your business leaders—the objectives and success measures for your initial implementation—will pay dividends in countless ways.

■ If you expect better efficiency or effectiveness in execution, then be sure to optimize the core sales, service, or marketing processes to drive the results you want, *before* beginning to design and configure the application.

■ Leverage the native functionality in the current release of CRM On Demand when designing your initial application configuration. If you have outlier requirements, consider deferring them until you can find the best technical approach to satisfy them.

■ Getting a modest solution into the hands of your user community quickly is always better than trying to build the perfect system. Starting with limited functionality that users can get their arms around and expanding capability in small increments has proven successful time and again.

■ Don't underestimate the change required of users to adopt CRM On Demand. Prepare the business community to use the application through effective communications and training.

Next, we'll dive into the design process for CRM On Demand and the best practices for configuring the application.

CHAPTER
5

Designing Oracle CRM On Demand

n effective CRM On Demand implementation is the result of a well-conceived design that includes modeling where information is stored (customers, contacts, products, opportunities, etc.), and how information flows through the system (business processes). CRM On Demand provides an out-of-the-box model for storing and accessing information, along with inherent business processes to support sales, marketing, and support functions.

Understanding the nuances of the native CRM On Demand functionality has important implications for you, the application designer. CRM On Demand is built with object model and business process best practices in mind. By taking the time to understand these best practices before you settle on a design, you will be able to improve system usability and performance while reducing costly customization and rework. Further, you will be able to effectively leverage as much of the inherent model as possible to accelerate your implementation.

In this chapter, we will review the basic design elements that make up the CRM On Demand application: the fundamental business model, the natively supported business processes, and the available data access and security controls. We'll discuss the underlying structure of each element, how it fits in the overall design, and how you can manipulate each element to meet your configuration needs. Understanding each of these elements is the start to a solid system design.

As you read about the CRM On Demand design elements, keep the following considerations in mind:

- Identify the features that closely fit your business. A feature is a close fit if the basic process steps, entity relationships, and data fields can be used or repurposed to meet your needs. If you find process or data gaps within your particular CRM On Demand edition, review the other industry editions first to see if they provide an existing feature to fit your needs.

- If a particular process is not a good match or is missing key data, you will need to determine whether to reconfigure the process using the CRM On Demand configuration tools or customize the application using custom objects, custom relationships, and possibly web services.

- The built-in analytics and data warehouse were not intended for data mining against large data sets. Rather, because CRM On Demand has optimized the Analytics subject areas to support the main business processes, they are best used for performance reporting and historical trending against the transactional data generated within CRM On Demand.

- Finally, make sure you take the necessary product training. Going into a design phase without a solid grounding in the basic product capabilities will likely result in missed opportunities and costly rework.

Designing the Object Model

The object model consists of the application business objects and their relationships to each other, as shown in Figure 5-1. Here, a business object refers to a representative data store, such as an Account, Contact, or Opportunity. An Account, for example, may have multiple related Contacts, whereas an Opportunity may relate to one Account and many Contacts. Each business object has primary relationships with other business objects and many have several secondary relationships. A Contact, for example, may relate to multiple Accounts, but only one may be the Primary Account.

Understanding the primary and secondary relationships is important when determining the appropriate design. For many companies, the standard Account-centric design will look familiar and easily fit their requirements. For some, a more critical look at the model will be required. As a best practice, strive to craft your deployment around the out-of-the-box objects and relationships. These should serve most requirements and allow flexibility to expand as future needs dictate.

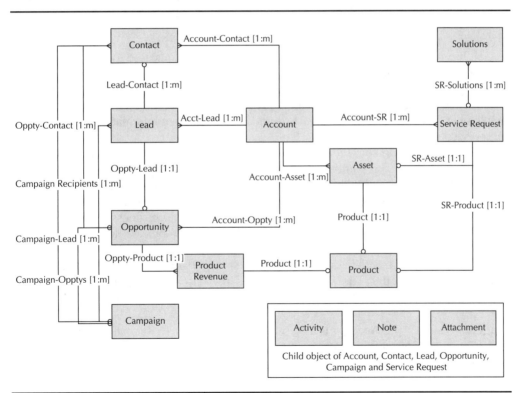

FIGURE 5-1. *CRM On Demand simplified object model*

Baseline Objects

CRM On Demand comes prepackaged with several "baseline" business objects. These objects form the core of the prebuilt sales, service, and marketing functions, and require no special configuration to access. Begin your system design by attempting to map your business records to the baseline objects.

In this and later chapters, we will refer to *repurposing* business objects. Repurposing means using an existing object for a purpose other than what it was intended for. An example is storing financial account information in the Contact Object.

For most predefined business objects, repurposing can be a bad idea. Several have special fields and relationships that make them ill-suited to other uses. Deciding whether to repurpose the Contact Object or use an industry-specific object, or a Custom Object, for example, will hinge on the degree to which the built-in relationships, fields, and processes support the particular business need.

Accounts

Accounts are the companies you do business with, compete with, and partner with. Any information about such business entities (address, annual revenue, industry, etc.) should be stored here.

Special Purpose Fields   The out-of-the-box Account Type field is used to distinguish among Customer, Partner, Competitor, and other types of businesses you may track. Several prebuilt Account Lists refer to this field. The field is also used to drive dynamic layouts, which change the display of onscreen information based on the field value. For example, a Customer Account can store and display different information than a Partner Account.

The values in the default Account Type picklist can be modified and extended through configuration and you can change the label. It is important to recognize that this field is the one field that drives the dynamic layout feature. Consider how dynamic layouts can be used in your design to enhance the user experience and what driving fields and values make the most sense within your business context.

The Reference checkbox field is used to drive the out-of-the-box All Referenceable Accounts List.

The Account Currency field determines the currency (USD, EURO, etc.) for values displayed for the Account. The value set here will also cascade to Opportunities created from the Account detail page.

Relational Design   The Account is a "top-level" record type. That is, other record types (Contacts, Opportunities, etc.) are children of an Account and can be summarized at the Account level.

Assets link an Account to a *Product* in the Product Catalog and represent goods or services that are owned by the Account. This feature may be used to track previous purchases. Assets have a special field labeled Notify Date, which, if populated, will create a reminder for the owner to follow up on the Asset. This reminder may be useful for assets that expire or represent a maintenance or renewal opportunity.

Accounts can have parent-child relationships with other Accounts to represent a subsidiary or branch relationship. This is defined via the Parent Account field. The number of levels in the hierarchy has no hard limit.

Considerations   When considering how to use the Account object, it is useful to think about how you view your customers. Who is the main entity you are selling to? How would you want to roll-up opportunities and activities to a single customer?

In most organizations, the Account is the central point of information about customers. As such, you should enter as much information as possible about your Accounts. Information such as region, territory, and industry can then be used in reports and lists to categorize customers and related information (such as Opportunities within an industry).

Essentially, think about what you want to report on as it relates to Accounts. How will you segment the Account, Sales, and Service information to drive your business toward its stated business objectives?

Contacts

Contacts are the people you interact with when conducting business. CRM On Demand allows users to synchronize personal contacts with their personal information management software (PIM) and track their interactions.

Special Purpose Fields   The out-of-the-box Contact Type field distinguishes among Prospect, Customer, Partner, Competitor, and other types of people you may track. This field is also used to drive dynamic layouts and prebuilt lists.

The E-mail Address field has built-in formatting validation ensuring a *name@ company*.com format. This field also functions as a link to launch the user's e-mail client.

Relational Design   Contacts are related to one primary Account. Contacts can be related to multiple Opportunities, Service Requests, Leads, and Campaigns.

Considerations   The Contact object is modeled to represent an individual. The data fields, the object's relationship to other objects, and the subject areas in reports all reflect the notion that the Contact represents a person. The Contact object should not be repurposed to represent something other than a person.

Opportunity

The *Opportunity* record type is the primary container for sales information. The Opportunity is typically the most dynamic and oft-accessed part of the system in a sales force automation (SFA) implementation and, therefore, deserves considerable attention in the design phase. Effective Opportunity design is a key to driving sales representative productivity and forecast accuracy.

Because the Opportunity is expected to change frequently, and because it serves such a core function, it is one of the business objects with an automated audit feature. Changes to selected fields will be stored in an audit trail, available for export and review.

Special Purpose Fields   The core of the Opportunity is the Sales process, driven by the Sales Stage field. This field is tied to the Sales Process Coach, a feature that provides automated workflow and activity creation. Although you can add and remove sales stages from the default list, you cannot remove or rename the Closed/ Won and Closed/Lost values. Even if your process uses different terminology, keeping these values is important, as they are used to drive automated metric calculations in Analytics.

The out-of-the-box Opportunity Type field distinguishes among Renewal, New Business, and other types of Opportunities you may track. This field is also used to drive dynamic layouts. The Expected Revenue field is a read-only calculated field that displays the Revenue × Probability. This value is rolled up in Forecasts to provide a likely revenue amount.

The Revenue, Close Date, and Sales Stage fields are used in multiple prebuilt reports, including trending analyses. The Forecast checkbox field flags an Opportunity for inclusion in the built-in Forecast.

Relational Design   Opportunities are related to one primary customer Account, multiple Contacts, and a single Lead. Opportunities can be related to additional Accounts as Competitors or Partners.

Product Revenues link an Opportunity to Products defined in the built-in Product Catalog. Multiple Product Revenues can be associated with a single Opportunity, each representing a potential product or service sale. Product Revenue line items each have their own revenue amount, which is the value of Quantity multiplied by Purchase Price. Revenue lines also support recurring revenue opportunities, such as monthly subscriptions.

The total of all the Product Revenues is calculated and written to the Opportunity Revenue field by clicking the Update Opportunity Totals button.

Considerations   Consider how your organization views the sales pipeline, how you forecast revenue, and what key information you need to gauge the quality and progress of an Opportunity.

Driven by the Sales Process Coach, the Opportunity should be the main point of entry for sales users. The Opportunity record should contain as much information as needed to provide a complete picture of the deal at any point in time. Consider how you want to segment and report on your sales pipeline and make sure to include the necessary fields. For example, if you want to view your pipeline based on a class of deal, such as Enterprise or Small Business, include this as a picklist. Keep in mind you can include Account fields in your Opportunity reports, so be cautious about duplicating information that is found in related records.

When designing the Opportunity object and relationships, keep in mind this will be where sales reps are asked to spend most of their time and contribute the most information. Strive for simplicity and ease-of-use to ensure compliance. Dynamic layouts should be used to present a tailored screen based on the Opportunity type, removing unnecessary fields from view. This will simplify opportunity management and improve user adoption.

Lead

A *Lead* is a person who represents an early-stage sales opportunity A Lead can contain a mix of Opportunity, Contact, and Account information. Leads also have prebuilt system functions, represented by the buttons across the top of the screen and are convertible to being an Account, Contact, and Opportunity. The process enabled by these buttons is explored in detail in "Designing the Business Process."

Relational Design   Leads can stand alone or may be related (usually through conversion) to a single Account, Contact, Opportunity, and multiple activities. Leads are typically associated with a Campaign as well, as many Leads originate through marketing activities.

These prebuilt relationships enable an end-to-end view of marketing effectiveness, which is captured in several out-of-the-box reports. For example, a company leveraging these relationships can see how many Leads were generated from each Campaign and the conversion rate of Leads to Opportunities. This provides insight into the overall contribution of various marketing activities.

Leads differ from other business objects in that the available relationships are somewhat more limited. A Lead may be linked to a single Account, Contact, Opportunity, and Campaign. Multiple Activities and Custom Objects can be associated to a single Lead.

Special Purpose Fields   The Status field value is set through the action buttons at the top of the Lead screen. For example, clicking Mark As Qualified on a Lead will change the Status to Qualified. Several prebuilt lists refer to this field along with out-of-the-box Analytics reports. The values cannot be directly edited.

The Source picklist field is used to drive dynamic layouts for the Lead detail screen. Values in this picklist can be changed or extended and the field label can be modified to reflect the best data to drive this feature.

Leads can link to two different Users via the standard Owner field and the Sales Person field. Sales Person is not a required field, but if it is populated, then the user specified will become the Owner of new records (Account, Contact, or Opportunity) created through conversion.

Considerations   Leads are best used as intended—to capture information at the early phase of a Sales process. Typically, Leads are owned and worked by inside sales users until qualification criteria are met or the Lead is disqualified. For all of these reasons, repurposing the Lead object is not recommended.

Because of the inherent relationship among Lead functions (qualify, archive, reject, etc.) and the values in the Status field, we highly recommend you use the existing Status field and values rather than create your own custom Status field.

 Campaign

A *Campaign* represents a marketing effort, often aimed at promoting a particular product or special offer. A Campaign may also be an event, such as a seminar or trade show. Campaign records contain information about the marketing effort, including budgeted cost, actual cost, and revenue target. This information is useful in analyzing the return on investment of marketing efforts.

Relational Design   Campaigns are related to multiple Contacts. The Contact-Campaign relationship is labeled Recipients. The Recipient relationship has additional attributes that track the Delivery Status and Response Status of the campaign vehicle to the individual. These attribute settings can be updated automatically via integration or using E-mail Marketing On Demand (EMOD).

Campaigns are related to multiple Leads. Leads represent the early stage Opportunities that result from Campaign activities. Multiple Opportunities may be related to a Campaign as well.

The Contact, Lead, and Opportunity relationships to a Campaign are important to maintain as they provide the basis for analyzing a campaign's effectiveness. Several prebuilt reports rely on these relationships to give a picture of marketing return on investment.

Special Purpose Fields   The out-of-the-box Campaign Type field distinguishes among various sorts of campaigns (such as Mailings, Seminars, etc.). This field is also used to drive dynamic layouts. The Status field is used to drive prebuilt lists and reports.

Considerations   The Campaign object should be configured to contain all the necessary detail describing the marketing effort. Consider how your effectiveness reporting can be segmented based on campaign attributes. Specific revenue and audience targets should be entered in the Campaign object so results can be measured accurately.

Service Request

Service Requests (SR) contain all information related to a particular support event, such as a product or service problem. Because Service Requests may change ownership (through front-line to specialized resources, for example), changes to SR records are captured in an audit history.

Service Requests are unique in that an Owner is not assigned or required by default. Assignment Manager can be used to automate the distribution of Service Requests based on any combination of attributes.

Relational Design   An SR can stand alone, with no required relationships to other business objects. An SR may be related to one Account and one Contact. Service Requests may also be linked to an Asset that is tied to the Account.

The *Solutions* business object is intended to contain answers to common questions and issues. One or more Solutions may be related to a Service Request. There is no relationship between a Service Request and Opportunities or Leads.

Special Purpose Fields   The out-of-the-box Service Request Type field should be customized to represent the major classes of SRs you expect to handle. This field is used to drive dynamic layouts. The Status field (Open, Closed, Open-Escalated, etc.) is used in multiple prebuilt lists and is used to calculate SR metrics in Analytics. The values in the Status field cannot be modified or extended.

Considerations   Service requests should be configured to capture enough information to allow service representatives to troubleshoot and resolve issues effectively. Consider adding attributes to the SR record to allow for detailed analysis of the types of problems being reported. Use caution when considering repurposing the object or default fields. Of particular note is the Status field. This field should be used as-is, even if your process differs slightly because all SR metrics and aging analysis are derived from it. For example, the average time to close a request is automatically calculated based on the Status changing from Open to Closed.

Vertical Objects

CRM On Demand includes several special-purpose business objects intended for use in specific vertical industry applications, as shown in Figure 5-2. These include financial services, high-tech, life sciences, and automotive verticals. Within these verticals, special business processes have been created, including partner fund management, householding, pharmaceutical samples management, and special event tracking.

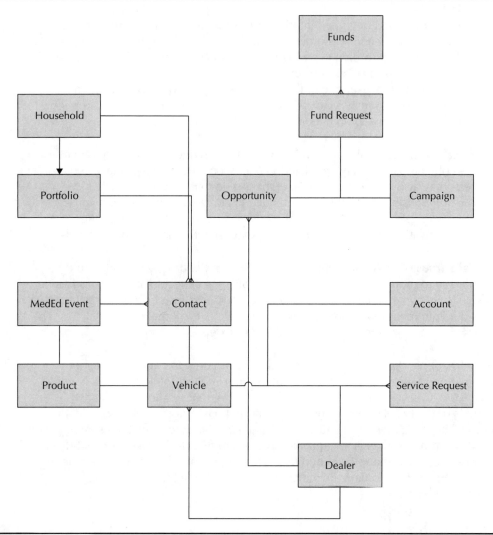

FIGURE 5-2. *CRM On Demand vertical object relationships (partial list)*

Considerations Vertical Objects may be repurposed for other means, but care should be taken to fully consider the supported relationships and built-in workflow. For example, *Funds* and *Fund Requests* have a strict parent-child relationship and an approval process workflow, which ties into the Fund Approval Limit value on the User record.

Fully exploring and understanding these processes before repurposing these objects is critical. Also, factor in reporting requirements when evaluating the suitability of an object for reuse. Investigate the available subject areas and analytics before committing to a nonstandard design.

Custom Objects

Custom Objects are generic business objects. Custom Objects are enabled upon request by Customer Support. These objects have no predefined business purpose and, therefore, represent a blank slate upon which to work. A Custom Object can represent a Quote, an Order, a distinct Asset class, or any other entity. Each company instance can use up to 15 Custom Objects. Custom Objects 1, 2, and 3 can be modeled to have one-to-one (1:1) or one-to-many (1:m) relationships with all other primary business objects.

Although a Custom Object may have many-to-many (m:m) relationships with other key record types (including additional Custom Objects), as shown in Figure 5-3, you are free to model the relationships as needed.

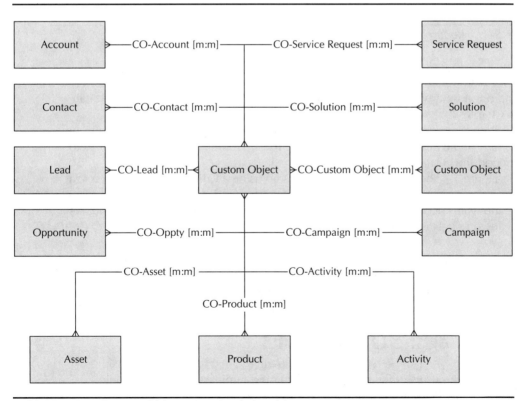

FIGURE 5-3. *Custom Objects 1 to 3 relationships*

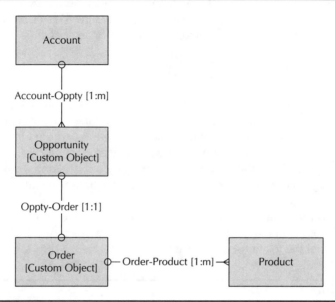

FIGURE 5-4. *Repurposing a Custom Object to be used as an Order record type*

It is important to note that Custom Objects 4+ support only one-to-one (1:1) and one-to-many (1:m) relationships. This distinction is covered in more detail in Chapter 7.

In most cases, your end-users will be exposed to very few of these relationships. As part of the design process, you should illustrate the required relationships to support the business.

Figure 5-4 shows a simplified relationship using a Custom Object to represent an Order record type. We selectively use one-to-one (1:1) and one-to-many (1:m) relationships between the Opportunity (one order per Opportunity) and Products (many products in an Order).

Considerations   Because Custom Objects are so open and malleable, special care should be taken in their design. Start simply; a simple data model drives higher user adoption rates. Just as too many data fields negatively impact usability, so, too, do a large number of business objects and related items.

Modifying the Object Model

Each record type can be renamed, thus allowing you to represent the business object to your users in the manner they are most familiar with. For example, Account may be more recognizable as Company.

The most common, and often most effective, means of modifying the object model is through adding, removing, and changing fields. As noted previously, each of the prebuilt business objects is tailored for a particular purpose; this includes a base set of fields that describe a "typical" Account, Opportunity, and so on. Nearly every company will find that they must modify this somewhat to accommodate its particular needs.

A less common means of modifying the object model is by adding, removing, or modifying the relationships between objects. This is most easily done with Custom Objects. Custom Objects are essentially blank containers. They can be associated with any other major object type simply by adding a Custom Object as a related applet in another object's detail page or by exposing the look-up field on the page.

For example, if a Custom Object is used to contain "Quote" information and you want multiple quotes to be associated to a single Opportunity, the Quote (Custom Object) should be added to Opportunity Related Items in the layout controls. Alternately, if a Custom Object represents an "Order" and you want only one order to be associated to an Opportunity, you could add an Order link/lookup to the Opportunity detail via the field setup layout control.

Modifying the native relationships among the core business objects can also be done by changing the nature of the linking fields and choosing what related information to expose. For example, if you wanted to eliminate the relationship between Opportunities and Accounts, you can deselect the Required checkbox for the Account fields on the Opportunity. The same can be done for Contacts. In this way, you can decouple the business objects.

Removing or adding related items can also change the object model and influence your business process. For example, adding the Opportunity Partners and Competitors applets exposes a secondary Account-Opportunity relationship. A more detailed exploration of configuring the object model will be covered in Chapter 7.

Best Practices for Object Model Design

Consider the following best practices when designing your CRM On Demand application:

- *Don't get hung up on names.* One customer saw the label Accounts and correlated that with his existing idea of Accounts—that of financial accounts held by banking customers. Applying this concept to the company's design was problematic as the inherent object relationships and processes did not adequately support the requirement. Considerable work was needed to customize the relationships.

- *Think about the relatives.* The key area to focus on is the relationships within the object model. As much as possible, leverage the primary relationships that match the business need. In the previous example, the desired relationship was one contact to many financial accounts. What other possible object model could have been applied? Perhaps modeling the financial accounts as an industry-specific or Custom Object would have been preferable.

■ *Renaming the data objects is usually trivial; rewiring the object relationships is not.* An Account can easily be renamed "Company" or "Business." Likewise, Opportunities can become "Deals," and Leads can become "Prospects." Consider the underlying purpose of these objects, as discussed earlier in the chapter, and their relationships to other objects, before creating new ones.

By using the existing objects and primary relationships, reporting and analysis is much easier. These are shown in Figure 5-1. Many secondary relationships are supported in CRM On Demand Analytics, but it is often more difficult to develop reports using secondary relationships. Out-of-the-box reports and the most well-developed Analytics subject areas give preference to the primary relationships.

■ *Pay close attention to the out-of-the-box fields and picklists before changing or creating custom fields.* You may find that an out-of-the-box field serves your needs with a simple label change. Note also that several baseline fields have a special purpose in CRM On Demand and changing or removing them may limit the effectiveness of some analytical reports, dashboards, and prebuilt lists.

For example, the Status field on Service Requests is used to calculate metrics such as # Of Open SRs, Average Days Open, and Average Time to Close. If you remove the Status field and replace it with a custom field, you will lose the use of these precalculated metrics and the advantages that go with them.

■ *Use caution when modifying the native relationships.* Removing relationships (such as making Account an optional entry in the Opportunity) may result in "orphaned" records that are difficult to find and may not appear in reports. Thoroughly review and understand the embedded business processes (examined later in this chapter) before changing the object model. These go hand-in-hand and should be a continuum of design.

■ *Start simply.* Above all, start with the simplest object model design that most closely matches your business needs. As gaps are identified, consider how other inherent relationships may be leveraged. Selectively expose expanded or secondary relationships as needed.

Customizing Business Processes via the Object Model and Workflow

As we've shown in our review of object models, CRM On Demand comes prebuilt with fundamental business elements. These elements are designed to cover the basic needs of most customers, though for some they may be simplistic. Every company will likely see a need to customize the objects and the processes to fit its needs. The important point here is that you should *first* have a solid understanding of the inherent design.

The best practice is to stay as close as possible to the out-of-the-box process design and augment only as needed. That is, do not try to change or modify a core design element fundamentally. For example, although your Sales process may seem substantially different from the model in CRM On Demand, you should retain the built-in Sales Stage field to reflect your process steps. Configure the discrete stages and related probabilities and coaching steps, but retain the fundamental concept of a driving process.

Staying close to the inherent process will reduce design time (much work has already been done for you), ensure support in integrations and analytics, and will be less confusing to end-users (built-in lists and documentation refer to these processes).

Designing the Business Process

CRM On Demand provides robust support for Marketing, Sales, and Support processes. Built upon the baseline business objects and relationships detailed in the previous section, these processes are reflected further in the out-of-the-box fields, workflow, and prebuilt lists, reports, and dashboards. A successful design will fully leverage the existing process and tune it, via configuration, to suit your particular business need.

Campaign Management Process

CRM On Demand provides Campaign Management capabilities to track the progress of a marketing event or project from inception to completion, as shown in Figure 5-5. Through the life of a marketing campaign, the Campaign record serves as the central point of data collection and should provide a snapshot of a campaign's state at any point in time.

- **Create Campaign**   A Campaign record is created directly in the application or via import. Basic information must be entered, including Campaign Name and Source Code. Planned start and end dates should be entered as well.

- **Add Campaign Details**   Add and update additional Campaign attributes as the campaign progresses. The out-of-the-box Status field is tied to the Campaign dashboard and should accurately reflect the Campaign state at

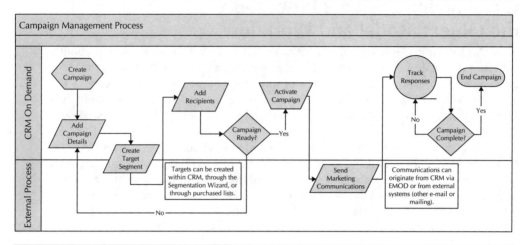

FIGURE 5-5. *The Campaign Management process*

any point in time. Cost, revenue targets, and Campaign Type further help to distinguish the campaign and provide attributes that can be leveraged for later analysis.

■ **Create Target Segments** CRM On Demand lists, reports, or the Segmentation Wizard can be used to build your target segment. You can also use external data sources. Create segments based on Lead or Contact attributes that meet the campaign's requirements. Leads can be loaded and linked to the Campaign via import. Contacts should be linked to Campaign via the Recipients relationship (see the next item).

■ **Add Recipients** Recipients are the Contacts who are receiving your marketing communications. This feature is most often used in conjunction with e-mail marketing. Once you have established your target list of Contacts, you can load it via import as Recipients. Using Recipients allows you to track the Delivery and Response Status of your communications.

■ **Activate Campaign** Once the Campaign record is fully (and accurately) defined, the marketing team determines if it is ready to be activated. This step can be simple, or you can use a workflow to create a more involved Campaign approval process. For example, the Status field can be restricted to specific user views, so only marketing managers can activate a campaign. Workflow events can spawn alerts or tasks based on Campaign attributes. These tools can be configured to facilitate collaboration among marketing users as campaigns are planned and executed. When ready, set the Status to Active and begin marketing activities.

- **Send Marketing Communications**   These activities occur outside of CRM On Demand and typically consist of e-mails, mailings, invitations, or other marketing communications sent to identified targets. Recipient's Delivery Status is updated either through integration or manually.

- **Track Responses**   Recipient Response Status can directly reflect the Recipient's action. The goal of a campaign, however, is to generate viable leads. As responses are received, Leads are created and updated. Leads can be entered programmatically through integration or manually by users.

- **Campaign Complete?**   When the campaign reaches its goal, change its Status to Completed, and the Campaign is considered closed.

Along the way, all activities related to the planning and execution of a marketing campaign are tracked. Once completed, the Campaign record provides a detailed history of the project and adds to the information repository available for analysis.

Considerations for the Campaign Management Process

Consider how your internal process matches or differs from the inherent process in CRM On Demand. What extra steps are part of your process? Where does the information that drives the process reside? What kind of approval process or workflow is employed by your marketing teams? How are your marketing efforts measured and reported?

Sales Process

In CRM On Demand, the Sales process can be visualized as a progression along two sub processes. The Sales process begins with Lead Management and continues in Opportunity Management. These processes are typically undertaken by different roles within an organization and each deserves significant attention in the design phase.

Lead Management Process

The Lead Management process in CRM On Demand encompasses all activities related to identifying and developing early-stage revenue opportunities. Figure 5-6 shows a basic Lead Management process. As discussed earlier, the Lead object is a flexible container of information about the Contact, Account, and Revenue potential.

- **Create & Assign Lead**   Leads may come from many sources such as trade shows, responses to marketing campaigns, and directly from reps. CRM On Demand provides multiple channels for Lead input. Leads can be created via direct input, import, or web services integration.

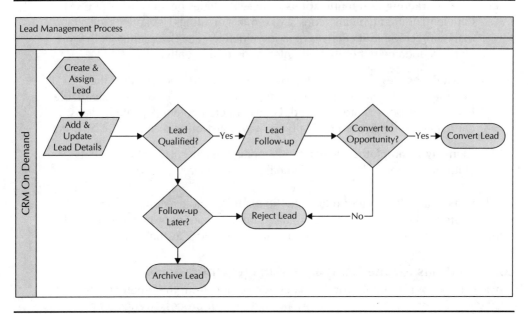

FIGURE 5-6. *The Lead Management Process*

- **Add & Update Lead Details** Often only sparse information is provided in the initial Lead input. For example, the initial lead could be a business card or an attendee badge from a trade show. Once a Lead is assigned (either directly or via Lead Assignment rules), the owner should begin to populate the Lead with additional information, such as product interest, revenue potential, and details about the company and person. This includes adding related information such as scheduled and completed appointments and tasks. New Leads are given a default Status of Qualifying.

- **Lead Qualified?** The built-in Lead Management process drives users to qualify a Lead. Lead Qualification criteria may differ from company to company and the user should understand this. Typically, qualifying the Lead involves validating the Lead details (Is the phone number/e-mail accurate? Is the Lead already a customer or opportunity?). Qualifying the Lead (by clicking the built-in button) changes the Lead's Status from Qualifying to Qualified. If a Lead is not qualified, it can be Archived (Archive Lead) or Rejected (Reject Lead). Again, the Status field will be changed to reflect this action.

- **Convert Lead** Qualified Leads may be further worked by the sales rep to confirm that a revenue opportunity exists (Convert to Opportunity?). Actions may include multiple interactions via phone or e-mail with the Lead. If the Lead is considered a viable opportunity, it should be converted to an Opportunity.

Choosing to convert the Lead creates (up to) three new records: an Account, a Contact, and an Opportunity. If the Sales Person field is populated, then that user will become the Owner of any newly created records. During the conversion process, the field values on the Lead are copied to fields in the target records.

The process can be further configured to require or exclude any of the three target record types. For example, conversion may require an Opportunity be created but not an Account. The option to create or link to any of the three record types may be removed through Lead process configuration.

Considerations for the Lead Management Process   The Lead Management process is not a good candidate for modification given the robust underlying processes "hard wired" into it. Augment the Lead information as needed, but consider working within the existing process. If the out-of-the-box process does not fit your requirements, then consider alternative approaches. For example, Leads can be tracked as part of the Opportunity process (as initial Sales Stages) or via a Custom object. Keep in mind, though, that employing an alternate object for the Lead will sacrifice the benefits offered by the prebuilt lists, Analytics, and performance metrics.

The Sales process continues with Opportunity Management.

Opportunity Management Process

The Opportunity Management process in CRM On Demand encompasses all activities related to developing revenue opportunities, as shown in Figure 5-7. The Opportunity record serves as a central collection point for details on the potential sales transaction. The driving field for Opportunity Management is the Sales Stage. The Sales Stage is the core of the Sales process and should be defined to match your organization's established or desired processes.

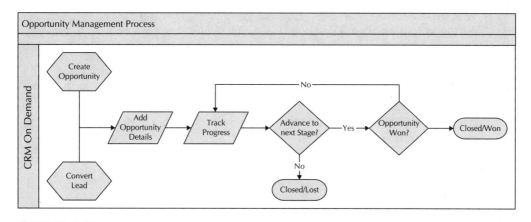

FIGURE 5-7.   *The Opportunity Management process*

A typical Sales process includes the following Sales Stages:

- **Qualified Lead**   Typically, the default stage for converted Leads.

- **Building Vision**   Sales activities are focused on defining needs and providing a fit for the solution.

- **Short List**   The prospect is seriously considering the solution.

- **Selected**   The prospect has accepted the solution and indicated a preference.

- **Negotiation**   Terms are shared, amended, and finalized.

- **Closed/Won**   The deal is completed, and the sale is won.

- **Closed/Lost**   The deal has been abandoned or lost to a competing provider.

Your Sales process could differ substantially from this example, but should represent a logical sequence from identifying the Opportunity (either directly or via a converted Lead) to closing (winning or losing). The Sales Stages should be detailed enough to provide management with a clear picture of where the deal is at anytime, yet remain broad enough to accommodate many different situations.

Closed/Won or Closed/Lost represents the last stage in the process and cannot be modified or removed, due to reporting and forecasting considerations. These stages should be used in every Sales process. The CRM On Demand Sales Process Coach allows management to further influence or dictate how an Opportunity is approached as it progresses from stage to stage. The Sales Process Coach provides the following for each Sales Stage:

- **Required fields**   Based on the stage, you may force the entry of information in Opportunity fields. For example, you can require an entry in a Reason Won text field when the Sales Stage is Closed/Won. The user cannot save the Opportunity with the updated stage until a value has been entered in the required field.

- **Sales Process Coach steps**   For each stage, provide specific instruction for the user. These instructions can help reinforce desired behavior throughout the Sales process. For example, during the Negotiation stage, the process steps may include direction on who to contact for contract templates and legal approvals. This feature can be especially useful as an aide in training new sales representatives and in distributing updates to sales policies. Note that the steps provide textual guidance and do not contain any logic to enforce recommended actions.

- **Automated tasks**   When a deal progresses to a new stage, tasks may be automatically created with default values and assigned to the sales user or another user related to the Opportunity or Account. These tasks can reinforce the actions specified in the coaching steps. For example, when a deal moves to the Negotiation stage, an automatic task can be scheduled for the user to contact Legal within 15 days.

- ■ **Useful resources**   Documents, web links, and other files may be loaded into the Sales Process Coach related to a specific stage. Again, these should be relevant to the steps and tasks implemented for the stage. During the Negotiation stage, to extend our example, a web link to an internal contract template repository may be added.

All of these features provide real-time feedback as an Opportunity moves through the process. Effective use of these features can improve compliance with business standards, reduce user training time/costs, and help managers to focus on other areas of sales development.

Throughout the Sales process, numerous interactions are likely taking place and changes to the deal occur as time passes. The Opportunity Detail page, showing the deal details, related activities, contacts, and partners, should give a comprehensive picture of the deal's state at any point in time.

Multiple Processes

CRM On Demand allows your company to set up multiple Sales processes—an entirely distinct set of stages and related actions, steps, and resources. When using multiple processes, each process must be associated to one or more Opportunity types.

For example, you may engage in separate selling procedures for new Opportunities vs. renewal Opportunities or small vs. large Opportunities. The steps a sales rep is expected to follow and all the related guidance can be completely unique. Furthermore, your sales users can be segmented so that one group works only with a specific process. In this way, you can enable a direct sales organization to work small, transactional opportunities, and a field organization to work large, multifaceted opportunities. Used in conjunction with dynamic layouts, the user's experience of each sales group can be uniquely tailored to his or her needs.

Sales Categories

When employing multiple sales processes, it is especially important to leverage Sales Categories. Each Sales Stage can be associated to a Sales Category. Think of Sales Categories as a "macro" sales process; the categories should be broad, universal buckets that help classify deals across the various types. For example, your Sales Categories may simply be Early, Middle, Late, signifying the broad sales process period the deal is in. Each category may itself contain several Sales Stages from each Sales process. By using the Sales Category, Opportunities can be grouped using a common method, so a combined view of strategic and transactional opportunities or deals across various business lines can be summarized based on their Sales Category, for example, if they are early or late stage deals.

Considerations for the Opportunity Management Process   The Opportunity object should be configured to capture the information most relevant to sales users and managers. Explore and utilize the Sales Process Coach to ensure that users are adhering to standard policies and procedures.

Do not employ a Custom Sales Stage picklist field; the built-in Sales Stages can be modified to meet most needs and these are wired into numerous reports and metrics. Because the business object and the process are purpose-built, the Opportunity object is a poor choice for repurposing.

Forecast Management Process

CRM On Demand has a built-in Forecast that automatically rolls up Opportunities and prepares a comprehensive report for management. The basic process is shown in Figure 5-8. Often, the native Forecast is supplemented by more detailed custom Analytics. For example, reports can be used to provide forecasting and pipeline reporting along various dimensions, such as region or market segment, which the native Forecast cannot.

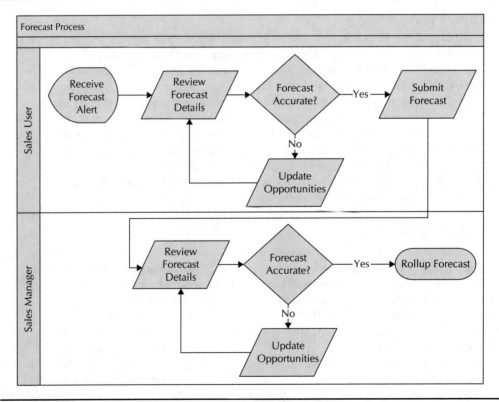

FIGURE 5-8.   *Forecast Management process*

Forecasts can be based on any of the following:

- Opportunity revenue

- Product revenue

- Product quantity

- Account revenue

- Contact revenue

The Forecast should be used to reinforce a process (for example, of reviewing and submitting commitments on a weekly basis) and to give management a high-level view of sales performance.

The Opportunity Revenue Forecast process includes the following steps:

1. **Automated Forecast Collection** On a predefined schedule (weekly or monthly), an automatic process runs that collects snapshots of the current disposition of all included records and users.

2. **Notification** Users included in the Forecast receive a notification and are directed to review their forecast.

3. **Forecast Review** Users review their Forecast detail, including the following fields:

   - **Forecast** The sum of all Opportunity revenue in the Forecast period, based on Close Date, where the Forecast checkbox is checked.

   - **Pipeline** The sum of all Opportunity revenue on all records included in the Forecast period.

   - **Closed Revenue** The sum of all Opportunity revenue where the Sales Stage is Closed/Won.

   - **Expected Revenue** The sum of Expected revenue on all Opportunities included in the Forecast period.

   - **Quota** The Forecast owner's quota for each month in the period, as defined by the administrator.

   - **Quota %** A calculated value of closed revenue divided by Quota.

4. **Forecast Updates** After reviewing the Forecast snapshot, users can update the forecast:

   - **Forecast** The Forecast field is pre-populated but can be overwritten by the user.

- **Best Case**   This is an open field available for providing an upside amount.

- **Opportunity Updates**   Underlying Opportunities can be individually updated.

- **Rollup**   To capture any changes in the underlying data, users can choose Rollup to refresh the snapshot.

5. **Forecast Submission**   Once a Forecast is ready, users click Submit to send the Forecast to their manager. Submitted Forecasts are no longer available for editing.

Managers have a slightly different view of Forecasts, which includes summaries for each of their subordinates by month and the ability to drill into each of their Forecasts. Forecast configuration allows managers to submit their Forecasts without waiting for all child forecasts to be submitted.

Considerations for the Forecast Process   The Forecast process relies on the user hierarchy, which is defined by each user's "reports to" relationship to other users. Forecasting works best when there is a clear hierarchy up to a single top level. Breaks in the hierarchy can cause the Forecast process to fail. Keep in mind that users are not directly added to the Forecast; rather, they are added by virtue of their Role. So all users in any included Role must have an intact management hierarchy.

Forecast offers few options for configuration once the initial settings are in place (Frequency, Forecast Type). For most organizations, this is sufficient. If the native Forecast detail screens do not meet your requirements, consider implementing Forecast Analytics reports or leveraging a Custom object.

Service Request Management Process

The Service Request Management process, shown in Figure 5-9, includes all data capture and activities related to a support incident. The Service Request record collects all information related to the incident, including the customer and contact information. A typical support process includes

- **Receive Customer Communication**   Communication from the customer can come through many channels—e-mail, phone, web, etc.

- **Create Service Request**   Initial entry into the system may occur automatically via web or e-mail integration, or via manual input by a support representative.

- **Enter/Update Details**   However the initial SR is entered, a support representative must review the information and ensure it is accurate and complete. Specific details about the incident, such as the products or versions involved, are added to the SR.

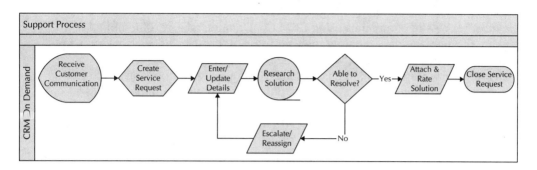

FIGURE 5-9. *Service Request Management process*

- **Research Solution** With detailed information in hand, the support representative seeks to find a resolution to the problem. This may involve searching an internal knowledge base or reaching out to other resources.

- **Able to Resolve?/Escalate/Reassign** If the support representative cannot resolve the SR, it may be reassigned to another user. Reassignment can be done by directly changing the owner, via SR Assignment Rules, or through a custom workflow. The latter two approaches allow a consistent logic to be applied in the routing decision. For example, an SR related to a specific product may be assigned to a product specialist when escalated.

- **Attach & Rate the Solutions** The Solutions business object houses information on answers to common problems posed via SRs. Solutions typically contain a summary title (suitable for quick searching) and a detailed description. Once SR details are collected, users can search the available Solutions for a possible answer.

  Once found, the Solution is linked to the SR. Solutions can be rated by users. The average rating is used to rank Solutions in the Highest Rated Solutions list (visible on the Solutions Home Page).

- **Close Service Request** When an SR is resolved, its Status is set to Closed.

Considerations for the Service Request Management Process

Generally, the Support object and Support process can be modified as needed to suit your requirements. Do not remove or attempt to override the native Support Status field. These values are used in CRM On Demand Analytics to calculate metrics such as average age and time to close. Add your own substatus field if needed.

Business Process Design Basics

The most successful companies using CRM On Demand take considerable time in thinking through and documenting their business processes. Using visual tools to model a workflow can be an effective way of validating a process prior to implementation. Starting with a basic process and adding components, such as activities to be logged into the system or "offline" tasks to perform, as well as approvals required, can offer clues about the detailed configuration needed. For example, a certain company uses Lead Quality as criteria for promoting Leads to Opportunities. There are half-dozen criteria that determine the Lead Quality. When moving into the configuration phase, the company will likely want these criteria on the Lead page (see Chapter 6 for more configuration best practices).

Overlay your user role onto the process. These overlays are often referred to as *swim lanes*. In Figure 5-10, each "lane" or horizontal box represents a person, role, or functional group. In most organizations, many people play a role in any one process.

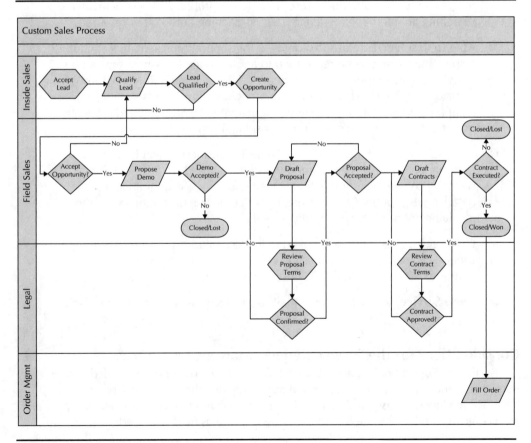

FIGURE 5-10. *Custom business process*

Opportunity Management may involve individuals from sales, marketing, product management, finance, legal, and executive staff. Each may have a part to play as the Opportunity progresses. By plotting the process across the swim lanes, it becomes apparent where workflow or other special configurations (such as a unique page layout for a particular user role) may be required.

Designing Data Access and Security

CRM On Demand employs a role-based access and visibility model. This means that the rules dictating what a user can and cannot do or see is defined in a Role. Roles such as Field Sales Rep, Executive, and Administrator are available out of the box. These Roles can be modified and new Roles created to achieve the necessary mix of privileges and access rights.

The advantage of the role-based model is that it allows you to apply a consistent set of privileges across an entire group of users very quickly. When a Role needs to change, an existing Role can be copied, modified, and tested, and then pushed out to users by simply changing one field in their User record. Role definitions should be thought of in context of the business processes you are enabling.

Most companies already have established roles/functional areas within their organization. This is a good starting point. When you cross those roles with the procedural business processes, you begin to see clues about how one role will need to be implemented differently from another.

For example, in our Opportunity Management process, we require a legal review if a deal has special terms. Only a user in Legal (i.e., with a Legal Role assigned) can indicate that a deal has been approved. This can be enforced by providing the Legal Role with access to fields that other users cannot see or update. Roles allow you to do this.

Functional Aspects of Roles

Roles dictate what a user can do and influence what data a user can see. Privileges are specific functions in the system, such as converting a Lead or running Analytics reports. Consider what a user will need to do in the system and provide the simplest possible mix of privileges (these can be extended later as needed).

The user experience can be tightly controlled via Role settings. Here are a selection of Role settings that should be carefully considered:

- **Default Sales Process**   In a multi-process environment (see the Sales process discussion previously), giving each user a starting point or default process is important. This is also defined at the Company level; if no user default is designated, the Company default will be used. For a user in Inside Sales, it is best to define their default Sales process as Inside Sales so when he or she creates a new Opportunity, the correct process is automatically applied.

■ **Record Type Access**   Within the Role setup, you can completely remove entire business objects from the user interface and define what can be created. These settings neatly bracket what a user can do and most fundamentally affect the user's experience. For a Sales user, Leads and Opportunities will be visible (Has Access) whereas Service Requests and Solutions may not. A user should have access to those business objects he or she interacts with; others should be hidden.

You can also make a single change to allow a Role to Read All Records of a specific type. Use the View All Records setting with caution: it may be the easiest way to give a group of users access to what they need, but consider it a blunt instrument. If any records, now or in the future, need to be protected, then this setting must be removed.

■ **Tab Access and Order**   Similar to above, this area of Role settings dictates what a user sees when he or she logs in. Should the user see only a few key tabs or a wide array? Again, err on the side of simplicity or least privilege; expose only what a user's Role requires to complete his or her job tasks. Areas that the user does not frequently access, but may require, can be hidden but available if needed.

■ **Page Layout Assignments**   Different Roles should have page layouts that reflect their part in a business process. Layouts can be shared across many Roles, but it is important to provide users with a view of information that is familiar and in context with their overall process.

A significant amount of process control and workflow can be driven purely from page layouts. As in the previous example, one role (Legal) is given a page layout that has been simplified to contain the information necessary to evaluate nonstandard terms. A picklist field may indicate if the deal has been submitted to legal, is pending approval, or has been approved or rejected. This field may be read-only to the Sales user but editable in the Legal Role layout. Furthermore, the Sales Process Coach could be used to restrict an Opportunity from moving beyond a particular stage until another field is populated—one that may only be accessible to another Role. Whenever considering the path a record takes along a business process, think of how the fields may be presented, protected, or hidden depending on the viewer.

Earlier in this chapter, we referred to "dynamic layouts," which are driven by special fields on the main business objects. Multiple dynamic layouts can be created for each object. When assigning Page Layouts to a Role, you can set layouts as static or dynamic. This combination allows for an incredible amount of customization, effectively tailoring the role ever more tightly to the job function.

■ **Access Profiles**   This setting discretely defines what a user can do with an object: Read, Write, Edit, Delete. It also extends to related information, so you can decide what a user can do with, for example, Contacts related to an Account the user owns, giving you a very fine degree of control over the user's actions. A single Access Profile can be shared among many roles. So changing one Access Profile may impact multiple roles and several roles may require only a handful of Access Profiles.

Considerations for Roles and Access Profiles

Start with the Roles and Access Profiles provided out of the box. Copy the one closest to your needs and refine the settings as required. Keep in mind that Owner Access Profiles affect how a user can interact with records he or she owns directly. Default Access Profiles are in effect when a user is viewing a record he or she does not own. We'll discuss the available access controls in more detail in Chapter 7.

Analytics Access

Access to data within Analytical reports can be controlled somewhat independently from general user interface access. At a company level, Analytics access can be set to honor Manager Visibility or Team Membership, or both (Full Visibility). If this access is specified at the individual user level, it will override the Company setting. The Role-Based Can Read All Records setting will honor the Read All option at the Role level. For example, if you enable a role to Read All Activity records then any user with that role will be able to run reports containing all Activities in the system. Care must be taken when considering reporting needs, as they may require an approach that is different from that employed in the general user interface.

Access All Data In Analytics, which is set in Admin: Role Management: <Role Name> : Privileges, effectively overrides any other Access Control scheme. With this privilege enabled, a user can see all records in a report. Note that this does not mean the user can get access to all records; it means that when he or she runs a report, there are no record-level access restrictions that are invoked. The information the user sees in the report is still a factor of the filters applied and the fields exposed.

To restrict access in reports when this privilege is enabled, here are a few tactics:

■ Restrict report access via Shared Custom Analyses Folders. In Content Management, administrators can grant access to shared folders by Role. Once a folder is associated with a Role, it is no longer visible to other Roles, with the exception of the Administrator Role (and any Role created as a Copy of Administrator).

■ Within shared reports, employ filters to ensure that private (nonpublic) data cannot be seen. For example, filter out Accounts in a particular Territory.

■ Also within the report, expose in the layout only those fields that are necessary to convey the information. Analytics reports typically consist of charts and graphs; these can convey a great deal of information without exposing a lot of data.

■ Disable drill-down in reports so users cannot get to the underlying data records. Some reports have a Default Interaction setting on Column Properties, which will enable click-thru to a more detailed level of data. Change this setting to No Interaction.

Considerations for Analytics Access

The Access All Data In Analytics setting is most often used for Management, Executive, or any Role that needs to access to high-level metrics from the application, or for analysts who are asked to provide such data. Be careful to grant this privilege only when needed and to a minimal number of Roles. If All Access is not granted, then the application will honor settings at the Company or User level. If there is a need to employ complex visibility rules in Analytics, allocate time for adequate testing and user training.

Best Practices for Designing Access and Security

Your data access scheme should enable the business processes outlined earlier in the chapter. That is, users must be able to interact with records in the manner required by the business process. Consider the functions users must perform during the process. Do they require the ability to create, edit, or delete records? Is Read-Only access enough?

Start with the most restrictive access—again employing the principle of least privilege. It is easier to add access to data, through any of the mechanisms described, than it is to take access away. Consider whether any user groups have data that is "off limits" to other users. If so, then this immediately eliminates the Can Read All Records option on all user roles. It is often harder to implement such an access scheme, so weigh the necessity of such restrictions against the effort required.

An overview of each access scheme is given here. A more detailed analysis of each is offered in Chapter 7.

■ **Manager Visibility**   This scheme is easy to implement as long as the user hierarchy is maintained. This scheme may be too simplistic for many organizations, such as those that have cross-functional roles like Sales Consultants or Product Specialists or alternate hierarchies such as Product- or Customer-based. Manager Visibility performs well for small to mid-sized organizations, but may degrade performance when reporting hierarchy exceeds five levels.

- **Teams** This scheme is good for ad hoc user assignment to Accounts, Contacts or Opportunities. Managing Teams can be difficult as they get larger, and there is limited automation for Team assignment.

- **Books of Business** This scheme supports automated assignment via workflow and hierarchical viewing (users can view subbooks) and is well adapted to modeling an organizational structure. Beware of implementing an overly complex Book hierarchy; the flexibility of the tool could make it harder for users to find data if not properly designed.

It is often a combination of available access schemes that is the right one. Understand exceptions but don't design to them; strive to arrive at a system that supports core needs and most common use cases.

Designing for Analytics

CRM On Demand's most compelling feature is its sophisticated business intelligence engine. The Reports and Dashboard tabs can serve as a window to information as simple as a list of accounts by territory to a detailed quarterly pipeline trending analysis. The Analytics tool is a topic unto itself and rightly the subject of advanced training and published materials. In this section, we will talk about some fundamental considerations for your Analytics design. Leveraging this powerful tool effectively relies on planning, training, and forethought.

Reports vs. Analytics

CRM On Demand provides two subject area groupings: Real-time Reports and Historical Analyses. In nearly every case, the recommendation is to build your reports from the Historical Analyses area.

Historical Reports pull from a data warehouse that is populated nightly. Data in the warehouse is optimized for faster reporting and has pre-calculated metrics that speed development time. Regular snapshots are held in the data warehouse to enable trend reporting in certain core areas, such as Opportunity Sales Stages.

Real-time Reports are run from the transactional database, where all the action occurs when entering, editing, and saving records. Consequently, it shares resources with all the daily user activities. Further, the data is optimized for access via the user interface, not analytical reports. These factors can combine to impact report performance negatively. Because real-time Reports compete for user interface resources, they are subject to a ten-minute time limit, which may be inadequate for a highly complex analysis.

Understand Baseline Analytics and Assumptions

The Reports tab contains a wealth of prebuilt reports and analyses (45 in all), conveniently grouped by business function. Run these reports before building new ones! Each of these reports is available through the Analytics tool and can be modified as needed and saved as a Custom Shared Report. So even if the prebuilt reports lack some metric or data field, you can save time by using them as starting points.

Take particular note of the trending reports. Historical Pipeline Analyses gives you a good idea of how key Opportunity fields, such as Close Date, Sales Stage, and Revenue are "wired." Sales Stage, in particular, provides great insight into your pipeline velocity. Every change in the Sales Stage is captured in the data warehouse, so the days required for each stage can be calculated and leveraged in rich analytical reports.

Considerations When Designing for Analytics

Designing for Analytics means understanding what you need to get out of the system as you are deciding what to put into it. That is, when you are designing the object model and the fields and picklists within each object, keep in mind how those data points will be reflected in reports.

- *Visualize the output.* Effective organizations already know what they need from the CRM system and rationalize their object model to ensure they can get it, for instance, by collecting examples of existing reports from legacy systems or by mocking up a "must have" report.

- *Know your metrics.* Most companies, and groups within companies, have key metrics or performance indicators that drive management oversight and action. For a sales organization, this may be the number of active deals, deals at a particular stage, or number of logged activities. Whatever the metric, it should be firmly understood and agreed to before the object model and process design is completed. Validate that the design supports the metrics: Does the Sales process reflect what management expects to see? Is the definition of an "active" deal the same for users and managers?

- *Ask the question.* What is the question your users are trying to answer? Approaching Analytics from this point of view can help focus your design efforts. Instead of "Show me a list of Opportunities closing in the quarter," frame the design around "What Opportunities should management be focusing on?" This question will beg others (what's the criteria for management involvement—revenue, customer size, or other attributes?), which can, in turn, further influence your overall design decisions.

■   *Design for action.* Many organizations start using Analytics as a data factory rather than a data mine. Lots of lists, tables, and charts can be produced to add to the mounds of data undoubtedly generated by other systems. When considering your overall design approach, think about the action an executive, manager, or user might take based on a report. Does seeing a list of deals result in action? Perhaps a list of deals with the top ten grossing customers? Or the percentage of deals across industry or geography? Add intelligence to Analytics by leveraging key attributes from the related business objects to enrich the data and move toward information. When information is actionable (the executive knows to call those top customers), then it is valued.

■   *Think visual.* Well-designed charts and graphs can paint a vivid picture that is harder to discern in a tabular format. When considering how the information will be interpreted, try out various visual approaches; pie charts and bar charts can tell a story that is harder to interpret from tables. Also consider using conditional formatting to set thresholds in the data. For example, to highlight poor performing territories, change the color of pipeline measures below a set amount.

■   *Anticipate performance.* As a general rule, the more data the report is running against and the more complex the query, the slower the report runs. When designing reports, anticipate the data volumes and user roles involved when the report goes into production. Often these are different than what exists at design-time. A report that runs quickly during implementation may be unacceptably slow or time out when production data has been loaded. The CRM On Demand help system and knowledge base contain numerous tips for ensuring and improving report performance.

Summary

In this chapter, we've covered a lot of ground, including the fundamental business model within the application, the natively supported business processes, and the available data access and security controls. Understanding each of these elements is the start to a solid system design. Paying special attention to the considerations and best practices we've outlined here will further increase your chances of a successful implementation. In the next chapter, we'll examine CRM On Demand designs that applied these best practices and were deployed by real companies in a cross-section of industries and specialties.

CHAPTER
6

Sample Oracle
CRM On Demand
Designs

hat makes a design effective? At its most basic, an effective design meets your business requirements, is easy to configure and maintain, performs and scales well over time, and is consistent with the application's intended use so it works well with future CRM On Demand features. The proof of an effective design is in the results—high adoption rates among your users, actionable information at your manager's fingertips, and business process flows that are efficient and effective.

In this chapter, we'll show you several implementations of a well-designed CRM On Demand application. We'll highlight implementations across a number of industries and for various business needs, as well as some unique solutions that were developed to meet specialty or niche requirements. These are idealized versions of customer configurations we've designed based on our experience working with multiple customers in a given industry. We'll highlight the unique business process needs that companies in these industries require and describe how these requirements translate into a CRM On Demand design element—object model, access and visibility, analytics, and integration and workflow.

Horizontal Solutions: Business to Business (B2B) Equipment and Service Sales

Sales Force Automation is a core function of CRM On Demand. As we've detailed in other chapters, this function provides support from generating Leads to tracking Opportunities to closing deals. Sales Force Automation is arguably the most common use of CRM systems in general and provides the backbone for full customer engagement.

In this scenario, we will review a design suited to a large business-to-business equipment producer. The producer is organized by a traditional territory model, with major regions defined geographically and subdivided to the individual sales representative level. Representatives target new accounts and service existing accounts. The equipment they sell can be complex, so product specialists are assigned to each region to assist as needed.

This organization does little direct marketing, but they use special promotions to help drive business in certain product groups. Sales representatives rely primarily on cold calls and face-to-face meetings. The Sales process is a simple one and generally not longer than three months.

Territory alignment is a key challenge. The sales staff experiences moderate turnover, requiring regular modifications to territory assignments. Although most assignments are based on certain rules, such as zip code and account classification, exceptions are frequently made and must be accommodated immediately.

Like most sales organizations, the main performance measure for this business equipment producer is the weekly forecast. Along with forecasted sales, representatives and managers track progress toward attaining quotas. To manage effectively, executives must maintain an accurate and timely forecast view across the organization.

Beyond the sales forecast, management is regularly seeking metrics on regional performance trends, sales by product, and new account penetration. For individual performance monitoring, managers seek details on the number of calls each representative is making and the number of new accounts opened versus the number of existing clients served. Where marketing promotions are used, Analytics are required to determine how effectively goals are met.

B2B Sales Process Flow

Figure 6-1 shows the Sales process in a B2B sales implementation. It begins with an Account, assigned to a Territory. Accounts represent both existing customers and potential business. Opportunities are identified by sales representatives and manually input into the system. Products are selected and deals are negotiated to closure.

Assigning Territory

Before any selling can begin, sales representatives and managers must know what their territories contain. Accounts are assigned to a territory based primarily on zip code, though ad hoc assignments are often required due to turnover and minor reorganization. Occasionally, executives will review the full territory structure and make more dramatic changes. Once territories are aligned and Accounts are populated, sales representatives can start selling.

Creating Opportunity

There are two main types of sales: servicing existing customers and prospecting for new business. An existing customer has already purchased equipment from the company and may be a candidate for additional units, upgrades, or add-on services. Sales representatives use CRM On Demand to identify Accounts with existing Assets that may be ready for retirement and can see what models have available add-on components. Once potential upgrades or add-ons are identified, sales representatives can create Opportunities and schedule calls or visits using Appointments related to the Accounts and Contacts.

For new business, the representative relies on Accounts and Contacts supplied by marketing. There is often very little information about these businesses—perhaps simply a name and address. The data may come from trade shows or purchased lists or even public directories. The sales representative's challenge is to contact as many of these companies through "cold-calling" as possible and quickly winnow them down to a list of leads. They will follow up with additional calls or visits. The representative then creates Opportunities for each one. The representative is also expected to fill out additional information about the Account and Contacts.

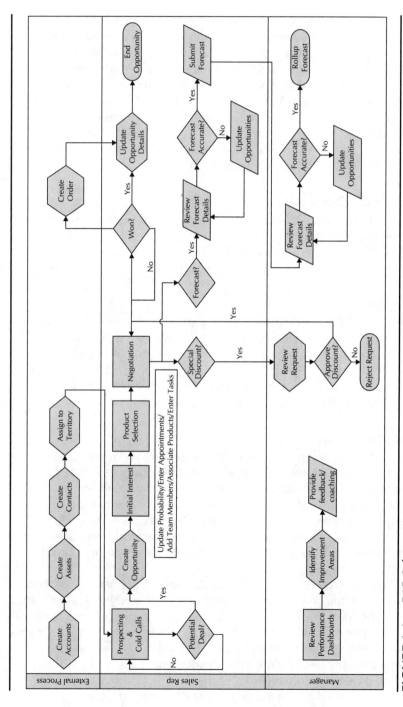

FIGURE 6-1. *B2B Sales process*

Once an Opportunity has been created, the representative selects the Opportunity Type, which is either New Business or Existing Customer. The selection made determines the fields displayed in the Opportunity Layout.

Developing Opportunity

The nascent Opportunities are developed through additional calls and meetings and each is recorded in CRM On Demand. During the Initial Interest stage, the sales representative confirms the client's interests and needs and establishes a relationship. The representative enters Account details and key Contacts in the system. The Opportunity probability defaults to 10 percent, and a rough revenue estimate is calculated.

Selecting a product is next and may require the help of a product specialist, who is then added to the Opportunity Team if needed. This process may involve multiple consultations and demonstrations. All appointments and tasks are tracked by the team in CRM On Demand and linked to the Opportunity. When the product or product mix is determined, the representative adds the products as revenue lines, inputting the expected price per unit. At that time, the Opportunity Revenue is updated with a more precise amount.

Now that the customer's needs have been confirmed and potential products identified, the deal enters the negotiation phase. This phase is typically where deals are won or lost, so the sales representative must provide additional information to ensure compliance with the corporate sales process. The representative must enter dates for expected installation and identify business competitors. Additional tasks are created for the representative, reminding him that Contracts needs advance notice for special terms and the factory needs 30 days for special configurations.

In certain situations, representatives may request discounts. CRM On Demand workflow automation is used to facilitate the approval process. Sales representatives cannot input a discount greater than 10 percent without manager approval. To request approval, the representative simply checks a box on the Opportunity Layout. This action alerts his or her manager who then sees the deal in the request queue. The manager can indicate approval via another checkbox on the record, which is hidden from the sales representative.

During the negotiations stage, the probability of winning the sale may rise or fall. This stage is also where the representative decides whether to include the Opportunity in his or her Forecast.

Closing the Deal

A price has been negotiated and final terms hammered out. At this point, the Opportunity has either been won or lost.

Upon winning the deal, the sales representative is required to enter one or more factors that led to winning the sale. The representative verifies the final details for the Opportunity and products before saving the record with the "Closed/Won" sales stage set. Winning a sale triggers an integration event, sending the key customer and product details to the back-office system for processing, which initiates an external process involving accounting, inventory, and manufacturing. When complete, an Order number appears on the Opportunity Layout along with a link to the Order details and status so the representative can check progress.

If a deal is lost, the representative is likewise required to enter one or more factors contributing to the lost sale. If lost to a competitor, the winner of the sale should be indicated.

Forecasting

Each week, the Forecasting process plays out among the sales representatives, managers, and executives. The representatives receive a notice each Monday that a new Forecast has been created. They know that their manager needs the updated Forecast by end of day. Their first task is to check the Forecast tab and review the numbers.

Before making any changes to the Forecast totals, the representative checks the included Opportunities and makes adjustments as needed to the revenue amounts or close dates. When satisfied, he refreshes the modified Opportunities on the Forecast page and then selects "Rollup" to capture those changes in the main Forecast. He can then adjust best case and forecast numbers if needed. By Monday afternoon, he is ready to submit the forecast to his manager.

First-line managers begin the Forecast review process on Tuesday morning, first verifying that their subordinates have all submitted Forecasts as required. Managers drill into each Forecast and confer with their representatives as needed to gain a clear picture of a region's performance. When satisfied, they make final adjustments to the best case and forecast and submit the Forecast to the next level.

The process continues up the management chain until Friday morning, when the vice president of sales reviews the final Forecast numbers with her team.

Management Activities

Besides the Forecast and discount approval processes noted, managers play an active role in coaching their representatives, assisting in developing key opportunities, and ensuring the Sales process is smooth within their region.

Regular one-on-one conversations with representatives keeps managers and their teams aligned on key initiatives and improvement plans. Managers come prepared to the meetings with reports detailing the representative's recent activities recorded in CRM On Demand. The manager can see the number of calls and appointments made compared to previous periods and against targets. The manager is also looking at the representative's pipeline, specifically the split between new business and existing customers. All of this information guides the discussion and coaching provided to the representative.

Managers also commonly deal with employee turnover. When a sales representative departs, the manager must ensure the territory is covered by a new or existing representative. The manager must quickly pull a list of all the representative's Accounts and have them transferred to another representative or distributed among several representatives. The final alignment data is then given to the CRM administrator who uploads the changes to the application.

CRM On Demand Design for B2B Sales

The design for this B2B Sales process leverages the following CRM On Demand core business objects: Accounts, Assets, Contacts, Opportunities, Products, and Revenues.

Object Design

Figure 6-2 shows the key objects and relationships. An Account is the customer or potential customer. For existing customers, their installed equipment or service contracts are listed as linked Assets. Contacts associated with an Account are the people you're dealing with throughout the sales cycle. Contacts may be directly linked to an Opportunity. The Opportunity stores all the relevant, timely information about the deal in play, including the Products being pitched, which are represented as Revenue line items.

Accounts, Contacts, and Opportunities exist within one or more Books of Business. Books of Business are flexible containers of data defined by the CRM On Demand administrators—in this case, designed to reflect the sales territory structure.

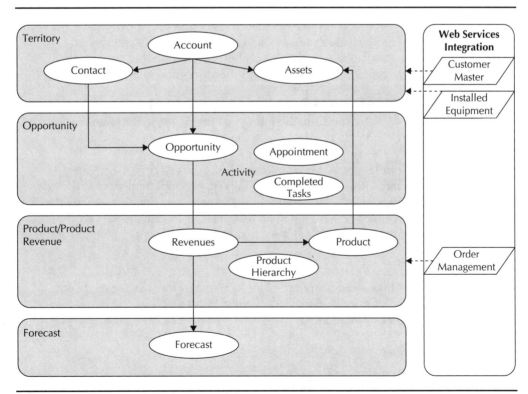

FIGURE 6-2. *B2B Sales Object model*

In our scenario, we also refer to Orders, which are not stored in CRM On Demand. These are linked records stored in a back-office system, but accessible through the CRM On Demand user interface.

Access and Visibility

Access to records in our example sales organization is tightly controlled. Sales representatives see only the Accounts, Contacts, and Opportunities in their territory. Managers see the same in their region and so forth up the chain. Special roles, such as administrative assistants, contract specialists, and inventory managers, need access to the regions they support. Product specialists see only the deals they are involved in directly.

To achieve this visibility model, they employed a combination of access control schemes. The main mechanism for sales representatives is simple Ownership. As the Owner of an Account, Contact, and Opportunity, the representative can see and edit the information as needed. Gaining ownership, however, may not be so simple. The Owner of each record is determined through territory assignment rules. These rules are maintained outside of CRM On Demand and only the final Ownership designation is applied in the system.

Books of Business are created for each Region, which, in turn, rolls up to a major Geography Book and then to a Corporate Book level. This structure allows managers and support specialists in the region to gain access to all Accounts and related information by simple association with the Region book. Administrative personnel are given Read-only Access to the Book, whereas managers and executives have Full Access.

Product specialists are included in deals through Opportunity Teams. Sales representatives manually select and add the individual specialists to the team as needed and give them Read-only or Edit Access. Once added, product specialists can view the deal details and add their activities.

For ease of use, all Roles are set up with Read All Records Access to Activities. This access ensures that all Roles can see the details of any appointment or task linked to their Accounts, Contacts, or Opportunities, even if they don't directly own the Activity record. Because access to the main records is restricted, the various Roles will not be able to access Activities outside of their territory easily.

Analytics

CRM On Demand provides a number of out-of-the-box reports for sales organizations, all of which can be used effectively in the design outlined here.

Pipeline Analysis reports include

- Pipeline Analysis
- Opportunity Revenue Analysis
- Pipeline Quality Analysis

- Team Pipeline Analysis

- Top Ten Opportunities

- Historical Pipeline Analysis

- Historical Expected Revenue Quarterly Analysis

- Historical Opportunity Revenue Quarterly Analysis

- Quarterly Closed Revenue Analysis

- Opportunity vs. Expected Revenue vs. Closed Revenue

- Sales Stage History Analysis

Sales Effectiveness reports include

- Top Performers List

- Quarterly Sales Effectiveness Analysis

- Team Sales Effectiveness Analysis

- Team Activity Analysis

- Team Win Rate Analysis

- Team Average Sales Cycle Analysis

As is evident from the report titles, many of these are built with managers in mind. Any of these analyses may provide a good starting point for a custom report as well. In our B2B scenario, it is important to see the distinction between new business and existing customers. For example, to see how the average sales cycle (in days) compares, the Opportunity Type can be added as a dimension to the Team Average Sales Cycle Analysis report.

For managers, collecting these key performance reports in a Dashboard is critical, so coaching discussions can be informed and effective and any necessary corrective action can be taken.

Integration and Workflow

Increasingly, CRM On Demand is part of an overall business systems environment that spans front-office and back-office functions. Strategic integration among the various applications within that environment can improve data reliability and user productivity.

In a B2B sales implementation, we commonly see several integration points. First, often the "master" source of customer information is external to CRM On

Demand in a data management or other back-office system. Any updates to the customer master occur only in this external system, which, in turn, feeds any other business system that references customer data. In our example, shown in Figure 6-3, batch integration is implemented using Web Services to insert and update Accounts from the customer master system each night. Only new and modified Accounts are included, keeping batch sizes to a minimum. A subset of Account fields is updated in this way, and each of these is locked down (for Read-only Access) for users. Therefore, updates are one-way as no changes to key Account data fields are allowed in CRM On Demand. Along with the key Account fields, any fulfilled orders are inserted as related Assets.

An area for integration referenced in the process overview is territory management. CRM On Demand automatically assigns Accounts based on rules. However, many companies need more advanced logic than the simple rule builder offered by CRM On Demand. Also, Assignment Manager runs asynchronously and may take several hours to complete. In our example scenario, the company needs updates as soon as possible. Therefore, a web services utility is developed to update record owners based on the output of an in-house territory management tool.

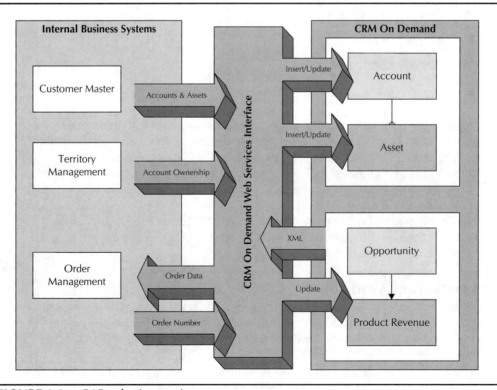

FIGURE 6-3. *B2B sales integration*

The actual integration process is simple: a file of Account IDs and Owners is provided, and the utility updates the Accounts and their associated child records (Contacts and Opportunities) with the new Owner values. The complex logic used to determine record ownership, along with ad hoc changes made by managers, lives in a tool that is purpose-built for the company.

Another integration mentioned earlier was order management. Like most companies, our B2B equipment producer uses a back-office order management system. Any new equipment orders must be entered and accepted into this system. When a new deal is closed, a workflow rule fires and enters an integration event in the queue. An external process periodically checks the queue via Web Services, retrieves new events, and clears the queue. With this information, an order can be created in the order management system. Once the order is verified, an order number is written back to the CRM On Demand Opportunity record via Web Services. Using a few basic integration points, our B2B sales implementation provides the right data, at the right time, to the right users and systems.

Within the application, a scripted workflow is also used to control certain processes. Field validation prevents a discount amount greater than 10 percent if a "manager approved" checkbox is not true. Representatives initiate an exception by checking a box that triggers a workflow, sending an e-mail to the representative's manager. The manager uses a saved list to view any pending approvals.

Once approved, another workflow fires, alerting the representative that she can now apply a higher discount. Field validation again evaluates the user input and verifies the approved amount. Workflow also comes in handy for managing the Books of Business. For each book, workflow rules are created to evaluate new or updated records and determine what Book or Books those records belong to.

Horizontal Solutions: Consumer Support Services

Oracle CRM On Demand provides the building blocks for a robust consumer support application. As discussed in the previous chapter, this centers on the inherent Service Request (SR) object model and associated processes. But a real-life support environment is likely more complex than basic SR tracking.

A consumer support organization will typically involve multiple, geographically dispersed teams of resources. Support requests come through many channels, both online and offline. Customers often have expectations of response times or even contractual guarantees (service-level agreements) that must be managed.

Performance measures in a support organization may include time to respond, time to resolution, and customer satisfaction scores. Support managers will look for metrics around the issues that drive support requests, the products involved, and the most common solutions.

Support Services Process Flow

Figure 6-4 describes the general process for support agents within CRM On Demand. First, a Service Request (SR) record is created. This comes through one of potentially many channels, either automatically entered or manually created. Information is collected within the SR so it can be initially dispositioned. An SR is assigned to an agent through intelligent routing or picked from a queue or some combination of the two. Next, a series of activities occur directed toward solving the reported problem, which may include continued dialog with the customer requesting service or researching a solution.

Most support organizations employ a defined escalation process. Escalation may be based on the time taken to resolve an issue, the stated severity of the issue, or specific details about the product involved. Escalations often result in the SR being reassigned based on business rules. Finally, when the SR is resolved, the customer is informed and the SR is closed. After closing the SR, many organizations now employ internal or third-party customer satisfaction surveys.

Outside of the core Service Request handling, an agent may be involved in multiple activities:

- Adding other agents, such as product specialists, to the SR

- Searching local or external knowledge bases for solutions

- Recording inbound and outbound communications with the customer

Let's examine each step in the process.

Creating and Assigning Service Requests

Service Requests originate through one of many possible channels: web site form submissions, e-mails, chat interactions, or direct phone calls. Today, electronic submissions comprise the majority of transactions. These transactions are automatically created through Web Services Integration.

By default, Service Requests may not have an owner. The record owner can be designated via a few mechanisms:

- Agents view a list of unassigned SRs and "claim" them by setting themselves as the owner.

- Assignment rules are invoked, which interrogate the SR field values and route to an owner based on the defined logic.

- Workflow rules can default the owner value upon a record being created or updated. Such rules can also assign SRs to Books of Business, which may be visible to a certain segment of agents.

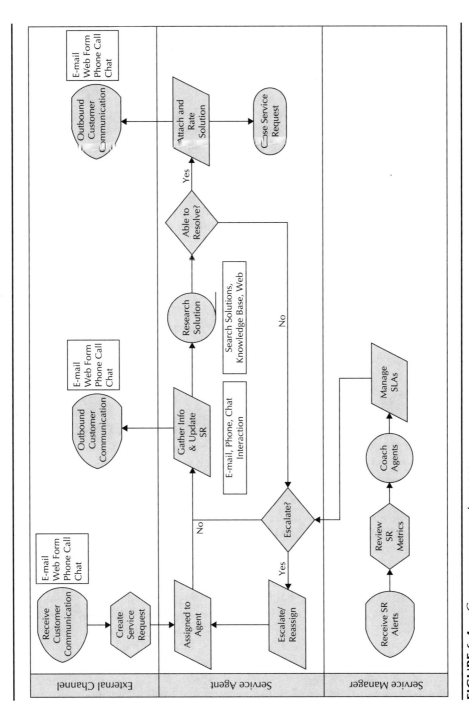

FIGURE 6-4. *Consumer support process*

Researching and Escalating Service Requests Research

An agent's first actions will be to gather enough information to resolve an issue, assuming it is not resolved immediately. The specific information needed will drive what custom fields and pick list values will be required for configuration. Key field value changes will be tracked in the Audit History.

Communications between the agent and the customer can be tracked as related Activities. Using Outlook E-mail Integration, all e-mail correspondence with the contact is logged as an Activity in CRM On Demand. When an agent cannot solve a Service Request, it may be escalated to a higher tier agent or group. The record may be manually reassigned or escalated through predefined workflow rules.

The Solutions tab provides access to a knowledgebase, used by agents to find quick answers to problems. Solution entries are approved and rated to make finding the right answer easy. If a solution is found, it is linked to the SR. If a new solution is determined, the agent enters it and submits the solution for approval. When a Service Request is resolved, its Status is changed to Closed.

Management Activities

While the research and escalation activities play out, Support Management is tracking the overall status and effectiveness of the agent group. Managers track the number of open and aging SRs. A custom workflow triggers manager alerts when SRs age beyond agreed time limits (often detailed in service-level agreements, or SLAs). Regularly reviewing open SRs and trends informs managers of needed initiatives for process improvement and agent development.

CRM On Demand Design for Support Services

In this section, we will discuss a sample support services design intended to maintain the process just described. This implementation is based on real-life designs used by sophisticated consumer support organizations.

Object Design

Figure 6-5 illustrates the support services object design. This design centers on the native Service Request and Solutions objects and their relationships to the Account, Contact, and Product objects. The main object is the Service Request, which stores all of the key information about the support incident. This information includes the priority and timing (date reported) of the request, as well as the problem area, potential causes, and any other information required to fully describe the problem. A Contact is related to a Service Request and represents an individual's basic information, such as name, personal information, and how to contact him or her (phone, e-mail, etc.). A Contact and Service Request may be associated to an Account, for instance, a company that has a contractual relationship with the service provider.

This service organization tracks a Product and Asset within the Service Request. These objects provide details about the product that may be the source of the problem

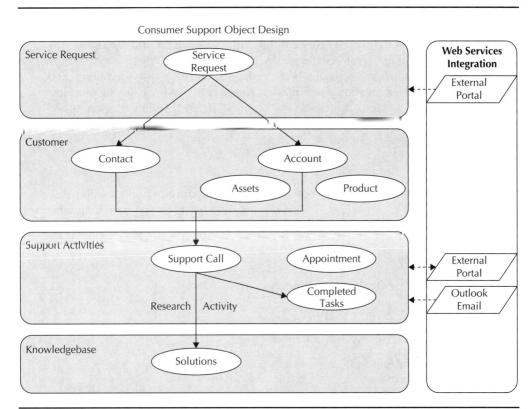

FIGURE 6-5. *SR object design*

or the specific asset located at the customer site. Finally, Solutions act as a knowledge base for agents to resolve Service Requests. One or more Solutions may be linked to a Service Request.

Access and Visibility

Access needs may vary among support organizations, but, in general, agents have Read access to most record types. An agent may need to work with any Account or Contact in the system. This access is easily set by selecting the Read All Records option for these record types in the agent Role settings. Access to Service Requests may be more restrictive and can be governed by ownership or Books of Business. In some organizations, agents may need access to all Service Requests, which can be granted at the Role level.

Access is an important area to consider in any support deployment. Support agents need to access their SRs and related records quickly and are often working multiple cases at any time. Access to all records in the system may be the simplest approach but could overwhelm an agent, and, in a high volume environment, contribute to declining performance.

Restricting access tightly may make it difficult for agents to find the right information and complete their assigned tasks. In a high-volume environment, where hundreds of thousands or millions of SRs are generated, access that is too open could impact searches and list creation. Finding ways to segment SRs logically, by product group, region, or other factor, can make such operations more efficient. Giving agents access to the right amount of data with the right level of access can improve productivity and decrease extra work.

Analytics

This design leverages the out-of-the-box objects and relationships, which will make reporting and analysis relatively easy. Several prebuilt reports can be used with little or no modification:

■ Service Analysis

■ Current Service Request Aging Analysis

■ Open Service Request Analysis

■ Number of Service Request Analysis

■ Team Service Analysis

For custom analyses, a Service Request History report exposes the key business object relationships among Service Requests, Accounts, Contacts, Products, and Assets. From here, various metrics can be constructed, including SRs by Product, by Contact, by Account Demographics, or by Installed Assets. Many organizations take advantage of Dashboards to combine multiple reports and analyses into a single view.

CRM On Demand precalculates metrics based on SR status. These include number of SRs per status (Open, Closed, Pending, and Canceled) and aging (Days/Minutes Open, Days/Minutes to Close). This design gets most of these metrics by using the out-of-the-box Status, Opened Time, and Closed Time fields.

Integration and Workflow

An effective support organization must interface with customers through multiple channels. The most common interfaces today are web forms and e-mail. A customer visits the company web site, clicks the support link, and enters a request. Many companies provide self-service tools as well, such as an online knowledge base and community-driven support forums. Having an integrated support environment is critical to achieving the level of service most customers expect and is an essential part of an efficient support organization.

Workflow in CRM On Demand allows for scripted control over business processes and automated enforcement of business rules. As SRs are entered and tracked, the workflow is used to ensure that service-level agreements are adhered to and corporate standards are met.

The starting point for integration within a support services deployment is Service Request input. As we've pointed out, SRs may come through any number of channels. Using CRM On Demand Web Services, any of these paths can integrate with the application. This integration must be in real time and highly dependable, so no SRs are lost or delayed.

Once SRs are in the system, agents can communicate with customers through e-mail or phone calls, each of which can be tracked by manual agent input. Oracle's prebuilt integration with Microsoft Outlook automatically captures outbound and inbound e-mails associated to an SR and Contact, storing them as related Activities. This plug-in is freely available to users as a client-side installation.

A more elaborate custom integration can tie CRM On Demand SRs to a customer facing web site. The full functionality of a support web portal is not native to CRM On Demand; however, the Web Services API allows the application to connect to any existing portal through custom development. Integration Events can be created based on workflow rules to "push" Service Request updates to any external interface. These events can extend from case initiation to status updates and interaction to publishing Solutions in a customer-accessible and searchable knowledge base.

CRM On Demand partners offer complete or partial solutions to support a customer interaction strategy. Partner offerings include prebuilt customer interaction portals, complete with knowledge base and community tools. Companies can use partner offerings to deploy web forms and integrate various communications channels rapidly. Additional partner offerings can be explored at www.crmondemand.com.

Workflow is used to automate escalation and communication to agents, support managers, and to customers. For example, when certain fields are updated on the SR record, a workflow is triggered, sending a formatted e-mail to the SR Contact to notify him or her of the change. Support management likewise receives e-mail alerts or automatic tasks based on the status of SRs. Field validation is implemented to enforce standard rules. For example, when an SR has a priority of High, it cannot be saved without additional information being added in the Type field.

Time-based workflow allows support organizations more control over their adherence to contractual service response times. When a High priority SR is created, for example, a workflow initiates an action to occur in 24 hours (or any specified period of time). When the time interval has passed, the SR is evaluated to determine if it is Closed. If not, an e-mail is sent to the agent's manager alerting him or her of the need to escalate the request. In this way, all internal response targets and external contractual obligations can be scripted into an escalation engine, driving the support organization toward greater compliance and efficiency.

Vertical Solutions: Retail Banking Sales and Service

Of all the companies and industries we've worked with, the design requirements for financial services firms tend to be one of the most technically complex and challenging. From a CRM design perspective, the challenge is integrating the numerous customer and transactional systems and consolidating vast amounts of data so the banker can see a complete view of the customer—the customer's current banking relationship, financial goals, history of interactions, and, of course, account details. The following design is for a retail bank that utilizes CRM On Demand as the integrated portal for customer interactions. The overall design approach, however, will have general implications for companies that require integrating disparate transactional systems, accessing large amounts of transactional data, and controlling access and visibility to sensitive data.

A banker's relationship with his or her customer is built on trust and expanded through effectively anticipating and servicing needs as clients go through life. Some of the unique client relationship challenges for a consumer retail banking firm include

- **Complete (360-degree) view of the customer**   A banker should have a complete view of a customer's details—personal data, familial relationships, as well as up-to-date information for each account the customer holds with the bank. Beyond these basics, a banker should have an understanding of a customer's expectations of the bank, for example, whether the customer cares most about price, convenience, or personal relationship. A banker should have a general understanding of the customer's financial goals and be aware of relationships the customer may have with other banks (for example, a customer keeps a checking account at your bank but savings at another).

- **Prompt response to customer requests**   From a systems perspective, this means

  - Real-time access to account-related information, such as credit card balance and payment status

  - Real-time confirmation of sales and service requests, such as check reorders

- **A measure of customer satisfaction**   Finally, the bank should measure customer satisfaction every time its customer interacts with the bank.

Figure 6-6 describes the typical customer sales and service interactions for a retail bank, where the customer interacts directly with a banker over the phone or at the bank branch. The interactions generally fall into three categories:

- **Inquiry**   A customer will request information about an existing product or service. For example, a customer may want to review his credit card

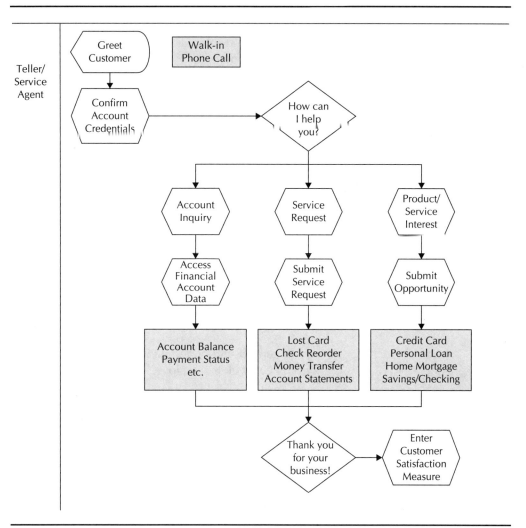

FIGURE 6-6. *Customer sales and service interactions at a retail bank*

balance, payment status, and new transactions or fees that may have been charged to his account.

- **Service Request** A customer will request help with a particular item. For example, she may need to replace a lost bank card, arrange for a wire transfer, or receive a copy of her bank statement.

- **Product inquiry** A customer may be interested in obtaining new banking services, such as a savings account, personal loan and mortgage services, or credit card.

A customer may request assistance for any number of these items during the course of a single customer interaction, with the expectation that each request will be handled quickly and efficiently. The banker's operational efficiency then becomes a critical factor in determining whether the customer is satisfied or disappointed with the interaction.

CRM On Demand Design for Retail Banking Sales and Service

Following is a sample design for a retail bank sales and service application. The design relies upon a tight integration between the CRM and transactional systems in order to present a 360-degree view of the customer. The designs uses the CRM On Demand Financial Services Edition and Custom Object extensions to track customer information and the customer's relationship to the bank, and the use of Web Services to integrate the core banking systems for accessing detailed account data.

Object Design

Figure 6-7 describes the retail banking object design. The design builds upon the CRM On Demand Financial Services objects, with additional Custom Objects to capture important customer relationship details. The key objects include

- The Contact represents the customer. Customers and their immediate family are organized into Households by connecting the Household Members.

- The Financial Profile (represented by Custom Object 4 in Figure 6-7) stores the status of the customer's banking relationship. It lists each account and financial product the customer keeps with the bank—checking, savings, mortgage, etc.—as well as other institutions the customer may work with. Note that we've chosen Custom Object 4 for a reason. This object has a one-to-many object relationship (a Contact can have multiple banking relationships), for which Custom Objects 4 to 15 are best. Refer back to Chapter 5 for an overview of Custom Objects.

- A customer's Financial Goals (represented by Custom Object 5) stores a summary of the customer's expectations and general financial objectives. Expectations are what the customer values in the bank; for example. a customer may value personal relationships more than price. Financial goals may include a list of objectives, such as the customer wants to own his or her own home within the next five years. Again, note that this is a one-to-many object relationship, for which Custom objects 4 to 15 are best used.

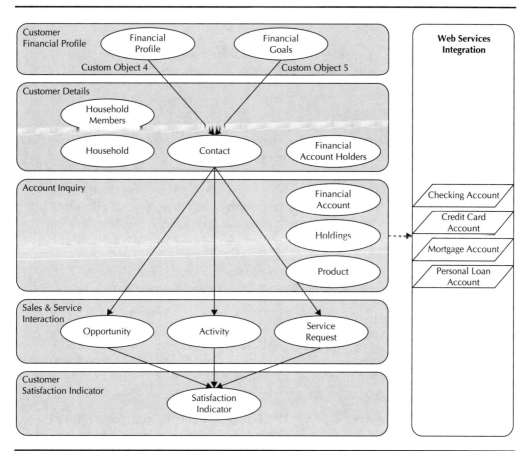

FIGURE 6-7. *Object design—retail banking sales and service*

- Financial Account/Holdings stores account summary information and the product holdings for each account. Note that these tables track summary information such as account names, numbers, products held, and, if needed for analytics, some monthly or weekly summary balances. Real-time account balance and transaction information are not held in these tables. Rather, these tables store the mapping information to allow CRM On Demand to link to the core banking systems to access this data directly.

- The Service Request tracks the service request detail requiring action, such as a check reorder, lost card, etc.

■ The Opportunity tracks the sales requests requiring action, such as a new account, personal loan, etc.

■ The Activity tracks appointments, individual tasks, and notes during the course of conducting a Service Request or following an Opportunity.

Access and Visibility

The regulatory nature of financial institutions requires a well-defined and implemented access model. There are three key components within CRM On Demand:

■ **Physical segmentation**   Many countries require banking firms to physically segregate customer data for each country in which they conduct business. Most companies have interpreted the regulations to mean that each country entity should be set up as a separate CRM On Demand instance; however, a smaller group of companies have deployed a consolidated company instance utilizing a Book of Business to segment each country's data. Technically, you can utilize either approach to fulfill this requirement.

■ **Data access**   Within a company instance, a Book of Business would be used to segment customer data further, for example, by market segment or branch. Within each Book, the various sales and service Roles will have broad visibility to the customer Contact and financial Account information in order to quickly and efficiently conduct their business (for example, users have Read/Edit Access for their market or branch Book).

■ **Audit trail extension**   CRM On Demand provides built-in auditing for the Opportunity and Service Request objects only. Audit records for additional objects can be simulated using a basic configuration technique that uses workflow to identify field-level changes for a given record and writes the prior and current values to a Custom Object. This approach, however, is fairly cumbersome and should only be used for tracking a small number of field updates for a particular object.

Analytics

Because the design utilizes standard objects, Analytics reports are easy to develop. The following types of reports are available from the data warehouse and real-time analytics:

■ Customer Segmentation Using Contact with Custom Object 4 (Financial Profile) or Custom Object 5 (Financial Goals)

- Customer Value Trending Analysis (Contact and Household History)

    - Number of Households

    - Products by Contact and Household

    - Percentage of Household members who have accounts

- Customer Satisfaction (real-time analysis)

    - This is a combined report utilizing Custom Object 6 (Customer Satisfaction Indicator) and either of the Service Request, Activity, or Opportunity subject areas

Integration

Why use Web Services to link to financial account data outside of CRM On Demand? Why not load the transactional data directly into CRM On Demand? A number of companies originally decided to load daily balances and related transactions into CRM On Demand. They wanted to utilize Analytics. The downside, however, is that there is generally a lot of financial transaction data; even a medium-size bank can easily manage millions of accounts. Setting up an integration to move all that data each day is very tricky; not only are there bottlenecks and points of failure, but also the sheer amount of data can cause performance issues in a number of areas, from loading the data warehouse nightly to degrading application and report performance.

In the end, CRM On Demand was designed to optimize sales and service execution. It is not meant to be a financial analysis application. The companies that originally loaded transactional data realized that the maintenance costs for moving this data outweighed any benefits they derived from Analytics.

Eventually, these companies revised their CRM On Demand design to integrate directly to the transaction systems utilizing Web Services Integration. The CRM On Demand Financial Account and Holdings objects store the internal identifiers that map to the appropriate transactional system and account data. Balance information can be presented in CRM On Demand using a related web applet. When a banker needs to execute a transaction, he or she links back to core banking to conduct the work. Data integration in CRM On Demand is limited to the customer data that is needed to enhance the 360-degree customer view.

Vertical Solutions: Pharmaceutical Sales Call Tracking

The selling process for pharmaceutical and healthcare service providers is very different from most industries. This sale is an influence sale, and the salesperson's objective is to educate and raise the awareness of the healthcare providers who ultimately prescribe a drug, device, or service to their patients. The life of a pharmaceutical sales representative revolves around the office visit (known as a "professional call"), and his or her effectiveness is measured by call reporting that tracks the frequency and coverage of professional calls made to physicians and healthcare professionals within his or her territory.

At its heart, pharmaceutical sales call reporting is nothing more than a specialized activity tracking process, but the metrics used to track and manage professional calls make it potentially applicable across other industries that use activity-based selling methodologies. In this section, we'll call out those cross-industry capabilities that you might want to consider for your implementation.

Before we discuss the call reporting process in detail, let's discuss how the pharmaceutical sales process works:

■ Salespeople are organized by product or service line. Companies generally have separate sales teams for each of their product lines. The product sales teams separately manage their own territory structure and reporting hierarchies.

■ A salesperson manages a territory of *referral sources,* which consists of Account-centric organizations such as hospitals, medical practices, or providers, or Contact-centric groups such as physicians, nurse practitioners, pharmacists, etc. Companies with multiple product or service lines generally overlap sales territories and thus multiple salespeople end up calling on the same Accounts and Contacts.

■ Each salesperson is expected to make a certain number of professional calls each day to a selected set of referral sources within his or her territory. The company classifies each referral source into different segments (rankings) based upon their relationship with the company and value to the product line or market. The Call Priority and Call Cycle (frequency of visits) will differ depending upon the segment type. For example, a salesperson may make monthly calls to a new physician group in order to develop a referral pipeline, compared to quarterly calls for an existing group with a strong relationship in place.

Pharmaceutical Sales Call Tracking Process Flow

Figure 6-8 describes the general call process for a primary care sales team. A salesperson will prepare a list of customers based on product interest and ranking and use this list to prepare their call schedule. A call route for a particular day may consist of a number of professional (physician) Contacts for a particular segment who have open office hours during that day. Prior to the call, the salesperson will

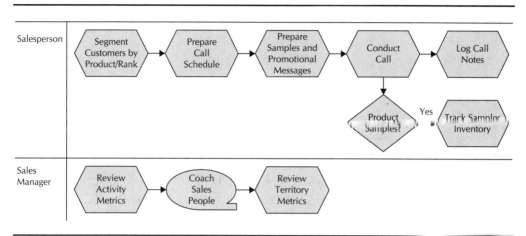

FIGURE 6-8. *Pharmaceutical sales call process flow*

prepare the product messages and samples. He or she may also review the call and prescribing habits for the Contact to see how often the other sales teams have been visiting the contact, what was discussed, and any other information gleaned from prior visits that may have bearing on the call. Next, the salesperson conducts the sales call, where he or she meets with the Contact and orients the Contact to their product efficacy. As part of the call, the salesperson may leave product samples. After the call, the salesperson will log his or her call activities for each physician visit, which details the products covered and/or samples given out and any other information relevant to management and fellow sales teams.

Sales management plays an active role throughout the process. Management reviews the call notes and provides coaching and mentoring to the salesperson to help improve the message, monitors salesperson call activity compared to the quotas set by the company, and monitors territory revenue performance and adjust activities as needed.

Typical management reports that support these activities are

- **Call Reports**   Number of calls made, products discussed, and/or samples given compared to quota

- **Territory Performance**   Total prescriptions, new prescriptions, and market share information for a particular territory

- **Sales Team Performance**   Trending information on the number of calls made for each segment

In addition these reports, there are a number of critical design items for marketing and operational-related activities that support the sales call process:

- Analyzing and ranking Accounts and Contacts

- Updating territory performance data and competitive information from the best available third-party information

CRM On Demand Design for Pharmaceutical Sales Call Tracking

Following is a sample activity tracking design for Account- or Contact-centric sales organizations in the life sciences industry. The design relies upon three key elements: the CRM On Demand Life Sciences Edition Activity Management features, the Book of Business data access model, and integrative feeds for competitive and revenue performance data. Note that this design only covers the sales call tracking portion of the pharmaceutical sales flow, which may have cross-industry applicability.

Object Design

Figure 6-9 describes a sample life sciences sales-call-tracking object design. This design starts with the CRM On Demand Life Sciences Edition objects, along with several Custom Objects needed to support integrations for supporting call tracking. The design is organized as follows:

- Referral sources consist of institutional Accounts (hospitals, physician groups, managed care organizations, etc.) and Contacts (physicians, nurse practitioners, pharmacists, and other non-prescribers).

- Each Account and Contact is assigned to a market segment. The Account Rank (represented by Custom Object 4) and Contact Rank (represented by Custom Object 5) contain the market segment type and related call frequency details. The Account Formulary (Custom Object 6) contains the approved product lists for the institutional accounts, including competitive product information.

- Accounts and Contacts can be linked to one another to represent the multiple affiliations among them.

- The Appointment object tracks the call schedule for each day. The schedule for Contacts will be based on a Contact's Best Time to Call.

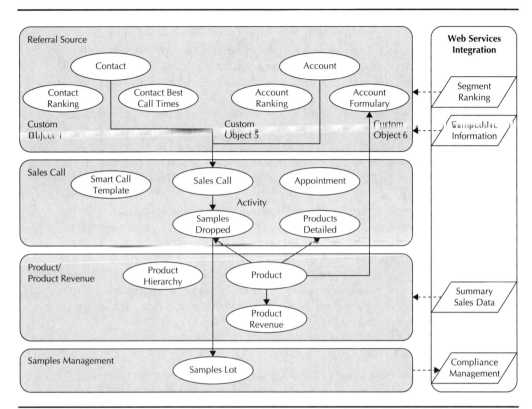

FIGURE 6-9. *Life sciences object design for pharmaceutical sales call tracking*

- Sales Call (the renamed Activity object) tracks the details for each visit, in other words who the salesperson visited, at what location, etc. Products Detailed tracks the products discussed during the call and the messages delivered. Samples Dropped tracks the product sample, lot number, and quantity provided as part of the visit.

- Product Revenue tracks summary script information that can be attributed to a particular Contact.

- Product Category groups related product information into product hierarchies for consolidated reporting.

- Smart Calls are an interesting feature for creating call templates. A salesperson can save a call as a private or public smart call and load it up later as a template to speed entry.

Access and Visibility

The Book of Business access model is best suited for building multiple seller, multiple territory models such as the one used as an example for this sales call process design. Each product line is set up as a separate Book structure. Individual Book leaves represent discrete sales territories. You then add as many rollup nodes as needed to represent the territory hierarchy structure—territory, district, region, sales organization, etc. Accounts, Contacts, and related items are assigned to one or more Books based on the territory criteria—postal code to territory alignment, named accounts, and so on. Each salesperson is then assigned to a particular Book. As part of the Book setup, each salesperson should have visibility access set to Edit/ View All Accounts and related items so he or she can view other sales team calls in order to coordinate efforts.

Territory management is often a burdensome activity for life sciences companies, as their sales teams tend to be quite volatile. In this design, territory management is done via Book assignment. To add new salespeople, simply set up the user, tie the user to a role, and assign the user to a Book. If the salesperson leaves, his or her existing Book can be quickly assigned to a replacement salesperson or to a manager in the interim. Book assignment can be done manually via the Administration screens, automatically within the system using Assignment Manager workflow, or managed completely outside the system using Web Services.

Analytics

Activity call types are critical for call activity reporting. The CRM On Demand Life Sciences Edition consolidates an extensive set of Activity metrics in the Call Activity History metrics subject area. Using this sample design, the following reports are available within the data warehouse:

- Call Analysis (utilizes the Call Activity History subject area):
  - Call analysis by product
  - Call analysis by segment
  - Call activity—number of calls by products detailed
  - Call activity—number of calls by samples dropped
  - Salesperson performance—call activity versus quota
- Territory Performance (utilizes the Account History and Contact History subject areas)
  - Script analysis by individual contact
  - Script analysis rollup by Book of Business hierarchy (territory, district, region)

Integration

The following integrations represent typical data feeds to enhance the sales call functionality. The integrations include

- **Syndicated data** Third-party summary script data used for sales performance tracking. This data can be loaded into the Product Revenue object with a reference to the relevant Contact. Note this data should be summary data only, as it is intended to support the sales management function.

- **Market segmentation** This process includes the segment ranking for a particular Account or Contact. The segment type is stored in a related Custom object to the Account and Contact, which can be loaded via Web Services or using the Import Wizard.

- **Competitive (formulary) data** This data also comes from independent third-party sources and can be loaded into the Account Formulary Custom Object.

Specialty Solutions: Delivering Relief to Families in an Emergency

Oracle CRM On Demand has been configured in many unique and interesting ways. One of the most beneficial uses we've seen has been for coordinating emergency relief for victims of a natural disaster. Several nonprofit and government entities have used CRM On Demand to track relief activities in the aftermath of a natural disaster. Given the unique deployment capabilities of the SaaS model, these organizations were able to configure and roll out a production-ready application within days to help coordinate efforts on very short notice.

It is important to note that this application is not meant for tracking emergency response activities, such as search and rescue, and emergency management operations. Rather, by simply creating a few roles, renaming a few objects, and populating a few records, agencies can deploy a simple but powerful tool to track post-response relief activities, including

- Tracking basic information and the disposition of individuals and families impacted by an emergency

- Tracking details of a family's short-term needs such as food, clothing, and housing

- Determining eligibility for emergency grants and other assistance

- Consolidating need requests for relief providers

- Assigning case workers and tracking ongoing activity

Emergency Relief Issue Tracking Process Flow

Figure 6-10 describes the general process for the front-line teams who coordinate the inbound and ongoing activities at a relief agency. To begin, an agent will meet with the impacted individuals, for example, a family who has been displaced by a natural disaster. The agent will capture the contact details about the family, their status/health, location, and how they can be reached. This information is the most critical to capture as people start looking for family and friends. Next, the family is assigned to a case worker who will determine their current disposition and detail their short-term needs, such as temporary housing, food, and clothing, and noncritical medical attention. The case worker will match these short-term needs to a relief service provider who will deliver the needed services. As the short-term needs have been addressed, a grant administrator will then work with the family to determine their eligibility for longer-term assistance such as government grants. If eligible, the grant administrator will work with the family to prepare the requisite paperwork and will track the request's progress.

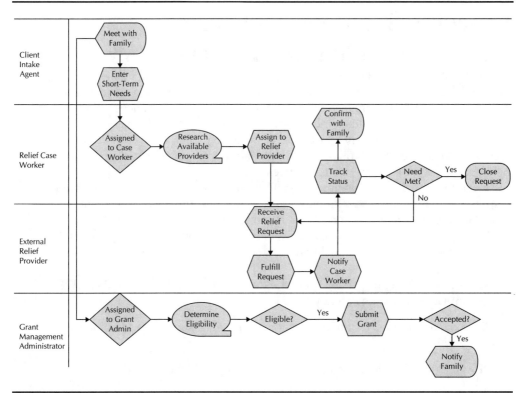

FIGURE 6-10. *Process flow for emergency relief tracking*

In addition, there are a number of operational-related activities that support the emergency relief process. These include

- Registering relief service providers and identifying the goods and services available for the relief effort

- Consolidating need requests

- Notifying relief service providers of need requests

- Tracking the status of open/closed need requests and grants

CRM On Demand Design for Emergency Relief

Following is a sample design for an emergency relief specialty application. The design relies upon the standard CRM On Demand Service Request and Solution applications to manage need requests and the Opportunity application to manage grant requests.

Object Design

Figure 6-11 shows the emergency relief object design. The design utilizes the standard CRM On Demand Account, Contact, Opportunity, and Service Request objects, which have been renamed to reflect the streamlined process and terminology needed for emergency relief. The key objects include

- A family is represented by a Household. Household Members make up the individuals within the family.

- A Contact contains an individual's basic information—name, basic personal information, and basic medical condition. In this design, the application tracks more additional information for the primary member of the household, such as the best phone number to contact.

- The primary Contact will also have a primary Contact Address, for example, the family's permanent address. If the Contact has been displaced, multiple temporary addresses can be tracked as well.

- Each Contact's short-term needs are tracked as a Service Request. A grant request is stored as an Opportunity. Grants can be tracked according to stage, just as a standard sales opportunity can be.

- The Opportunity Assessment stores eligibility rules for a particular grant type. The assessment can be attached to the individual grant request.

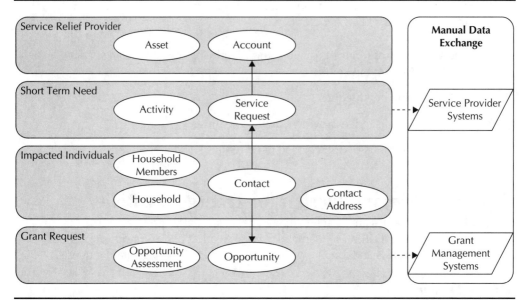

FIGURE 6-11. *Object design for emergency relief implementation*

- Account stores the relief service provider details. These are the organizations that will service the short-term need requests. A need is matched to a service provider by assigning the Contact Service Request to the relief service provider account.

- Asset stores the goods and services available for each service provider.

Access and Visibility
Given the fluid and short-term nature of a relief effort, each user within the application has full visibility to all records, so agency workers can quickly access any information they need. If more restrictions are required, then you can update the user roles to enforce visibility through record ownership.

Analytics
Because the design utilizes the standard objects, Analytics reports are easy to develop. The following types of reports are available from the data warehouse:

- Client Status (utilizes the Contact History subject area)
  - Client summary by city

- ■ Individual client disposition

- ■ Unassigned clients

- ■ Short-Term Needs Analysis (utilizes the Service Request History subject area)

  - ■ Current short-term needs aging analysis

  - ■ Current short-term needs assigned by service provider

  - ■ Short-term needs not assigned to a service provider

- ■ Grants Analysis (utilizes the Opportunity History subject area)

  - ■ Grant request summary

  - ■ Current open grants aging analysis

Another benefit of this simple design is that you can use the Printer Friendly links on the Detail Layouts to get a quick printout of virtually all of the information associated with the Household.

Integration

Most relief service providers and grant organizations will want to use their own tracking systems, so the coordination among organizations is managed through reporting. If tighter systems integration is possible, you can always set up a data exchange using Web Services or manual import/export.

Specialty Solutions: Account Planning

The following design is for a basic account planning process, which many organizations consider essential for effective customer account management. This design utilizes Custom Objects to create a simple application. The application consists of a basic situational analysis for an account, an objective-based account plan, and activity tracking for each of the objectives.

Each company claims a unique process for conducting account planning, but the basic process consists of similar elements. First, a company will gather intelligence from direct (interviews and surveys) and indirect methods in order to establish an objective assessment of their customer's disposition. They will then analyze the intelligence to determine the overall status of the company's relationship with the customer. Generally, the analysis will categorize the relationship into strengths, weaknesses, opportunities, and threats. Based on the assessment, a company will then identify a set of objectives that they want to accomplish with the customer over a period of time. Once approved, these plans are then tasked to an owner and the progress monitored.

CRM On Demand Design for Account Planning

The following is a basic account plan design. The design makes extensive use of Custom Objects to model the account analysis and planning process. The key to this design is to choose the right Custom Object types in order to benefit from their built-in functionality.

Object Design

Figure 6-12 describes the object design. The design consists of six Custom Objects that model the account analysis and plan/objectives. The design is organized as follows:

■ The Account represents the customer.

■ The Account relationship consists of four dimensions (represented by Custom Objects 4–7)

  ■ Expectations a customer has for the company. For example, high-quality products and consistent on-time delivery.

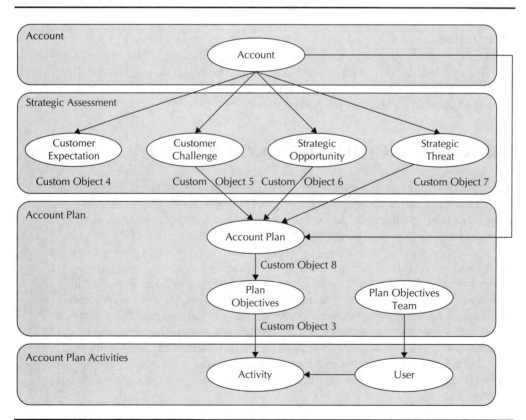

FIGURE 6-12. *Account plan object design*

- Challenges or issues that impede the relationship with the customer. For example, a recent negotiation ended poorly, damaging a relationship with senior management.

- Strategic Opportunities that the company has identified. For example, the customer is expanding its manufacturing next year and will be looking for a strategic vendor.

- Strategic Threats that may undermine the relationship. For example, the recently failed negotiation resulted in a major competitor winning the business, giving the competitor its first inroad with this customer and putting the expansion opportunity at risk.

- Each Challenge, Strategic Opportunity, or Strategic Threat is assigned to one or more Account Plans (represented by Custom Object 8). This link provides the purpose for putting an Account plan into place—either to exploit an Opportunity or to mitigate a Threat.

- An Account Plan consists of one or more Plan Objectives (represented by Custom Object 3). For example, an Objective tied to a Challenge-based Account Plan may be to establish quarterly visits designed to develop stronger relationships with customer management.

- Each Objective is assigned to one or more Users on the Plan Objective Team. This Team object is a prebuilt object that comes with Custom Objects 1 to 3. Refer to Chapter 5 for an overview of Custom objects.

- Users then log Activities against their assigned Objectives to track their progress.

Access and Visibility

By setting up these objects as related items under the Account object, the account plan application will mirror the Account access model we've set up for this example company. If a user has access to an Account, either through Ownership, Account teams, or Book of Business, he or she will see the related items under the account plan application.

Analytics

Because the design utilizes Custom Objects, you will need to use Real-Time Reporting to access the advanced Custom Object subject areas. The following types of reports are available:

Account Analysis reports available include

- Expectations by Account

- Opportunities by Account

- Threats by Account

- Challenges by Account

Note that you can consolidate the above reports into a single Strategic Assessment report using Combined Analysis.

Activity Reporting reports include

- Activities by Account Plan Objective

Summary

In this chapter, we've shown you example CRM On Demand designs created for a range of industries and business processes. These designs are based on what we've learned working with many customers over the years to meet common types of needs. We encourage you to take these designs and apply them to your needs as appropriate. As with all designs, you will need to test and confirm their applicability to your particular business need. And, to get the best out of any design, you will need to configure them according to the CRM On Demand best practices. We'll discuss these best practices in detail in the next chapter.

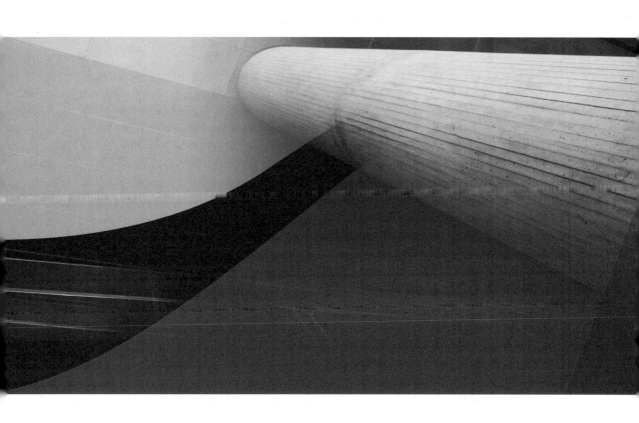

CHAPTER
7

Best Practices
for Configuring
CRM On Demand

ow that you've gone through the rigorous process of designing your CRM On Demand application to meet your particular business needs, you can begin to apply the configuration changes necessary to represent that design in the system. Just as the overall CRM design should adhere to best practices, the configuration should hold to those practices as well. In this chapter, we'll discuss how to achieve an effective configuration by applying proven best practices.

CRM On Demand provides administrators with numerous tools for configuring the application to support a business process. These include field configuration (relabeling, adding, and removing fields, creating cascading picklists, and performing advanced field management), Page Layouts, Custom Objects, data access controls, and workflow management. A high-quality configuration starts with understanding the available tools and options, as well as their limits. Configuring within the constraints of the application and avoiding extensive customization will result in a system that is easy to maintain and upgrade.

Field Configuration

CRM On Demand is configured to meet a particular business need primarily through field configuration. Adding, relabeling, and removing fields on the various business objects is a simple but effective means of making CRM On Demand work for you. For some companies, this configuration may be the only alteration they make to the out-of-the-box system.

CRM On Demand allows you to add Custom Fields of various types to your Screen Layouts. The number of available fields is predetermined; therefore, take care in allocating the field types you need. Table 7-1 lists the number and types of fields that are available for each record type (Accounts, Contacts, etc.), unless an exception is noted. Use Table 7-1 when planning your field configuration to ensure that you stay within field number and length limits. Refer to the application's online help for the most up-to-date field limits in your version. Just as we've said previously, a simple and direct data model and design is best, so fewer fields on screen result in higher user adoption rates.

Of particular note are *Indexed Custom Fields.* These fields are easily identified by their default labels (Indexed Picklist 1, etc.) and differ from other Custom Fields in that they are visible immediately in the application without selecting the New button; they are simply modified to suit a particular need by changing the field label.

These fields, as the name implies, are preindexed for optimal performance. When deciding on how to use the available indexed fields, consider which fields will be searched and sorted on most often. These fields should be indexed to ensure the best user experience. For example, you might want to use a picklist to note the Product Interest of an Opportunity, as you know sales reps will search on or report on this field regularly. Rather than create a new Custom Picklist field, you would find the next available indexed picklist, Indexed Picklist 1, and then rename it and add your values.

	Field Type	Length Limit (characters)	Number Available	Considerations/Exceptions
1	Checkbox	N/A	35	Consider using a picklist with the values of Yes and No. Picklists have the advantage of showing three states (Yes, No, and Not Selected) and can be more easily validated through workflows.
2	Currency	15	25	Accounts support 80 Currency fields.
3	Date	25	25	
4	Date/Time	25	25	Date/Time fields may slow down your lists and reports. Consider a Date field if you don't need time accuracy.
5	Integer	10	35	Whole numbers only, no decimals.
6	Multi-select picklist	30	10	Multi-select lists are supported on Accounts, Contacts, Opportunities, Leads, Activities, Service Requests, and Custom Objects 1 and 2. These lists only appear in Historical Analytics.
7	Number	10	33	Numbers will have a decimal.
8	Percent	16	30	
9	Picklist	30	100	Picklists can include up to 1,000 items (both active and inactive). Once added, values cannot be deleted but can be renamed. Initial values become the language-independent ID for that value and cannot be changed.
10	Phone	35	10	Custom Objects allows 20 Phone fields.
11	Text (Short)	40	45	Contacts and Opportunities allow 70 custom Short Text fields. Custom Objects 1–3 allows 60 fields. Custom Objects 4–*n* allows 90 fields. Short text fields are popular for storing ad hoc information but are not well suited for repetitive indicators that provide the basis for reporting or lists. Consider picklists in these cases.
12	Text (Long)	255	30	Position Long Text fields in the left column with no field in the right column. This placement will allow the field to expand as more text is added.
13	Weblink	N/A	100	Weblinks can be used to link to external sites, internal Analytics, or to invoke web services integration. See Chapter 8 for more detail.

TABLE 7-1. *Number and Types of Fields Available for Each Record Type*

Once you create a field, you cannot change its type. So, for example, a Custom Picklist cannot become an Indexed Picklist. Although you can modify your design later by copying field values from a custom list to an indexed one, this is a manual process and must be carefully planned.

The following Indexed Custom Fields are available on the main business objects. Note the fields for this may differ for some objects; refer to the online help for details.

- Indexed Checkbox

- Indexed Currency

- Indexed Date (note this is a Date/Time field)

- Indexed Long Text

- Indexed Number

- Indexed Picklist 1

- Indexed Picklist 2

- Indexed Picklist 3

- Indexed Picklist 4

- Indexed Picklist 5

- Indexed Picklist 6

- Indexed Short Text 1

- Indexed Short Text 2

Cascading Picklists

Cascading picklists can constrain the choices available in one picklist based on the value selected in another picklist. For example, consider how Service Requests are categorized. Each Service Request has an Area picklist. Each Area has several values: Hardware, Software, and Network. Now let's say you want to be a little more granular in classifying the Service Requests, so you have a field called Sub-Area. The Sub-Area field will have lots of values, including Printer, Desktop, Laptop, Operating System, Office Automation Software, Antivirus, Web Browser, and so on. You don't want all of those software options appearing, however, if the user selects Hardware for the Area. To limit and guide the user's Sub-Area selection, you can make the Sub-Area a cascading picklist linked to the Area field to determine what the user should see. When the user selects Hardware, only the Sub-Area values that correspond to Hardware will show up as field options. This example is shown in Figure 7-1.

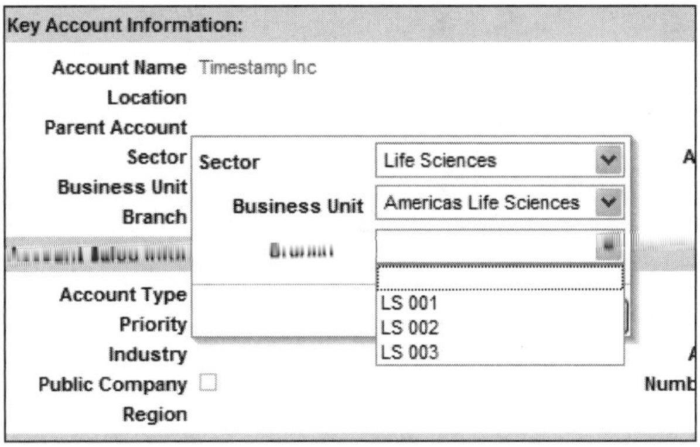

FIGURE 7-1. *A cascading picklist*

Consider using cascading picklists when you expect a picklist to exceed a hundred or more entries. But beware of stringing together too many picklists, as this can become confusing to end users and may result in redundant data. Three lists is an optimal upper limit for usability. Also carefully consider the total number of picklists available and allocate to your needs accordingly.

General Field Configuration Considerations

Adding fields to CRM On Demand is a very simple process. Take care to plan and document your field needs prior to implementation. Use the Field Setup Template Excel spreadsheet, shown in Figure 7-2 and provided by Oracle through Oracle Support, or create your own spreadsheet to list the fields you need, per object and by type. Cross-reference the fields by the Role that needs the field. Note if the field will be Required or Read Only for that Role.

As we've pointed out in previous chapters, Oracle online help provides many details not covered here. The help system is updated with each product upgrade, so always refer to it for the most accurate information.

Consider the following as you embark on your field configurations:

- Strive to present the end user with the minimum number of fields possible. Ask yourself this question, "Why is this field necessary?" and "How does this field support the business process?" If you've followed the recommendations in the earlier chapters, then you should be able to reference your business process flows to answer these questions.

- Avoid picklists with too many values (the upper limit is 1000); keep lists to less than a 100 values. Forcing users to scroll through hundreds of values can lead to frustration and impair usability. Consider how cascading picklists can be leveraged to keep picklists to a manageable length.

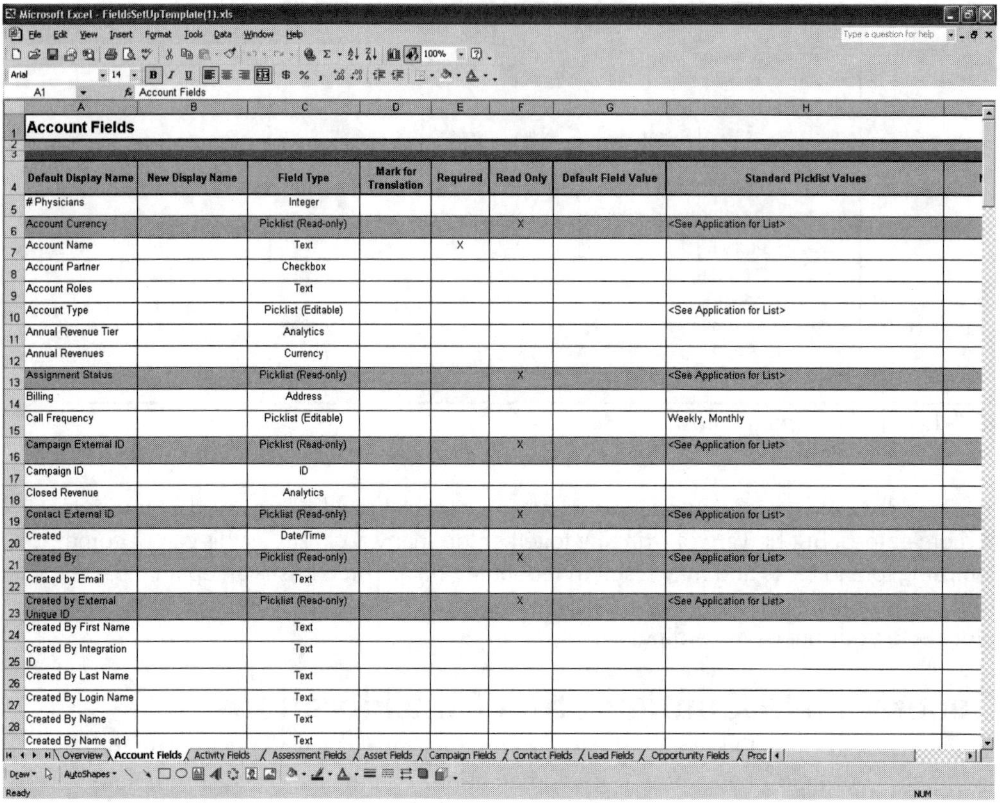

Default Display Name	New Display Name	Field Type	Mark for Translation	Required	Read Only	Default Field Value	Standard Picklist Values
# Physicians		Integer					
Account Currency		Picklist (Read-only)			X		<See Application for List>
Account Name		Text		X			
Account Partner		Checkbox					
Account Roles		Text					
Account Type		Picklist (Editable)					<See Application for List>
Annual Revenue Tier		Analytics					
Annual Revenues		Currency					
Assignment Status		Picklist (Read-only)			X		<See Application for List>
Billing		Address					
Call Frequency		Picklist (Editable)					Weekly, Monthly
Campaign External ID		Picklist (Read-only)			X		<See Application for List>
Campaign ID		ID					
Closed Revenue		Analytics					
Contact External ID		Picklist (Read-only)			X		<See Application for List>
Created		Date/Time					
Created By		Picklist (Read-only)			X		<See Application for List>
Created by Email		Text					
Created by External Unique ID		Picklist (Read-only)			X		<See Application for List>
Created By First Name		Text					
Created By Integration ID		Text					
Created By Last Name		Text					
Created By Login Name		Text					
Created By Name		Text					
Created By Name and		Text					

FIGURE 7-2. *Field Setup Template*

- Strive to keep the full content of a record detail page within one browser page, without requiring any scrolling.
- Use the out-of-the-box fields as much as possible. Creating a new Custom Field to represent Status on a Service Request, for instance, is usually unnecessary and may diminish the value of prebuilt lists and reports or force later rework. Many out-of-the-box fields are also used in built-in workflow and precalculated metrics. Discarding the original field will render these unusable.
- Fully examine the available out-of-the-box fields before adding a Custom Field. Many existing fields can be repurposed.

Field Management

Selecting the Edit option for any field brings you to the Field Management screen, as shown in Figure 7-3. From here, you can mark the field as Read Only. As you would expect, Read Only will prevent the field from being edited. Fields can also be marked as Required. This option forces users to input a value wherever this field appears and prevents a record from being saved without a value. The Copy Enabled checkbox will indicate that the value in this field will be copied to a new record. Note that this option is checked by default. When these options are selected in Field Management, they are applied throughout the application for all users.

CAUTION
Setting the Read Only and Required options at the Field Management level allows for no exceptions and could negatively impact some operations, such as web services integration. The same options can also be set within Page Layouts, as you'll see later in this chapter, and affect only specific roles.

Performing Advanced Field Management

Advanced field management allows administrators to specify default values and validation rules for a particular field. This feature can be used to ensure compliance with corporate standards and drive other workflow processes. Advanced field management can also be used to perform calculations based on other field values.

At its most basic level, advanced field management allows you to enter a *default value* that appears in the field when new records are created. For example, let's say you want to auto-populate the Total Discount that will be applied to an Opportunity. The Discount Amount is a percentage of the Opportunity Revenue. To calculate the Total Discount, you multiply the Revenue times the Discount Amount. This formula is used to populate the Default Value field within the Total Discount field.

Key Information

Display Name* Branch	Field Type* Picklist (Editable)
Mark for Translation ☐	

Additional Information

Required ☐	Default Value _____ *fx*
Read Only ☐	Post Default ☐
Copy Enabled ☑	Field Validation _____ *fx*
	Field Validation Error Message _____

FIGURE 7-3.   *Field Management screen*

By checking the Post Default checkbox (see Figure 7-3), the default value specified will not appear in the field when creating a new record, but will be populated when the record is saved if the user enters no other value. CRM On Demand's Expression Builder provides a basic scripting language suited to mathematical calculations and data-based logic. When your record is saved, the calculation is performed and the resulting value appears in the field.

Advanced field management can also be used to *validate field entry*. Validation allows you to create rules that enforce compliance with data entry standards set by your company. For example, a simple validation rule may check to determine if an entered value is long enough. Proceeding from the previous example, let's suppose a discount code is expected to be four characters. A validation rule can check the length of the value and force an error message to appear if the code is too long or too short.

More complex validation rules can be written to interrogate other field values to ensure the overall data entry is compliant. For example, when Opportunity Revenue is greater than $100,000, the Priority field should be set to High.

Note that Field Validation does not directly set or update field values; Default Value and Workflow can be used for that. Field Validation checks the state of the record before saving it and prevents noncompliant data from being saved. An error message can be specified to give the user an indication of why saving the record failed and what action, if any, he or she needs to take.

More detailed examples of setting up Default Values and Field Validations are in the Appendix.

Field Management Considerations

Be aware that the Default Value option only takes effect when you create a record. The Default Value is not enforced when you update a record. Validation rules, however, will be invoked when you save a new record and update existing records.

In many cases, you will need to use a combination of field management and workflow to achieve the desired results. For example, use field management to set an initial Default Value, and then use workflow to update the value as needed when the record is modified.

Field management settings are not role-specific, so they are in effect for all users at all times, unless there is logic within the expression itself that excludes a Role. One Field Validation expression is allowed per field. You may use Expression Builder to check several fields and conditions for the record at once, but only one error message will be displayed. Use a generic error message in these cases to assist users.

Page Layouts

Once you have created the fields required for your business, they must be arranged in a logical sequence on screen. Page Layouts are tied to a user Role. A single Page Layout may be shared among several Roles. Although minimizing the number of

Page Layouts you create in order to reduce maintenance overhead may be desirable, this alone should not drive decisions on the "right" number of layouts.

Layouts should present the data in the best possible way for the user. Justification for a new layout may be the inclusion of a different field or simply a unique arrangement of fields. For example, system administrators may need to see record ID fields to verify external integration processes. These fields would not be appropriate or necessary for an end-user layout. Inside sales reps may need qualification fields that collect data not used by field sales reps. In each case, a separate layout should be created to tailor the information shown to the user.

Page Layouts have the following attributes that you need to consider when deciding how best to apply them.

Sections   Each Page Layout contains sections that divide the detail page into groups of fields. A detail page may have up to six sections, each with a header (Key Account Information, Sales Information, etc.). If no fields are placed in a section, then the section does not appear.

Include your key fields under the first section header as these are the fields that will display when using the Preview option (the preview pops up when you hover on the record name). By default, the major business objects (Account, Contact, etc.) have three sections. If possible, keep the fields in each section to no more than 12 (6 in each column). This number provides optimal readability. Group your fields by purpose and function under the appropriate section header.

Field Setup   Each field can be marked Required or Read Only. System fields, such as auto timestamps, or key fields, such as primary name fields, cannot be marked as such. Note that the Required and Read Only checkboxes for layouts are the same as those for field management, which we discussed earlier in the chapter. Choosing those settings on this screen invokes these controls only within the chosen layout (and, therefore, only for the Role or Roles to which the layout is associated). Often this is a better approach than using field management, as it allows more flexibility.

Field Layout   This area allows you to specify the position of each field on the screen and within the available sections. Give serious thought to the appropriate "flow" of information on the screen. Core, often-accessed information should be at the top. High-value critical information should be next, followed by less critical information in subsequent sections.

The last section of information may contain creation and modification timestamps. The last field on any detail screen is the long Description field. The Description field can neither be moved on the layout nor removed from it. Note that not all available sections need be populated with fields. A blank section will not appear in the record detail.

Related Information   Sometimes the most important and useful information on a record detail is part of the Related Information, or *applets*. For example, on an

Opportunity Detail page, viewing the list of recent related Activities gives users a good bit of information about how a deal is progressing. Adding the right related information should be considered just as important as field layout.

Be careful not to overwhelm the user with unnecessary applets. We recommend that, at most, you include four to five key applets in the displayed column. If necessary, you can always add more applets to the Available Information column, and allow users to choose them for display if they really have to have them. As a rule of thumb, avoid creating pages that require scrolling more than two screen lengths.

Related Information Layout   For each Related Information applet, you also choose a field layout. These layouts are created in the Related Information Layout section of Page Layout Management. Take advantage of this step to further enhance the usability of detail pages. Choose the fields that are most relevant for users, so they get useful information "at a glance" without having to click into the related record. Note that not all fields are available in all related layouts. Administrators should verify that the fields are available before committing to any configuration changes.

Considerations for Page Layouts

In general, strive for simplicity in your layouts. Fewer fields means greater usability. Consider what information is important to each user Role and pare back less important data. Using dynamic, type-driven layouts can provide a way to contextualize the information on screen at any point in time. For data that is needed but not that frequently, consider other approaches to maintaining and presenting it. For example, if a sales rep occasionally wants to view several Marketing fields for a given Account, don't put those fields on the layout. Rather, create a custom report with those fields and then expose that report as a web link in the Account Detail.

Validate the usability and flow of information on screen by seeking user feedback or observing user behavior. Subtle changes in field arrangement and grouping can have a marked impact on usability and productivity.

Web Applets

Web applets are a type of Related Information that can be added to a record detail page. Web applets allow you to create an information pane from external information sources, custom views of CRM On Demand data driven by web services or Analytics, or any other web-accessible content. Because the contents are completely under your control, you can define the look and feel as well as the interactivity of the page, such as clicking through to another web site or drilling into details.

If you choose to use web applets, set them up to present information in context with the page on which they appear. Fields from the record, such as the Account Name or Account ID, can be passed as a URL parameter. A very simple example is shown in Figure 7-4. This web applet will display search results from Google within the applet pane by passing the Account Name field as a search parameter on the URL.

FIGURE 7-4.   *Google search results in a web applet*

Embedded Analytics via a Web Applet

CRM On Demand Analytics allows you to create detailed reports and charts based on your CRM On Demand data. Adding these reports contextually to a record detail page gives users instant access to actionable information. For example, adding a sales trend chart, as shown in Figure 7-5, to an Account Detail page may provide more insight into the Account than a simple list of Opportunities could achieve.

Keep in mind that each web applet added to a detail page layout will have to be loaded and rendered. This can potentially require several Internet connections and downloads. Multiple applets can slow down the response time for the full detail page to load, so keep applets to a reasonable number. If load times become unacceptable, consider using web links to access the same information.

Dynamic Layouts

Dynamic layouts give you another layer of control over how information is presented to users. Although a layout may be tailored to a particular Role, the information required for collection or display may vary based on the record type. Here, we are referring to the type field that distinguishes, for example, a Customer Account from a Partner Account.

Dynamic layouts have a *driving* picklist field that determines which layout is displayed. In most cases, this is a type field (Account Type, Contact Type, etc.). Vertical Objects sometimes differ. Table 7-2 shows the business objects that support dynamic layouts and the driving field for each layout. The driving field is predefined and cannot be changed. Note you can change the label of the driving picklist field

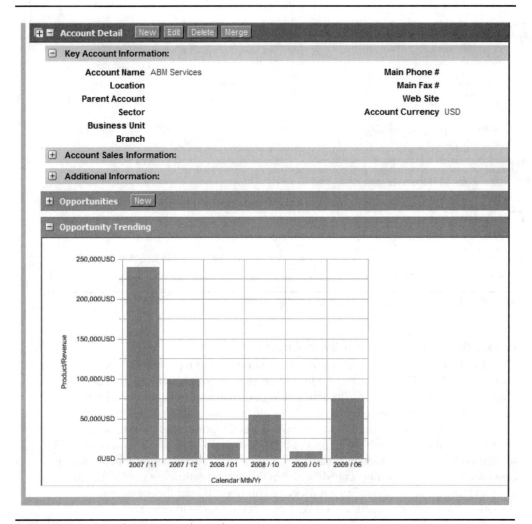

FIGURE 7-5. *Analysis in a web applet*

to suit your particular approach. For example, Opportunity "Channel" for partner, reseller, or distributor may drive what fields should appear. In this case, rename Opportunity Type to Opportunity Channel and set the appropriate values.

Considerations for Dynamic Layouts

As with static layouts, dynamic layouts can be applied to a Role. Multiple dynamic layouts can be created for a single business object and applied to different Roles. In this way, you can tailor the experience around the user and his or her particular needs regarding various types of records.

Business Object	Driving Picklist
Account	Account Type
Activity (Task & Appointment)	Type
Contact	Contact Type
Campaign	Campaign Type
Dealer (vertical object)	Status
Household (vertical object)	Segment
Lead	Source
MedEd Event (vertical object)	Type
Opportunity	Opportunity Type
Portfolio (vertical object)	Account Type
Service Request	Type
Solution	Status
Vehicle (vertical object)	Used/New

TABLE 7-2.   *Driving Picklists for Dynamic Layouts*

Consider your default layout. To build your dynamic layout scheme, you first need to create the layouts you will associate with each value in the driving picklist. The first screen displayed to the user, however, will be whatever you choose as a default. You should build this layout to display a minimal set of information—perhaps just the record name and the driving picklist. Keep the layout as simple as possible so it is clear the user is expected to provide a value in the driving picklist before continuing on.

Use consistent field placement. Each layout within your dynamic layout scheme can be completely different—but the differences shouldn't be jarring. Keeping fields that are consistent from layout to layout in the same section and in the same location reduces the visual impact of any change and focuses attention on the sections and fields that are different. For example, regardless of its type, all of your Accounts will have an Account Name. Keep this field in the same general area across all layouts.

Custom Objects

CRM On Demand can be extended to encompass additional business entities by employing Custom Objects. Custom Objects are essentially generic business objects that can be defined by relabeling or adding Custom Fields and picklists to model your specific needs. These objects differ from the out-of-the-box objects in that they have no predefined purpose and no inherent business process behind them.

Custom Objects are made available through a request to Oracle Support. Although Custom Objects can stand alone as a separate record type, they are most often used in relationship to other business objects. For example, you may want to store order information in CRM On Demand. Orders have no predefined record type. A Custom Object can be used to contain all information about the order. Each Order is a record that contains fields for the Order Type, Amount, Delivery Date, and so on.

As a stand-alone record, the Order isn't very useful. What is needed is a relationship between this Order and the Account that placed the Order. You can define this relationship as one-to-many (one Account may have many Orders). Furthermore, this Order is likely the result of an Opportunity. If so, the Order should be linked to the Opportunity. Each Opportunity produces only one Order (in this example) so this relationship is one-to-one.

To realize this configuration, you'll first configure the Custom Object. Follow these steps:

1. Provision Custom Object 1 through Oracle Support.

2. Rename Custom Object 1 as **Order**.

3. Configure the Order object.

   A. Relabel or add custom fields to contain all the order detail.

   B. Create a new Page Layout containing the new fields. Include the Opportunity Name on the layout to allow an Order to be linked to a single Opportunity.

   C. Consider using the following special-purpose fields:

   ■ **Name** This is the main label for the record and will be the link to the record in all views. You can relabel this field Order Name or Order Number.

   ■ **Quick Search 1 and Quick Search 2** These short text fields are optimized for searching and are displayed on the Action Bar if Targeted Search is used.

Next, you need to make changes to the Opportunity configuration. In this case, you're specifying a one-to-one relationship, so you only add the Order Name field to the Opportunity Page Layout. This change has the effect of adding a lookup tool and link.

You'll also need to update the Account Page Layout. Because many Orders are related to an Account, make Orders a Related Item rather than simply a lookup field. This setting will allow you to link multiple Orders to a single Account.

Finally, you will need to make changes to Roles and Access Profiles to expose this new functionality to the end user. For each Role requiring access, several updates are required:

1. Under Role Management: Record Type Access, select Has Access?. If users are required to enter Orders directly, then you should also select Can Create?. In this example, Orders will be imported from another system, so you can leave this deselected.

2. Orders will not be owned by a sales user. Unless you provide access to them via Teams or Books, users will not be able to see the orders. Therefore, you will select Can Read All Records?. Because the Orders will only be accessible through Accounts and Opportunities, the user's access to those business records will determine which Orders he or she can easily view.

3. Under Role Management: Page Layout Assignment, select the configured Page Layout for Orders.

4. If new Page Layouts were created for Accounts and Opportunities to expose the Orders, then select these layouts.

5. Optional: If Orders are accessed via a tab, under Role Management: Tab Access & Order, add the Orders tab to the available or selected Tabs. In this example, Orders will only be viewable as a child of Accounts and Opportunities.

6. Modify Access Profiles for the impacted Roles. Under Step 2: Specify Access Levels, set the appropriate level for Orders. The default is Read Only. For this example, users will not be changing Orders so you'll leave this alone.

7. On Account Related Information, set the Access Level for Orders to Read Only.

Users with the updated Role will now see an Orders applet on the Account Detail page and an Orders link/lookup field on the Opportunity Detail page.

Advanced Custom Objects

There are important functional differences between Custom Objects 1–3 and Custom Objects 4–15; therefore, we will refer to Custom Objects 4–15 as *Advanced Custom Objects (ACO)*.

Advanced Custom Objects have the following attributes:

- Single Activities section (combines Open and Completed Activities)

- No attachments

- No dynamic layouts

■ No Notes

■ No multi-select picklists

■ No Team support

Another key distinction of Advanced Custom Objects is the way they can be related to other business objects. Unlike Custom Objects 1–3, which can have many-to-many relationships with all other objects, ACOs support one-to-many relationships with all other objects.

To enable a one-to-one relationship with another business object (including another Advanced Custom Object), simply add the lookup field for that object to the ACO Page Layout. To create a one-to-many relationship, an ACO should be added as a Related Item on the Page Layout for another business object. What differs here is that the applet displays a New button, but not an Add button. This restricts the relationship and prevents a many-to-many association.

We do not recommend adding both the lookup field and the Related Item to the layout because it will create essentially two independent links and confuse users.

Many-to-many relationships between ACOs and other business objects are possible using an intermediary object. In essence, you can model the relationship using an ACO as a link between other objects. This approach actually has some interesting advantages. Because the relationship is a full-fledged object, you can add Custom Fields to it, allowing for enhanced attributes to be tracked. Also, the relationship itself can be viewed as a top-level object, or tab, and searched directly.

Note that the features available in Advanced Custom Objects are likely to change with new updates, so always refer to the online documentation for the latest information.

A detailed example of creating many-to-many relationships using Advanced Custom Objects is shown in the Appendix.

Considerations for Custom Objects

With Custom Objects, you can model complex relationships that support a business process. Note that the most usable and successful CRM On Demand implementations leverage the simplest data model to meet key business needs. As shown in the previous examples, Custom Objects allow you to model business objects that are not native to the CRM On Demand application and, therefore, enable entirely unique business processes.

When designing and configuring your Custom Objects, understand what features, such as Analytics, field types, and relationships, are supported, as these may differ from other object types. Thoroughly document and validate the process design and the intended relationship model early on to avoid missteps.

Data Access and Security

In Chapter 5, we discussed the data access and security scheme. A well-designed system gives users access to the data they need to see when they need to see it, and provides the minimum level of access (Read-Only, Edit, Delete) required to complete their work.

Access Controls

CRM On Demand provides several means of controlling access. Data access and security is configured through a combination of settings at the Company, Role, and User level. Achieving the security scheme that is right for your company may involve a combination of these settings.

Manager Visibility

Manager Visibility is enabled for your company in the Company Profile. When Manager Visibility is enabled for your company, then the user hierarchy (via the User Reports To setting) influences data visibility. A manager essentially becomes the "owner" of his or her subordinates' data; the Owner Access Profile for her Role dictates her level of access.

For example, a Sales Executive has three Regional Managers who each manage several salespeople. The Sales users can see only the data they own. The Regional Managers can see their data, plus the data owned by their direct subordinates (but not each other), and the Sales Executive can see all the Regional Managers and her subordinates' data. Most organizations employ Manager Visibility because of its simplicity and ease of implementation. It can be effectively combined with Teams and Books to accommodate situations that fall outside the normal user hierarchy.

For optimal performance, keep the management hierarchy to no more than five (5) levels. Larger/deeper hierarchies generate long queries that tend to slow down access at the higher levels. In large organizations (more than a few hundred users), where the hierarchy is deeper, consider using Manager Visibility at the lower levels and giving executives Read All access or access via Books of Business.

Team-based Access

Account, Contact, and Opportunity Teams allow data to be discretely shared among various users. The Owner of an Account or Opportunity can choose to add individual users to the Team and grant them certain access levels (Read, Edit, and Full). The Team access levels are themselves Access Profiles, which can be copied or modified as needed. Teams are good for enabling small ad hoc groups to collaborate on accounts and deals. Larger teams or constant groupings may be a better candidate for Books of Business.

Pay careful attention to the Enable Team Inheritance setting in the Company Profile. When this box is checked, the members of the Account Team with access to Contacts and Opportunities will automatically be added to the team of any related Contacts and Opportunities. If this is not desired, then you should deselect this option and instruct users to add team members manually for these records.

Teams can be automated via Assignment Manager, though this will also affect the record owner. That is, when an assignment rule runs, it will always update the record owner. Also, team members can only be added through assignment rules, never removed. More thorough team automation is possible through web services. Teams apply to Accounts, Contacts, Opportunities, and Custom Objects 1–3, so access to other records will rely on Manager Visibility or another access approach.

Books of Business

Books are custom-defined containers of data. Each Book can hold records of any type. Users can be associated to Books with various access levels—Read, Edit, Full. Again, these levels are controlled via Access Profiles. These represent by far the most flexible means of controlling your data access.

Books allow you to create a batch of records that are viewable to a particular group of users. Books can also be part of a hierarchical parent-child structure. For example, a company with a regional structure may create books that match its territory alignment. The Books may group users from across the organization—sales users, sales consultants, product specialists, and so on—who typically work together. Books of Business has an advantage over Teams in that you need only assign the Book once and the users come along with it, rather than having to assign users one by one.

A few key considerations for Books:

■ Books have the advantage of being automated. On Demand Workflow allows Book assignments to be rules-based. An Account country or state, for example, could be evaluated in a rule that determines the appropriate Book. Any attribute, or combination of attributes, can form the basis for your assignment workflow, as long as the information resides on the record.

■ Keep the volume of records in a Book at a reasonable level. Although there is no hard limit to the number of records you can put in a single Book, we've found that flat book structures that limit the number of records contained in any one book perform best.

■ Plan your Book structure carefully. Consider how users interact with data and where they spend most of their time in the application. Are they always searching for records? Do they work against predefined lists? Strive to define Books that encompass a typical workload.

■ Remember that a single user can be assigned to multiple Books. Each Book the user has access to will appear in their Look-in Selector. A single Book need not contain all the data each user can see; users should be trained to use the Look-in Selector as an additional filter to target their searches and lists.

■ Books work slightly differently in Real-Time Reports vs. Analytics. In Analytics, when the Company Profile setting for Historical Subject Areas is Full Visibility, Books will work as they do in the user interface. However, Books work at only one level in Real-Time reports. That is, the user will only see data in the currently selected Book and not in any sub-Books. Note that Books will not be invoked at all if the user Role has the "Access All Data in Analytics" privilege enabled.

■ Keep your Book structure flat and avoid parent books completely, if possible. If you do use a hierarchy, keep data in only the lowest level or "leaf nodes" of your Book structure while leaving the "branches" bare. Only check the Can Contain Data option on Books that will hold records (as opposed to empty parent and branching books). These choices can have a noticeable impact on performance when running searches, lists, or reports.

Groups

Groups were an early implementation of predetermined Teams. By assigning a record to a Group, the members of the Group become automatically assigned to the Account Team. Groups have generally been replaced by Books of Business and are not recommended for continued use as an access control mechanism. Groups do offer an advantage in Calendar sharing, however; groups allow you to provide several users with access to each other's calendar.

Delegation

Delegation is a mechanism to grant one user the Owner visibility rights of another user. Users and Administrators can both add and remove Delegates from the User Detail page. Delegation is limited in several ways. It applies only to Owner access; the delegated user does not gain the primary user's default access. Delegation does not override a No Access setting on the user's Role. The delegated user must also have Can Create enabled to create a record of a particular type; this right is not inherited from the primary user. Delegation neither grants Books of Business access nor does it apply to Analytics.

Delegation is not a candidate for inclusion in an organizational access design. It can be used for specific point purposes, but should not be relied on as part of a broader access strategy.

Role Management

In Chapter 5, we discussed how Roles are an important part of your CRM On Demand design. Within Roles, you can define Record Access. This setting specifies, per record type, what the user can do. Within this area, administrators can select Read All Records. This option effectively makes all records of that type visible to all users with that Role. For this setting to apply in Reports, you will need to enable the Role-Based Can Read All Records option in the Company Profile.

CAUTION
This setting overrides any other discrete settings and allows for no exceptions. Keep in mind this setting could negatively impact performance for users when conducting searches, running lists, or viewing reports.

With those cautions in mind, this setting has valid uses. An example is Activity access. In most organizations, access to Accounts, Contacts, and Opportunities may be restricted, but there is a general need to see the Activities associated with these records regardless of who created or owns them. In this case, selecting Read All Records for Activity records simplifies the access model (you don't have to set up explicit controls for Activities) and meets the business requirement.

Access Profiles, associated with Roles, give finer control over what a user can do with the records accessible to him or her. Note that the access settings for Related Information (such as Opportunities related to Accounts) have special options:

- **View**   This applies the setting from the main record, as specified within the same Access Profile.

- **Inherit Primary**   This option will apply the user access settings to related lists. For example, when viewing an Account Detail screen, the user will only see the related Opportunities which he or she has access to. We recommend you apply this setting throughout the system.

It is important to understand that different Access Profiles may be invoked at different times. An Owner Access Profile is applied when the record is directly owned by the user viewing it or by his or her manager when Manager Visibility is enabled. A Default Access Profile applies when the user has access via the Read All Records setting. Different Access Profiles can be applied for Team and Book access, determined by the Grantable to Team Members and Grantable to Book Users options on the profile setup. Ensure you have set the appropriate options in each of the applicable profiles.

Considerations for Access Controls

During system design, as covered in Chapter 5, you should have considered the types of records each user needs access to as part of an overall business process. With the detailed understanding of each available access scheme covered here, you should select the approach that best fits your business need.

Keep in mind that the best approach may be a combination of access controls. For example, most organizations start with Manager Visibility (because managers often need to see their subordinates' records). As ad hoc teaming is deemed necessary, Account and Opportunity Teams are employed. Finally, when groups emerge that consistently work together, Books of Business are added. This variety of controls works well together and is transparent to the end user.

The user's ability to see, edit, or delete a record will be determined ultimately by the most "liberal" permissions allowed through the access controls in effect. For example, if a user has Read Only access via Teams but has Edit access through Books, then he or she has Edit access on the record.

Workflow Management

CRM On Demand allows you to configure trigger conditions and actions that can add automation and validation to your business processes. Workflow uses the same scripting syntax as advanced field management, but allows for a broad range of actions. Workflows can be set to fire when records are updated, created, or deleted.

Workflow actions can include creating tasks, initiating time-based sequences, assigning Books, updating fields, sending e-mail alerts, or integrating events. The details of workflow creation are covered in the CRM On Demand online help and will not be discussed here, although you will find several examples in the Appendix.

Considerations for Workflow Management

Workflows offer a powerful tool for CRM On Demand designers and developers for adding dynamism to the system as well as a means of enforcing desired business processes. Although much can be done with workflows, you should be wary of excessive automation. Automating for every possible exception could result in a system that is unwieldy to use and administer. Weigh the benefits and drawbacks of each automation step against the cost and benefits of thorough training and end-user support.

Workflow rules represent one area of development, along with web services integration, that should be tested in a staging or alternate environment prior to deployment. Once a workflow rule is active, it is active for all users immediately. Therefore, take care to ensure that it works properly and does not conflict with other existing workflow rules.

Automatic Books of Business assignment is a particularly useful feature and should be leveraged if Books are enabled. Remember that automated Book assignment works on one record type per rule—so multiple rules will be needed to assign an Account and its related Contacts and Opportunities to a Book. Further, "create" and "modify" actions represent different rules. In a large organization with several Books, the number of assignment rules can quickly multiply. While this is not in itself a problem, be prepared for the ramifications of maintaining the rule set and consider how the Book structure or visibility model may be simplified. For example, perhaps Contacts could be Open access for most Roles since Contacts are typically arrived at via the Account record, thereby reducing the number of Book assignment rules required.

Keep in mind that evaluating and executing workflow rules employs system resources. Generally this load is minimal, but a high number of workflows triggering all at once could result in delayed actions. You should determine if you require workflows to fire only when triggered by human interaction. Employ the **ExcludeChannel( )** function to prevent a rule from activating via import or web services.

When using Wait actions, limit the use of one-minute timers. Wait actions are evaluated sequentially so a large number of actions in a queue can incur a delay in processing. It is best to use hourly increments or higher.

Summary

By adhering to the guidelines provided in this chapter, you can avoid common pitfalls and apply hard-learned lessons when configuring your CRM On Demand application. Review this chapter before starting the configuration phase and keep it on hand when implementing your system settings. These best practices will ensure a highly usable system that is easily maintained and seamlessly upgraded.

With a solid configuration, coupled with a system design founded upon the principles and guidance supplied in Chapters 5 and 6, you are well on your way to a successful deployment. Extending your design and configuration through integration can complete the picture, as you'll see in the next chapter.

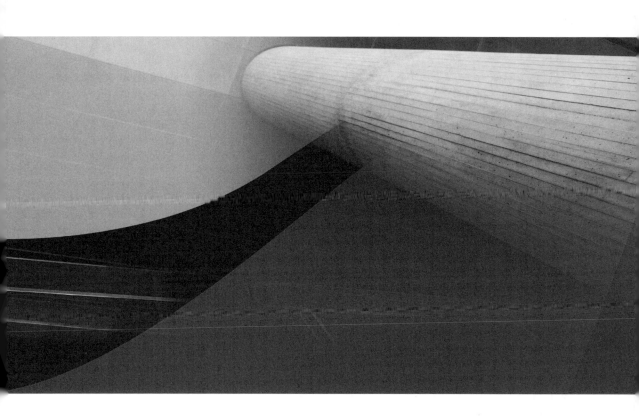

CHAPTER
8

Integration in Oracle
CRM On Demand

RM On Demand's flexible interface allows designers and developers to extend the application through front-end configuration, third-party add-ons, or custom programming. The extensive Web Services application programming interface (API) is commonly used to build batch or real-time integrations between other front- and back-office systems. The goal of integration in your design is to put the right information in the right place, available to the right user at the right time. In this chapter, we will examine the available integration options, from simple to complex, that can meet this goal, and point out the key considerations for each option.

Integration does not always mean middleware, coding, or expensive development. In fact, many companies leverage embedded external content and contextual links to deploy highly integrated applications with little or no coding at all. CRM On Demand provides the framework for integration at several levels to meet a variety of business needs.

We will explore three opportunities for integration. First, the CRM On Demand user interface provides basic tools for embedding external web content and pushing CRM content out. Second, built-in data integration tools can easily import and export records. Finally, the CRM On Demand Web Services API allows for ultimate flexibility in designing and building complex integrations and business logic.

User Interface Integration

The CRM On Demand user interface, or UI, is tailored to provide an elegant, seamless experience for users working with sales, marketing, or service functions. You can also manipulate the UI in surprising ways to augment the basic information resident in CRM On Demand with more dynamic data.

CRM On Demand's UI can be viewed as an open source tool for extending the application's capability. Often referred to as *mashups,* the technique of combining multiple sources of data and capabilities into a single presentation has often been used in consumer applications and web sites. Applying these same techniques to a business application like CRM On Demand can improve usability and user effectiveness with minimal effort.

Web Tabs

CRM On Demand's tab-based interface provides intuitive navigation for users, giving them one-click access to the major areas in which they work every day. This tab scheme can be expanded to include content from sources external to the application.

When a user accesses a web tab, the familiar On Demand interface stays in place, allowing the user to navigate easily between the CRM areas and the integrated content. This content might include your corporate intranet or expense entry system or other frequently accessed web sites.

Defining a web tab is as simple as copying and pasting the URL. For access to restricted internal resources, single sign-on (SSO) logic can be embedded in the web tab. Once created, a web tab becomes a seamless part of the CRM On Demand interface.

Web Linking

The simplest way to provide users with easy access to content and services outside of CRM On Demand is through a hyperlink. Although no longer revolutionary, hyperlinks remain the primary means of navigating across the Internet.

With CRM On Demand's intelligent web links, a hyperlink can do more than simply launch a new web page. With contextual content added to a link, it can carry additional information for the target web site. A simple example of this is linking to a search engine such as Google. As shown in Figure 8-1, the Account Name can be passed along in the URL as a parameter.

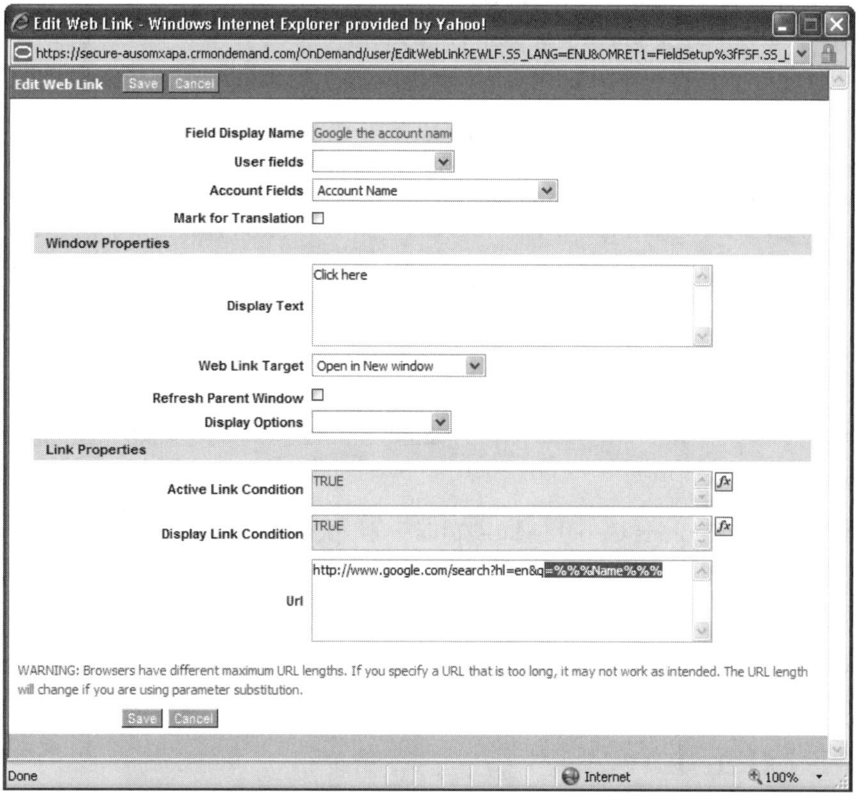

FIGURE 8-1. *A web link to a search engine*

When placed on an Account detail page, this link field will replace the generic parameter "%%%Name%%%" with the current Account Name. This type of parameterized URL isn't just for simple searching, however. Web links can serve as the primary mechanism for initiating complex integrations or retrieving information from other web-enabled internal systems.

The concept of adding parameters to a URL link is carried over to web applets. Web applets and web links each have their advantages. *Web applets* put information directly on the page; no user action is required to retrieve the information. *Web links* allow users to choose what information they need, when they need it. This ability can be advantageous if your detail page layouts are becoming long or the load time for external applets is slow or unpredictable.

RSS Feeds

One challenge many companies face is keeping users current on the most recent customer activities. Putting news and announcements regarding an Account in front of users can help prepare them for the next sales call and provide a compelling reason to revisit the system. RSS feeds are a simple and popular method for accessing news on just about any company or topic. RSS feeds may be very similar to other web content, but are usually simpler in format. Feed readers will check for updated content periodically.

CRM On Demand can act as an RSS reader when you embed a feed URL into the UI. Embedded content can reside in global or record-specific applets. When an applet is defined as type "feed," it will automatically interpret the provided URL as an RSS feed and display it appropriately. This process is simple, as shown in Figure 8-2, requiring that you only know the feed URL. Once created, web applets can be placed on the Home Page, as shown in Figure 8-3.

Web Application Integration

The web today is awash in custom utilities and applications—some very simple and some very complex. Much of what you consume on the Internet is made available for free or at low cost. Just about any such service can be leveraged within CRM On Demand's flexible interface.

A common example is Google Maps. This web application may already be the tool of choice for sales reps planning their site visits. By embedding the map application directly in the user interface, as shown in Figure 8-4, you can extend CRM On Demand without coding or complex data integration.

Your web applications aren't limited to maps or search engines, but can include proprietary or custom-built services as well.

HTML Extensions

When creating a web applet, you aren't limited to RSS feeds or URLs. You can also directly embed HTML code, including JavaScript, into the page, thus giving you

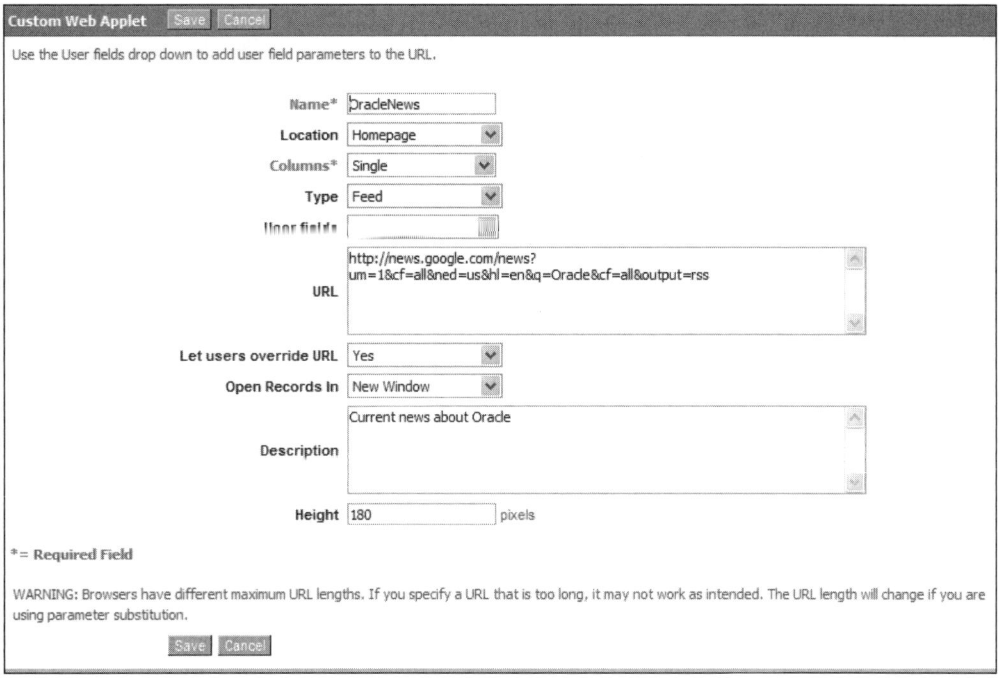

FIGURE 8-2. *Adding an RSS feed web applet to CRM On Demand*

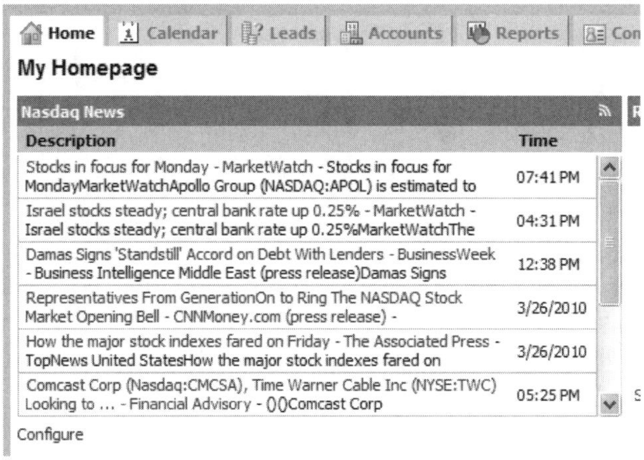

FIGURE 8-3. *An RSS feed displayed on the Home Page*

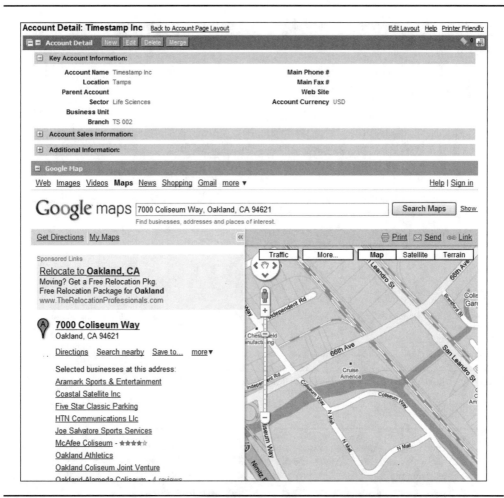

FIGURE 8-4. *A Google Map embedded on the Account Detail page*

tremendous flexibility in defining applet content. This feature also allows you to build complex calculations and logic into the application with client-side scripting. The resulting content is rendered in the applet just as with the RSS feed and URL applets described previously.

With JavaScript coding, administrators can further manipulate the user interface by adding or removing buttons.

External Portal Integration

Bringing content into CRM On Demand via web links and applets can extend the application beyond a business system and toward a portal solution. Many users, however, may have already established personalized portals. Adding CRM On Demand content into the user's portal allows the user to gain value from the system wherever he or she happens to work.

Through their personal setup, users can choose to embed CRM content elsewhere as widgets. These *widgets* are bits of information delivered within the iFrame standard, which is accepted by most portal providers including Google.

Widget content can include

- User-defined Favorite Lists

- Pre-built lists

- Message Center content

- Any accessible report

As seen in Figure 8-5, CRM On Demand makes accessing widgets very easy. The application-generated code can be copied into your portal or added to Google with a single click. When users access their portal page, they will see live interactive data from CRM On Demand.

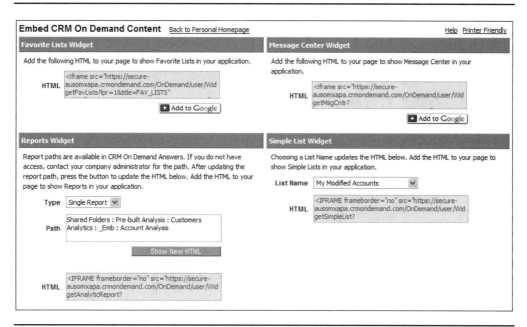

FIGURE 8-5. *CRM On Demand widgets*

Considerations for User Interface Integration

The integration methods discussed thus far occur at the web-browser level. No custom coding or external hosting is needed to leverage these approaches and no tinkering at the application or database level is required. Although simple to employ, these mechanisms may be combined with more complex business logic to extend CRM On Demand.

When assessing UI integration, consider the following questions:

- *Is the information you need web accessible?* UI integration is a good choice, allowing any web content to be easily included in a mashup.

- *Does the information change often?* External content is always accessed real-time via UI integration, so inserting links to frequently changing content is preferable to high-frequency integrations.

- *Is the data required for comprehensive Analytics?* UI integration leaves the data outside of CRM On Demand and, therefore, inaccessible to CRM On Demand Analytics. If the data is critical to the reports built into CRM On Demand, then you'll want to use the data integration tools or web services to bring the data into the application.

Browser-based integration has the advantage of putting information where the user needs it and making it accessible when it is relevant. The data itself, however, remains detached from CRM On Demand. Now let's look at the mechanisms that actually move data in and out of the application.

Data Integration

When business requirements dictate that external data needs to be included in CRM On Demand or that CRM data is needed in an external system, the application offers choices ranging from simple to complex.

Web-based Data Import

The most common—and simplest—way to bring data into CRM On Demand or to maintain that data once loaded is through the built-in Data Import tool. All objects, including Custom Objects, are supported. Data files in comma-separated (csv) format can be loaded and visually mapped to target fields through a point-and-click interface. Through the use of unique identifiers, existing data records can be updated with new information through the same process.

Although simple to use, data imports should be carefully planned and tested. No undo option is available, so once you've committed an import, you cannot back out of it. Administrators and developers should be familiar with the import process, including the field types and associated limits, before attempting an import. Most important, any new data import should be tested with a small number of records to assess errors and allow for corrections in the final data files.

The Data Import tool is suitable for relatively modest batches of records; most objects allow 30,000 records per submission. Repetitive data loads move quickly thanks to reusable mapping files generated during each load. Because the tool provides detailed error handling and reporting, it is the tool of choice for loading initial launch data. The manual nature of the tool makes it a poor option for handling high frequency incremental data loads and updates, however.

Oracle Data Loader

Another option for data import is the Oracle Data Loader. The Oracle Data Loader is a downloadable desktop application that uses Web Services to import and update records.

NOTE
Users leveraging this tool will need to have Web Services access and Administrator Import privileges activated for their role.

Most of the restrictions noted for web-based imports are removed with the Data Loader. There is no limit on the number of records processed per batch. The same file formats and mapping files used in the web-based import can be employed with the Data Loader, and all of the objects supported by the web-based tool are supported by the Data Loader. Once the files and mappings are prepared, you can save the command-line parameters in a .bat file and use it in conjunction with a job scheduling tool to automate the import process. Active and completed import jobs appear in the Import Request Queue so administrators can monitor progress and retrieve error logs.

For most large and repetitive data imports, the Data Loader is an excellent option. It does require some level of technical sophistication to set up; it is not a click-driven process. The command-line interface can be intimidating to some, although the parameters available for defining your data loads are largely self-explanatory and well documented. When considering this tool, keep in mind that it supports only simple logic and does not do any data transformations. If these features are required, you will need to consider custom Web Services, addressed later in the chapter.

Data Export

All major objects can be exported from CRM On Demand using the web-based Export tool. By simply checking boxes and paging through the Export wizard, users and administrators can request their data. Export requests are queued for processing and, therefore, do not impact the application's performance. Request results are made available from the Export Request Queue in .csv format, zipped for compact file sizes.

Export is easy to use but offers few options. All fields are included in the export, and you can only filter records on the Modified Date. Many companies use this feature as a back-up mechanism, periodically pulling all of their business-critical data for offsite storage. Note that companies are limited to one full export every seven days. Because this process is manual, it is not suited for high-frequency integrations.

Considerations for Data Integration

As you've seen, CRM On Demand anticipates the need for data from external sources or data needed in external data stores. The Data Import tool is the preferred method for initially loading your main business objects, primarily due to its ease of use and robust error reporting. Even very large data volumes can be successfully managed with adequate planning.

In any situation where data is required for comprehensive Analytics within CRM On Demand, the data must be imported. Prior to loading any records, you must fully prepare the target destination. That is, if you are mapping external data to a Custom Object or another record type, make sure it's part of a fully fleshed-out design.

The tools we've explored in this section are available to all CRM On Demand subscribers and require minimal technical expertise. They are built to accommodate the needs of most customers. When your integration strategy calls for more complex embedded logic or frequent data movement, however, consider Web Services.

Web Services

The most flexible and extensible method of data integration is CRM On Demand Web Services. The Web Services API provides full Create/Read/Update/Delete (CRUD) access to all data records. The API supports industry standards for secure communication between web applications.

Developers have long taken advantage of this API to integrate disparate systems, extend native product capabilities, and build entirely new custom applications. Leveraging this capability requires skill and experience in the particular tool. Beyond basic programming expertise, working with Web Services also requires an awareness of the target SaaS system's behavior and general network issues.

Designing a Web Services implementation starts with understanding the native CRM On Demand data model, which we discussed in Chapter 5. The inherent relationships and key field restrictions apply to external Web Services access as well, so the implementation team must factor these into the design.

Web Services Architecture

Interaction with the Web Services API is done through Extensible Markup Language (XML). XML provides a message structure that facilitates the communication of data and actions among software applications, giving developers a standard they can use to build integrations. For example, a developer can construct a request message in XML to search for a particular Account. CRM On Demand will respond with an XML message containing the results.

All XML transactions (sending and receiving) are done via HTTPS, a secure web transaction protocol. Web Services requests must be authenticated using either a userid and password or a single sign-on (SSO) token. All role settings and access rights associated with the authenticated user account are enforced when performing actions via Web Services.

The core business objects (Accounts, Contacts, etc.) are each exposed via the Web Services Description Language (WSDL) files. These are XML-formatted files that define the fields, methods, message structures, and network addresses needed to interact with CRM On Demand objects. WSDLs can be downloaded directly from the application and used within an integrated development environment.

Underlying the XML messaging, CRM On Demand relies on the Simple Object Access Protocol (SOAP) for the basic messaging framework. This protocol defines the message format (XML) and the message transmission medium (HTTPS). SOAP is platform- and language-independent and, therefore, offers the developer flexibility in choosing the development environment most suitable to the business need.

Common Uses for Web Services

Let's explore some common integration scenarios and how CRM On Demand Web Services is used to enable them.

Batch Data Updates

Businesses commonly require that data resident in disparate systems be synchronized. An organization maintains its client master in an onsite system. This data can change frequently throughout the day, via direct updates and integration with other systems. At the end of each day, any additions and updates to client information can be pushed out to CRM On Demand.

To enable this type of update, a common key must exist that ties a record in one system to its mirror in another. In this example, all Accounts in CRM On Demand have an External Unique ID, which is matched in the external client master system, allowing you to match existing client records confidently.

Two processes are needed at the client master. One queries the system for modified records and builds an extract file based on the results. The second queries new records and builds a similar extract file.

Each file is then placed in a specified location accessible to the Web Services application. The application launches at a scheduled time, reads the update file, and transforms the data into an XML message. A secure connection to CRM On Demand is established via HTTPS, and a session is created. Using the session identifier, update requests are sent to CRM On Demand in batches of 20 records. Upon receiving a successful response from CRM On Demand, the next batch is updated. Once the full update is complete, the Web Services session is closed.

Real-time Data Integration to CRM On Demand

Another common requirement is for real-time integration between systems. Let's say a customer has a separate customer interaction portal that records support requests. To ensure that support representatives receive customer requests immediately, real-time integration is needed between the portal and CRM On Demand.

As service tickets are entered and updated in the portal, they are carried to CRM On Demand as Service Requests. All Service Requests in CRM On Demand have an External Unique ID, which is then matched in the external system. Records can thus be confidently linked.

As new SRs are entered and existing ones updated in the portal, a process is invoked that transforms the data entered into an XML message. A Web Services application initiates a session with CRM On Demand. In a high-frequency environment, the application maintains a "session pool"—a listing of active, valid sessions that can be reused. This ability speeds up integration by removing the overhead required for logging in and establishing a new session.

Additionally, this integration benefits from multithreading. By using multiple sessions, the application can send and process multiple requests simultaneously as independent processes.

Real-time Integration out of CRM On Demand

Updates from CRM On Demand are commonly needed in other systems. For instance, the customer requires closed Opportunities in CRM On Demand to flow immediately into a separate Order Management system.

Workflow rules are scripted to trigger when an Opportunity is modified (that is, when a modified record has been saved). The rule checks the Sales Stage value to determine if it has changed to Closed/Won. If true, an Integration Event action is invoked. This event contains the Opportunity ID and key information such as Account, Revenue and any other fields that have been selected.

A Web Services application is scheduled to query the Integration Event queue periodically. Querying can occur at a configurable interval, from once an hour to every few seconds, enabling near real-time integration. Since the customer's polling frequency is set at several times per minute, the Web Services application maintains an active session, so login and authentication overhead is eliminated when checking the queue. If an event is found, the application evaluates and transforms it into an

Order in the Order Management system. The application then issues a request to clear the processed events from the queue, and the process continues.

User Interface Extension

Finally, companies often require the capability to search for Accounts across all of the CRM On Demand data, plus across an onsite customer master system. Further, visibility is limited to Accounts the user owns or is on a team for, but the search must scan the entire system to avoid possible data duplication. In this case, the Web Services application takes the form of a user interface extension embedded in the native user interface using a custom web tab.

This web tab is labeled Account Search and is populated by a web page from the company's internal servers. This page is a form with basic Account search fields. Submitting information via the form initiates a Web Services session that takes the form data and transforms it into an XML request. Because the Web Services application is linked to a user account that has access to all Account records, the search scans the entire CRM On Demand system. A separate thread connects to the onsite system and performs a similar search.

The combined results are presented on the web tab, allowing the user to choose an Account to work with or to proceed with creating a new Account. Because the contents of the window are completely customized, the amount of data presented to the user can be controlled for those Accounts users do not own. If the account does not exist in CRM On Demand, key information can be transferred to the system real-time via an insert Web Services call.

Web Services Best Practices

In our examples of various integration scenarios, we've highlighted a few design principles appropriate for each. As with other aspects of the application, Web Services capabilities are constantly evolving and improving. Always refer to the most recent Web Services guides, samples, and WSDLs before commencing a new project.

Know the Limits

CRM On Demand is a shared environment, which means the resources available for processing information may be leveraged by many customers at once. To ensure that any one customer does not impair the functioning of others, boundaries have been established. For Web Services developers, knowing these limits and anticipating them in the development process is critical to success.

■ **Session time-outs**   A Web Service session will expire after 10 minutes of inactivity. For solutions using session pooling, you will need to automate some activity to prevent sessions from expiring.

- **Rate of requests** The number of requests per second for a session is limited to 20 per second, or a minimum wait time of 1/20th second between requests. Constant requests could be indicative of a runaway process or an intentional denial of service attack and are, therefore, terminated by Oracle. You should ensure that a wait time of greater than 1/20th second is included in your integration.

- **Request size limit** An HTTP request sent to CRM On Demand cannot exceed a maximum of 14 MB. Consider splitting requests into smaller segments if required.

- **Maximum objects in a request** A single XML request can include up to 20 objects. If more objects are required, consider splitting the requests.

- **Maximum records returned** Each request can return up to 100 records per page. However, all valid records can be retrieved by requesting the next page and so on, until all records are retrieved.

Batch Processing

In our first use case example, "Batch Data Updates," a batch process is used to perform nightly updates. When constructing each Web Service request, up to 20 top-level records can be included.

Developers must consider that if the operation on a single record within the batch fails, the changes for the entire batch will be rolled back. The application should be programmed to anticipate such a failure and perform recursive retries, splitting the batch into smaller chunks, until the failed record is identified, logged, and then excluded, or handled appropriately. Ensure you log enough information that you can go back later and identify the failed record and the reason for the failure.

Batch calls are best used in cases of broad synchronization operations, such as nightly updates from a customer master system. This approach is not suitable for real-time user-driven actions.

Client Optimization

Web Services performance is impacted by numerous factors, including the size and shape of the data involved, the complexity of the queries, the capability of the hosting hardware and network, and the efficiency of the application itself. One of the best ways to accelerate Web Services performance in terms of record throughput is to employ multithreading.

Each Web Service request in a session is handled synchronously—that is, a request is sent and the application waits for a response; then another request can be sent, and so on. A Web Services application using a single thread is, therefore, limited to the batch size of each request processed linearly. In a high-transaction environment, this limitation could mean that new requests have to wait in line for others to complete. By initiating multiple threads, each with a unique session, a web application effectively becomes asynchronous, allowing multiple requests to be sent simultaneously. This multiplies the throughput dramatically.

Note that an effective multithreading implementation requires that the underlying application is developed with this in mind. Simply starting multiple copies of a Web Services application may result in database contention and row-locking. Employ developers knowledgeable in these techniques and budget additional time for quality testing.

An often-overlooked opportunity for optimization is the hardware and network where the Web Services application resides. Typically, Web Services applications operate within the corporate IT infrastructure, but many simple utilities may work from a desktop PC or laptop. Expect the application's performance to vary with the speed of the local processor, the available memory on the machine, and the bandwidth available on the network.

Error Handling and Logging

The CRM On Demand Web Services framework provides a set of error messages in SOAP responses. These error codes are further documented in the CRM On Demand Web Services guides. Effective error handling is essential in a business-critical application. Each error should generate logs containing as much detail as possible, so you can identify the root cause. Looking at the information in the SOAP requests and responses can point to a solution and can also be useful when working with Oracle support.

A production application must handle failures, wherever they occur, elegantly. This typically means logging the error and determining if the problem is with the data, the network, or the application. If the data is the cause, the application should be built to stop or to skip to another record. If the network connection is lost, the application should attempt to log in and retry. Retry attempts should respect the rate of request limit of 20 per second. Failure to implement a wait time between retries may result in the appearance of a denial of service attack.

Finally, recognize that at times CRM On Demand Web Services is unavailable due to planned or unplanned maintenance. An "always on" application should be able to persist until the Web Services becomes available again. The strategy employed will depend on the particular business case, but recognizing this need during the design phase will save time and frustration downstream.

Summary

The information in this chapter should give you a good grounding for starting an exploration into CRM On Demand Web Services and other integration techniques. but it is by no means an exhaustive analysis. The most recent guides, sample code, and best practices are available directly from the CRM On Demand interface and support portal. A successful integration strategy depends on a deep understanding of the tools as well as the quality of the work itself.

CHAPTER
9

Ongoing Maintenance
and Administration

ongratulations! If you have made it this far into the book, you are no doubt celebrating your successful design and well-executed deployment. After you take a few weeks off for your tropical island holiday—paid for by the company, of course—you are now ready to enter what the Europeans call "business as usual," or the ongoing maintenance and upkeep of the application as it enters into a production state. This chapter will discuss how to maintain a highly-functioning application, and how to continually improve your application by deploying new functionality and capabilities over time. The key areas of ongoing maintenance include:

- Monitoring user adoption

- Identifying and addressing performance-related issues

- Preparing for patches and upgrades

- Developing and deploying new features and customizations

We'll address each of these items in the following sections.

Monitoring User Adoption

In Chapter 4, we discussed how user adoption planning is critical to implementation success. A key component of adoption planning is to define expectations for how users and managers will use CRM On Demand as part of their everyday job activities. For example, if you are a direct sales organization that measures productivity by the number of outbound calls made each day, you need to set expectations for how you want your salespeople to track their call activity. You also need to communicate what metrics will be used to measure call productivity; these metrics should reflect the type of information you want people to enter. The same goes for your managers: define what metrics will be captured, what reports will be used, and how often to review productivity metrics with their team.

Monitoring User Adoption by Monitoring Data Quality

In addition to developing reports that provide insight into business performance, you should also track how well your people use the application. Many companies mistake usage monitoring with tracking login activity and focus their attention on how frequently people access the application. But monitoring login activity is akin to monitoring face-time at the office—you're tracking attendance instead of adoption. What you really want to know is that people use the application in the manner you expect, they provide the data needed to support the process, and they keep this data accurate and up-to-date. A good way to measure adoption is to monitor how often people access the system and the type and quality of data they enter. Examples include:

- **When someone last accessed CRM On Demand**

- **The amount of data entered** Companies that track activity-based metrics can quickly determine how active a user has been by tracking how much data has been entered.

- **The frequency of updates to key information** Tracking the last update for open Opportunities, Account plans, and Contact Profiles will give you a good sense of how diligent users have been with keeping this information fresh.

- **Whether important date information is being maintained** Monitoring the aging of expected close dates for a sales Opportunity, or for system-created activities that are past due, will give you a good sense of how accurately users maintain the data that is critical to your business processes.

- **Whether data is complete** Monitoring for missing records in child objects is also a good indicator of how thoroughly users update and maintain their data. For example, you may want to track whether product revenue lines are being maintained for each opportunity that reaches a certain sales stage.

Table 9-1 shows a list of sample metrics for monitoring user adoption by measuring data quality. All of these metrics are available using CRM On Demand Analytics. In addition to the sample metrics in this table, you can use Analytics to measure and compare information for any of the major objects: Accounts, Contacts, Opportunities, etc., as well as Custom Objects.

How should you use these metrics? First, establish a set of expectations for typical usage in your organization: how often people log in to the system, what data should be maintained, and how much data should be entered. These numbers will vary by company and industry; for example, a telesales organization may want to track call activity each day, whereas a strategic sales team may want to track deal progress and relationship activities on a weekly or monthly basis.

Once you've established usage expectations, monitor actual usage behavior for a period of time to establish baseline metrics. Finally, work with management to establish a process for reviewing actual user performance against these metrics, taking appropriate action to address any discrepancies when that performance varies with the baseline expectations. Some organizations have gone as far as creating a user adoption dashboard so managers are constantly aware of their team's user adoption status.

Login Activity	Amount of Data	Update Frequency	Data Accuracy	Data Completeness
Last sign-in	# of Accounts	Modified dates for:	Dates past due	# Accounts with/without Opportunities
	# of Opportunities	Account	Opportunity expected close date	
	# of Leads	Account Plan		# of Opportunities with/without Products
	# of Contacts	Opportunity	Activity due date	
	# of Service Requests	Opportunity-Product	Lead estimated close date	# Records missing key fields
	# of activities	Opportunity-Partner		
	# of calls	Opportunity-Competitor		
	# of calls with products	Contact		
	# of calls with samples	Household		
		Portfolio		
		Service Request		

TABLE 9-1. *Sample Metrics for Tracking User Adoption*

In the end, it is not unusual for usage adoption to ebb and flow during the normal course of business. Some of this has to do with seasonality and other external factors affecting your business, and you will need to adjust your expectation metrics to account for such nuances. Most of the variance, however, will likely have to do with typical human behavior, which will require constant monitoring and consistent follow-up and correction.

Identifying and Addressing Performance-related Issues

Measuring the quality of the end-user experience is another vital component of your post-deployment monitoring. In addition to measuring the effectiveness of your design, you will want to keep a close eye on application performance. In particular, you will want to focus on three key areas of application responsiveness:

- Navigation (accessing the home pages executing tasks, and navigating from tab to tab)

- List performance

- Report performance

CRM On Demand Performance Characteristics

In order to understand how to troubleshoot performance issues, you first need to understand the performance characteristics of CRM On Demand. As a browser-based application that accesses its data over the Internet, CRM On Demand is built to have a very light footprint, that is, HTML page size. A typical detail page, including data and client-side JavaScript, takes up approximately 30KB in size. Homepages are slightly larger. You can verify your actual page size using a web page analyzer, which is available as a free plug-in for your browser. Most of the static content images, servlets, and the Adobe Flash Player components needed to render the Analytics interactive graphics—are stored locally in the browser cache. These components are downloaded as part of a user's first login and total approximately 250KB in size. What this means is that as a user interacts with the application, very little traffic is generated across the network.

Given the small network overhead, you only need to take a small set of actions on the user desktop if you come across any performance issues:

■ First, make sure the desktop meets the minimum system requirements, including the proper operating system, browser version, display, and browser component requirements. Check the CRM On Demand site (http://crmondemand.oracle.com) for a list of the latest hardware and software requirements as well as a self-test to check your browser's compatibility.

■ Second, disable your browser's automated "Clear Cache" option so static content doesn't need to be downloaded each time a user logs in to the application. This will reduce complaints of persistently slow login issues.

■ Finally, you will want to check for slow Internet connections. Use a network sniffer to check the number of network hops between your offices and the CRM On Demand data center. Users outside of your network, particularly if they are located in remote international locations, will want to check with their Internet service provider to verify that the correct Domain Name Server (DNS) record caching and proxy settings have been set up.

For some corporations, firewalls and spam filters may cause unexpected performance problems. Most issues like these are usually found during implementation; however, you should always be aware of changes to the network infrastructure that could impact the performance of external applications like CRM On Demand. For example, some companies utilize network monitoring systems that reset the network connection whenever it detects a user accessing an unapproved (but not blacklisted) web page too often. You can imagine how difficult it might be to troubleshoot such an issue if you were unaware of this monitoring tool. To resolve this issue, simply add CRM On Demand to the approved access list.

In the end, the configuration of a CRM On Demand application will have the greatest impact on performance. Field validation, workflow and assignment rules, list comparisons, report calculations, visibility, and access operations are all processed in Oracle's data center before sending you a very small set of data to view on your browser.

CRM On Demand spends considerable time ensuring the application is well tuned, and extensive monitoring is in place to identify performance problems within the computing infrastructure quickly. However, companies sometimes introduce poorly designed configurations that can cause slow performing homepages/lists/reports within their particular company instance. There are a number of best practices that you should employ to make sure the application runs well. These include use of indexed fields, efficiently defined lists and reports, and clearly designed screens and homepages.

Troubleshooting CRM On Demand Performance Issues

Chapter 7 discussed how to configure CRM On Demand to optimize performance. In this section, we'll review the key concepts to assist you in troubleshooting particular performance issues.

In all of these cases, the same general process should be followed:

- *Duplicate and isolate the problem.* Make sure you actually have a systemic problem before deciding how to proceed. If possible, duplicate the problem with another user ID in another role and, ideally, from another location. Doing this may eliminate the local network as a potential problem and reduce the possibility that the specific user is doing something unique to cause the problem.

- *Troubleshoot the problem.* In most cases, slow response times can be tracked back to two basic problems: the action is working with too much data or the action is using a poorly defined filter or query. If, for example, you created a slow-running list that returns tens of thousands of records, then you're probably trying to pull too much data in the list and need to add more filters to reduce the amount of data returned. If, for example, you defined a slow-running report that queries across multiple objects, or navigates several sets of Books, or crosses multiple management hierarchies, then you should look to simplify the query. In the following sections, we'll address specific troubleshooting steps for each case, but the problem generally goes back to one of these two issues.

- *Follow best practices in application configuration.* If you determine that a specific action is inhibiting performance, refer to the best practices in the CRM On Demand knowledge base for design and configuration advice for the application feature related to your problem. The CRM On Demand

Help, Oracle Support knowledge base, and online training offer guidance on approaches to resolve most of the performance issues you will encounter. Refer to Chapter 3 for more information on the available resources.

■ *When all else fails, submit a Service Request.* If you've gone through the isolation, validation, and troubleshooting steps and still can't track down the source of the problem, submit a Service Request to Oracle. Oracle may be aware of other issues contributing to your problem, and can offer advice on how best to resolve the issue.

With this general process in mind, let's look at the most common performance issues that you might encounter in your CRM On Demand application.

Slow Running Homepages

Problem   Users complain of slow navigation between tabs or slow rendering homepages. Sometimes a user will report sluggish login performance, when, in fact, the default homepage is performing slowly. Usually, you will hear about these types of performance issues right after you deploy the application, complete a large data load, or change the visibility settings for a Role configuration.

Solution   With homepages, CRM On Demand renders each of the individual sections on the page before sending the completed page to your browser. Just one poorly performing section, therefore, will slow down the entire homepage. If a homepage runs slowly, check for the following:

■ Embedded list sections that are poorly configured. A typical configuration error is to embed a section on the homepage that accesses a large set of records. Examples include the "All" record lists, or lists that filter on large sets of data using nonindexed fields. To improve performance, consider swapping the poorly performing section with a faster one from the default list of available sections or writing an Analytics report as a replacement.

■ Embedded reports that are poorly configured or access large sets of data. Consider using default values for prompted reports. If the report is complex or runs against large sets of data, it may take longer than a few seconds to render, which is fine for a report but not for a homepage. Consider moving the report to its own dashboard and setting expectations with users about how long they should expect the report to run.

■ Poorly designed homepage layouts. Homepages sometimes run slowly when they have been overloaded with too many sections or attempt to provide a one-size fits all approach to meet the needs of multiple Roles. To improve performance, consider Role-specific dashboards that show only what is needed.

Slow Running Lists

Problem   Users report slow running lists. Typically, users who report these issues are managers and administrators, the lists were self-created by the users, and the lists return large sets of data.

Solution   Lists are essentially simple reports that run against the transactional database. In most cases, list reports run very quickly regardless of how they've been created. Performance can degrade, however, when a poorly configured list runs against a large data set. If a list runs slowly, check for the following:

- Sort Orders that use a picklist value or nonindexed custom field. To improve performance, consider adding an indexed field to the display column and sorting against that field.

- Search Criteria that have been improperly configured. Consider using simple queries of two conditions or less. Always use indexed fields for your conditions and filters, and avoid using the "Contains ..." or "Or" conditions as these tend to perform more slowly than "Like" and "And." Finally, remove unnecessary display fields from the list.

- Improperly using lists to export large sets of data. Lists do not perform well as export tools. Rather, let the user access the standard export tools available within CRM On Demand.

- Improperly using lists for complex reporting. When users utilize lists for exception reporting or to spot-check particular information, performance can be slow. Generally, this type of reporting is better accomplished with Analytics reports or graphical dashboards. Not only will performance be much faster, but also the information can be presented in a richer format.

Slow Running Reports

Problem   Users report that their reports run slowly. Typically, these are real-time reports that summarize large sets of data. Usually, you will hear about these types of issues after a large data load, sometimes even after the initial production load. Occasionally, a summary report that has performed well in production will slow down over time as the database grows.

Solution   CRM On Demand Analytics offers both real-time and historical reporting. The real-time reports run against the transactional database and provide real-time access to the operational data. Real-time reports are not meant for complex analysis;

rather, they provide quick access to simple consolidated reports based on current information—data entered or updated within the last 24 hours. Real-time reports will run slowly when you try to summarize large sets of data or trend against historical data. If you want to conduct complex analysis or long-term trending, then you should look to historical rather than real-time reporting.

If a real-time report is running slowly, check for the following:

- Column sets that do not include unique identifiers in the column criteria. Generally, reports will return data more quickly if you include a record key field in the column criteria list (Account ID, Contact ID, etc.).

- Filters that use nonindexed fields.

- Superfluous or excluded query columns, particularly in pivot tables and chart view.

- Prompted reports that do not use default values.

- For reports that return a large list of data, design your report in layers. Start with a high-level summary report, and then drill to more detailed reports as needed.

Slow Overall Application Performance for Executive and Manager User Roles

Problem   This problem is a user-adoption killer if not addressed quickly. If you find that performance deteriorates the higher you get in the reporting structure, this usually indicates that your access roles have not been optimized. Managers, by definition, have access not only to their own data but also to subordinates' data. If you're not careful when you set up their role configuration, managers will have to slog through everyone's data to get to the information they need. Most often, you see this issue for configurations that have the company flag "Manager Visibility" enabled.

Solution   If you see performance issues with manager setup, check the following:

- Grant the higher levels (managers and executives) Read All access to necessary record types. If their view of data is essentially all the data and your security policies allow for them to access all the data, the Read All setting effectively bypasses the filters generated by the Manager Visibility setting. Carefully consider if this approach will be acceptable given your business culture and any restrictions on exposing information within the management hierarchy.

■ Augment Manager Visibility with Books of Business. Set up a book for each executive that includes her subordinates' records. You can train managers and executives to use the Look in Selector more effectively to reduce the scope of a query or list. If an executive wants to view a particular user's records or just a subset of the hierarchy, she can choose that point in the hierarchy from the Look in Selector. This will improve performance by reducing the overall complexity of the query.

■ Finally, for executives who work primarily from Reports, you should consider providing them with interactive reports that give them their daily snapshot of information and allow them to selectively drill into the data. A direct link to summary data is more efficient than running a list or search query.

Preparing for Patches and Upgrades

The following sections describe how the CRM On Demand maintenance and upgrade process works and how to prepare for these relatively frequent activities.

Production Pod Maintenance

CRM On Demand maintenance follows a consistent and predictable schedule. The Production Pod maintenance occurs during a standard maintenance window, which, for most pods, is Friday evening 21:00 local time for the U.S. Central (GMT −6), UK (GMT), or Hong Kong (GMT +8) time zones. Standard maintenance generally occurs once a month, during which time CRM On Demand applies security and application patches, upgrades and replaces hardware, and tunes the database. CRM On Demand reserves up to eight hours for the maintenance window, though the actual time varies depending upon the type of maintenance conducted.

CRM On Demand publishes the maintenance calendar for your Production Pod many weeks in advance. You can see your pod's maintenance schedule by following the Service Information link at the bottom of any CRM On Demand page. You will generally see three types of maintenance events posted on the schedule. *Standard* denotes infrastructure maintenance, and, for security reasons, little detail is provided as to the nature of the activity. *Patch* denotes application updates. These types of activities are generally accompanied by release notes that detail what defects have been fixed. You can access a copy of the release notes from the Oracle Support knowledge base. Finally, *upgrade* denotes an upcoming release of new software functionality—an upgrade. We'll talk more about the upgrade process in a moment.

As a rule of thumb, you should plan for your Production Pod to be unavailable for the entire length of the maintenance window—one day each month for eight hours. While the actual maintenance time will vary, it is better to be conservative and set appropriate expectations with your users and IT support teams who work with the CRM On Demand service. In addition, make sure your users take the maintenance window into account when planning their activities, specifically:

- Web Service integrations should not attempt to access CRM On Demand during the window.

- Sales Forecast and Call Report submission deadlines should be adjusted to account for system maintenance. To avoid incomplete submissions, most organizations adjust their deadlines to give users one to two days before or after a maintenance window to complete their reporting obligations.

- Make sure your managers and executives are aware of the maintenance calendar, so they are not surprised if they cannot access CRM On Demand or run reports during scheduled maintenance.

Stage Pod Maintenance

The Stage Pod maintenance process is slightly different. As we discussed in Chapter 2, each Stage Pod is paired to a Production Pod and contains a quarterly snapshot copy of the Production Pod's configuration and data. The Stage Pod is an Oracle-owned environment, which is used for technical support troubleshooting and to test software patches and upgrades. When Oracle is not using the Stage Pod, customers can use it as a development environment, subject to certain restrictions. What are these restrictions?

- CRM On Demand reserves a weekly eight-hour window for patching and support troubleshooting. The window is generally set mid-week U.S. Central Time and is usually several days before the Production Pod's maintenance window.

- CRM On Demand first applies all application patches to the Stage Pod in order to verify there are no issues before applying them to the Production Pod.

- Once CRM On Demand confirms the patch in the Stage Pod, they will generally apply the patch to the Production Pod during the next maintenance window to keep the two environments synchronized.

- Not all patches will be of interest to you; however, for those patches that contain fixes that are relevant, you have the option to validate the fix in the Stage Pod prior to your Production Pod maintenance.

- As an Oracle-owned environment, CRM On Demand reserves the right to restrict access to the environment in order to conduct maintenance, test patches and upgrades, or complete emergency troubleshooting.

The key thing to remember is that there is absolutely no Service Level Agreement for your Stage Pod. If you use the Stage Pod environment for development, keep a close eye on the maintenance calendar and refresh schedule and plan around these maintenance events. In particular, make sure you move your new advanced customizations at least one week prior to the planned Stage Pod refresh or else risk having your customizations overwritten.

Upgrades

An inherent benefit to SaaS-based applications is the frequent release of new functionality. CRM On Demand is no different. Since its inception in 2004, CRM On Demand has released new functionality every 6 to 12 months. CRM On Demand delivers new functionality in two ways:

- **Major releases**   Delivered every 12 months or so, these software releases contain significant new features and enhancements.

- **Innovation packs**   Typically small functionality releases; these come every 3 to 6 months in between a major release.

The CRM On Demand upgrade process is very different than traditional software upgrades. Although there is quite a bit of advance preparation, the upgrade itself occurs over a weekend—generally lasting 12 to 24 hours depending upon the size of the release. The upgrades are intended to be seamless: you log out Friday night on the old release, sign in Monday on the new release, and your application and data look exactly as you left it. CRM On Demand does not expose new features with an upgrade; rather the features remain turned off by default, and it is up to your company administrator to enable whatever new capabilities you want to use. As a result, you maintain complete control over your application configuration and have the flexibility to release new features at your discretion and on your timetable, independent of the CRM On Demand release schedule.

CRM On Demand Upgrade Timeline

You also don't have to worry about testing new features during a release, since they will remain hidden to users until you decide to make them available. You do, however, need to verify that the new release works with your current set of configurations and customizations (what CRM On Demand calls the *Customer Validation Process*). A typical upgrade process is shown in Figure 9-1.

- Approximately six months prior to a release, CRM On Demand will release a *Statement of Direction,* summarizing the key features to be delivered. You can request this document from Oracle Support.

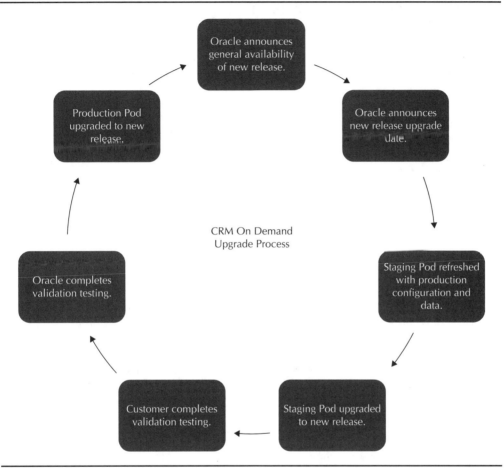

FIGURE 9-1.   *CRM On Demand upgrade process*

■ Two to three months prior to the upgrade, CRM On Demand will announce the general release dates; the actual date for your upgrade won't be announced until later. Single Tenant and @Customer subscribers will work with Oracle to schedule an upgrade date that best works with their business calendar. Multi-Tenant subscribers will be assigned an upgrade date by Oracle.

■ Approximately eight weeks prior to your upgrade, Oracle will announce your Production Pod upgrade schedule, and provide access to detailed product information and new feature training.

■ Approximately four weeks prior to the Production Pod upgrade, Oracle upgrades your Stage Pod.

Customer Validation Testing Process

During the last few weeks leading up to the Production Pod upgrade, you are invited to conduct verification testing of your configuration. You will also want to test your integration programs or third-party applications as well. At a minimum, you should conduct the following validation tests to confirm there are no issues with your existing configuration:

- For each Role, navigate through the application and ensure there are no changes to the configuration. Conduct a few routine tasks and make sure you can complete them in the new version. Run a sample report to ensure it returns the expected data.

- If you integrate data with CRM On Demand, conduct a sample set of transactions to confirm the integration program's authentication, data access, and read/update capabilities are working as expected.

- If you encounter an issue with your existing configuration, submit a Service Request to Oracle Support immediately.

You generally have a couple of weeks to conduct verification testing. Once the testing window closes, Oracle takes a week or so to complete its own internal testing and apply any patches for critical issues identified during customer validation. Assuming the validation has gone as planned, Oracle will send out the final upgrade announcement about a week before the upgrade date, with any last instructions and estimates for how long the upgrade should take.

Deploying New Features and Customizations

As we discussed earlier in the chapter, the company Administrator is responsible for deploying new features to the user community based on a schedule that works best for the business. Deployments may consist of new features from the latest CRM On Demand release, updates to your company-configured layouts, newly developed Analytics reports, or advanced customizations utilizing Custom Objects.

Most companies apply some type of software change control management process for deploying new CRM On Demand capabilities. The process consists of developing and testing the feature in a nonproduction environment and then promoting the changes to the Production Pod. CRM On Demand Administration provides a built-in migration tool that allows you to move configuration setup between environments.

The tool set is limited in the types of configurations that can be moved, which should be factored into your development and testing activities. The migration tool can extract and insert the following type of configurations:

■ Renamed fields

■ Custom fields

■ Pick-list values

■ Access profiles

We'll now review how the configuration migration process works for three scenarios: deploying standard features, advanced customizations, and custom Analytics.

Deploying Standard Features

To configure and deploy a new out-of-the box feature, the process is as follows:

1. Start from a test environment (your Stage Pod or a Customer Test Environment).

2. Complete your standard configuration steps, adding the feature to a user role, configuring fields and layouts, and defining field validation and workflow.

3. Conduct your system and acceptance testing.

4. Use the Configuration Migration Tool to extract the field definitions, picklist values, and new/updated user profiles, and import them to your Production Pod.

5. Move any other configuration settings to your Production Pod.

6. Conduct a quick validation test to confirm the configuration settings migrated.

7. Add the feature to the appropriate user roles. It is now available for production use.

Deploying Advanced Customizations

Advanced customizations include Custom Objects, Web Tabs, and Web Applets. The process for deploying advanced customizations is essentially manual. Except for your field and Access Profile definitions, you will have to re-create your advanced configurations between your test and production environments.

Deploying Custom Reports

Custom reports include those developed by your Administrator, as well as reports developed by users that you want to standardize and deploy companywide. At present, CRM On Demand does not have a migration tool for reports. As such, the best approach is to develop your report on the Production Pod and test against a small data set to confirm the report's accuracy. To test a report for accuracy, try the following:

■ Add temporary row count and footer totals to the report so you can check the amounts.

■ Spot check the report against the application data. If the data set is small, you can compare the report data against the detail screens. For larger data sets, utilize list reports or download the data to an external spreadsheet to compare values.

Once a custom report is ready for production use, the Administrator can move it to the companywide folders for distribution. How do you promote a user report? Temporarily grant the user Administrator rights, and have him or her move the report to the companywide folder. Then you can move the report to your workspace and prepare it for general use.

Summary

In this chapter, we've discussed the steps to maintain a properly functioning application and how to take advantage of continuous improvement through the deployment of new functionality and capabilities over time. Remember, the initial rollout is just the beginning of an ongoing journey. The dynamics of your business are constantly changing and Oracle continues to improve CRM On Demand. In order to return the most value possible from CRM On Demand, we recommend that you perform the following activities:

■ Measure user adoption and incorporate usage monitoring into the management review process. Instead of monitoring sign-in statistics (e.g., attendance), measure user performance against business objectives.

■ Monitor and address performance problems quickly. Apply your understanding of the CRM On Demand performance characteristics to target the likely root cause of any systemic issue. If a configuration setting is the cause of a performance problem, check your setup against documented best practices.

- Review the CRM On Demand maintenance calendar and plan work activity around scheduled maintenance events. For upgrades, be prepared to validate your configurations and integrations during the announced testing period.

- Understand how CRM On Demand administrative tools can support your change management process.

- Most importantly, educate yourself on the new capabilities introduced with each upgrade. Stay connected with your business leaders to understand their vision, and proactively seek user and manager input to understand how the application can be improved. Then plan to deploy new features and customizations, as often as needed, to meet your evolving business needs.

We hope you've found the guide to be helpful. We wish you continued success with CRM On Demand. Enjoy the journey!

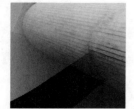

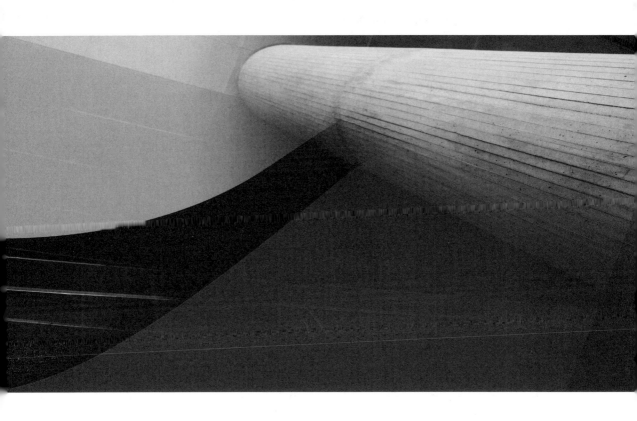

APPENDIX

Advanced Configuration
with CRM On Demand

hroughout this book, we've offered insights and examples of well-conceived and executed designs for CRM On Demand. We've delved into the best practices for configuration and integration that play a key role in supporting your design. Here, we're going to detail more advanced techniques that you can use to configure CRM On Demand to support your business requirements and get the most out of the system.

Creating Relationships

CRM On Demand core objects have inherent relationships among them. These relationships are predefined in most cases, such as the relationship between an Account and Contacts or between Contacts and Opportunities. Although most companies leverage these relationships with great success, in some cases you may find it necessary to employ Custom Objects and create custom relationships. This section reviews the different types of relationships and how they can be represented with the Custom Objects in CRM On Demand, and it provides examples of how to implement them.

Creating One-to-Many Relationships

When one record has links to many records of a different type, this is considered a *one-to-many* relationship. Natively, CRM On Demand supports several examples of this type of relationship, such as Opportunities to Revenues or Account to Assets. One-to-many relationships are seen in CRM On Demand as a list in the Related Items area on a detail page. In the case of Accounts and Assets, you'll see a list of Assets on the Account Detail page. To enable a one-to-many relationship among Custom Objects 1–3, you can simply add the "many" object to the Related Items section of the "one" object page layout, as shown in Figure A-1. In this example, a single Custom Object 01 record can be associated to multiple Contacts.

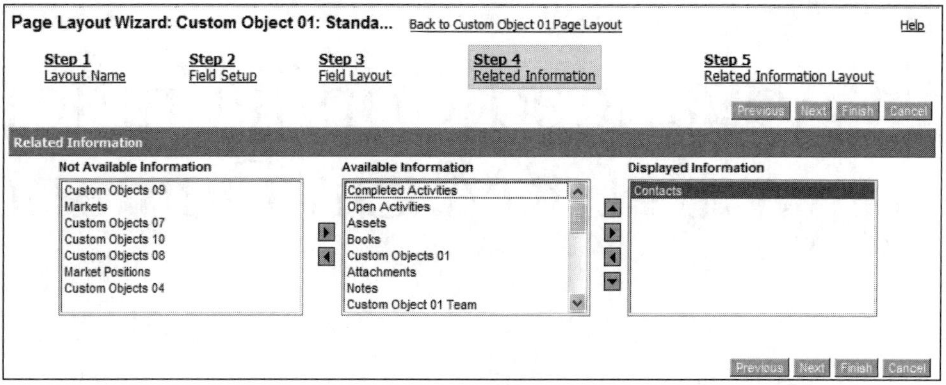

Page Layout Wizard: Custom Object 01: Standa...   Back to Custom Object 01 Page Layout   Help

| **Step 1** | **Step 2** | **Step 3** | **Step 4** | **Step 5** |
| Layout Name | Field Setup | Field Layout | Related Information | Related Information Layout |

Previous | Next | Finish | Cancel

Related Information

Not Available Information	Available Information	Displayed Information
Custom Objects 09 Markets Custom Objects 07 Custom Objects 10 Custom Objects 08 Market Positions Custom Objects 04	Completed Activities Open Activities Assets Books Custom Objects 01 Attachments Notes Custom Object 01 Team	Contacts

Previous | Next | Finish | Cancel

FIGURE A-1.   *Creating a one-to-many relationship with Custom Object 01 and Contacts*

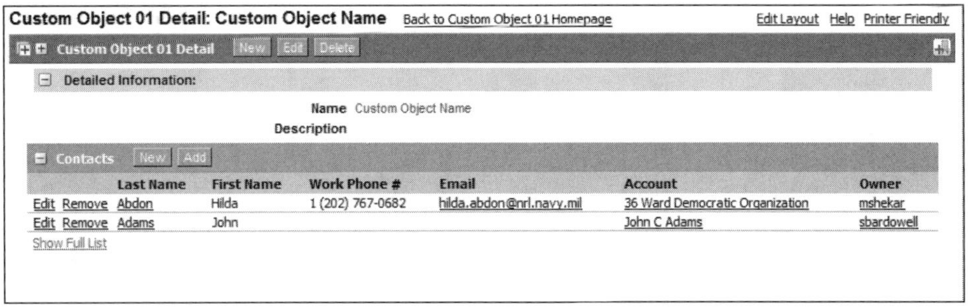

| Custom Object 01 Detail: Custom Object Name | Back to Custom Object 01 Homepage | | | Edit Layout | Help | Printer Friendly |

Custom Object 01 Detail   New Edit Delete

Detailed Information:

Name Custom Object Name
Description

Contacts   New   Add

		Last Name	First Name	Work Phone #	Email	Account	Owner
Edit	Remove	Abdon	Hilda	1 (202) 767-0682	hilda.abdon@nrl.navy.mil	36 Ward Democratic Organization	mshekar
Edit	Remove	Adams	John			John C Adams	sbardowell

Show Full List

FIGURE A-2. *Detail screen of a Custom Object 01 record with multiple related Contacts*

The supported relationships are apparent from the items available in the lists (Not Available Information and Available Information). If an object's name does not appear in the list, then its relationship type is not supported. Note that in the case of Custom Objects and Vertical Objects, the record type must first be activated by Oracle Support.

In this case, the company needs to track all Contacts associated with a particular mailing. The administrator enables Custom Object 01 to represent a piece of marketing collateral. He establishes a relationship with Contacts to show all of the Contacts who are scheduled to receive this particular flyer. Here, in Figure A-2, you see the final result: Custom Object 01 now has Contacts as a Related Item, establishing the one-to-many relationship.

Creating Many-to-Many Relationships

Many-to-many relationships are enabled when one object can be related to many of another type and vice versa. An example of a many-to-many relationship is Contact-Opportunity. A single Contact can be related to multiple Opportunities, and a single Opportunity can be related to multiple Contacts.

This type of relationship can be enabled just as described in the previous section on one-to-many relationships. However, it can be applied to both sides of the relationship (on both object page layouts). To extend the previous example, Custom Object 01 is added to the Contact Related Information section, as shown in Figure A-3. Now the company can associate a single Contact to multiple mailings.

Creating One-to-One Relationships

In some cases, only one link should be established. An example of a *one-to-one relationship* is Asset to Product. One Asset record will be linked to one Product.

One-to-one relationships are viewed through look-up fields (identified by a magnifying glass icon). Adding the Related Object field to the Page Layout, Field

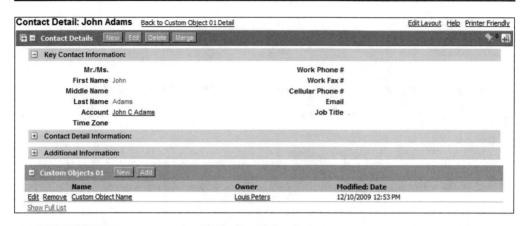

FIGURE A-3. *A Contact record detail with related Custom Object 01s*

Layout setup automatically creates the relationship. In this example, Custom Object 1 is related to a single Account. Figure A-4 shows how this can be done through Field Layout.

The result, shown in Figure A-5, is a standard magnifying glass look-up and link to a single Account record.

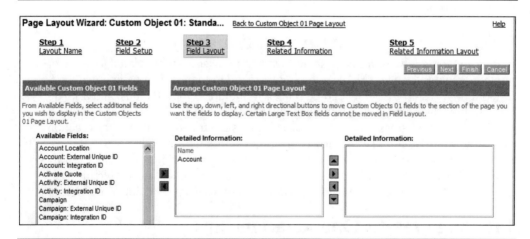

FIGURE A-4. *Adding a one-to-one relationship to Account on Custom Object 01 through Field Layout*

FIGURE A-5. *A magnifying glass link to an Account from a Custom Object 01 record*

Creating Many-to-Many Relationships Using Advanced Custom Objects

Custom Objects 4–15 support a more limited native set of relationships, yet they may still be used to model most of the complex relationships just described.

For example, let's say we're required to track various markets. A Market has custom attributes and, therefore, will be stored in an Advanced Custom Object record. In this example, the Market record contains simply a Name and Region, as shown in Figure A-6.

A Market may contain several Accounts. Markets, in this example, are defined as overlapping concepts, so a single Account may belong to multiple Markets. An Account may have a particular position within a Market, which itself may have several attributes. Therefore, the relationship between an Account and a Market will be modeled as another Advanced Custom Object called *Market Position*. Figure A-7 shows how a single Market can be related to multiple Accounts via the Market Position record.

Using Advanced Custom Objects in this manner allows you to create many-to-many relationships between various record types. Advanced Custom Objects also allow you to configure and track attributes of the relationship itself.

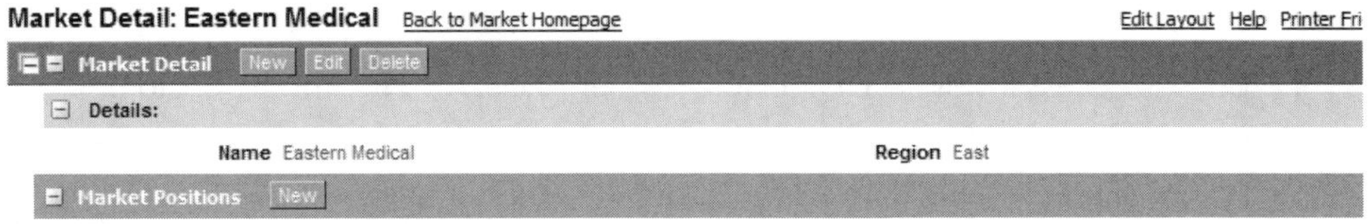

Market Detail: Eastern Medical Back to Market Homepage Edit Layout Help Printer Fri

Market Detail New Edit Delete

Details:

Name Eastern Medical Region East

Market Positions New

FIGURE A-6. *An advanced Custom Object record*

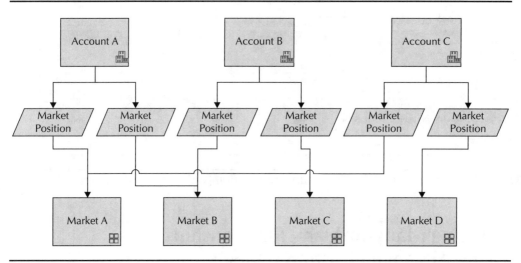

FIGURE A-7. *Advanced Custom Objects in a many-to-many relationship with Accounts*

For this example, use the following steps:

1. Rename Custom Objects for Market and Market Positions.

2. Set up Fields and Page Layouts:

    A. Configure Fields on Market and Market Position.

    B. Create Page Layouts and Related Information Layouts.

    C. Add Market Position to Related Information on the Account and Market Page Layouts.

3. Apply Role changes.

    A. Role Management: Record Type Access: Market Position: Has Access? = Y

    B. Role Management: Record Type Access: Market: Has Access? = Y

    C. Assign new Account, Market, and Market Position Page Layouts.

4. Change access levels on Default and Owner Access Profiles for the Custom Objects:

    A. Account: Related information: Market Position = View

    B. Market: Related Information: Market Position = View

FIGURE A-8. *Account detail with Market Positions and Markets using Advanced Custom Objects*

5. Create or import Market records.

6. From Account, add Market Positions as intersection with Markets.

Figure A-8 shows the result. From the Account Detail page, a user can now see all the Markets and Market Positions for this Account. By clicking New, a new Market Position can be created and linked to an existing Market.

Embedded Analytics

You can add rich information to a detail page by employing CRM On Demand Analytics in a context with a specific record. This capability can go beyond a simple listing of data to incorporate interactivity, such as pivot tables, column selectors, and links. Here, we will walk you through an example of building a web applet that provides an interactive analysis of recent Account activities.

The first step is to create the report that will ultimately become the web applet. The criteria and columns we're using are simple, but should provide a visual and informative view—far more so than a simple list of activities. We want to show the number of activities by various attributes: by Month, by Type, and by Status.

The basic report design is shown in Figure A-9 and includes only minimal information. This report is built from the Activity subject area. A single filter is applied to the Account ID field: Is Prompted. This filter allows us to pass the filter value as a parameter in a URL, as you'll see later.

FIGURE A-9. *Designing an Activity report for a web applet*

Notice that the report only contains the Calendar Month/Year attribute. In order to use the single report to view activities by Status and by Type, we use Column Selector view, as shown in Figure A-10, one of the advanced views available in Analytics.

Column Selector allows you to enable one or more columns in the report as a selectable option. In effect, this gives the user control over what columns are included. This technique allows a single simple report to serve multiple purposes.

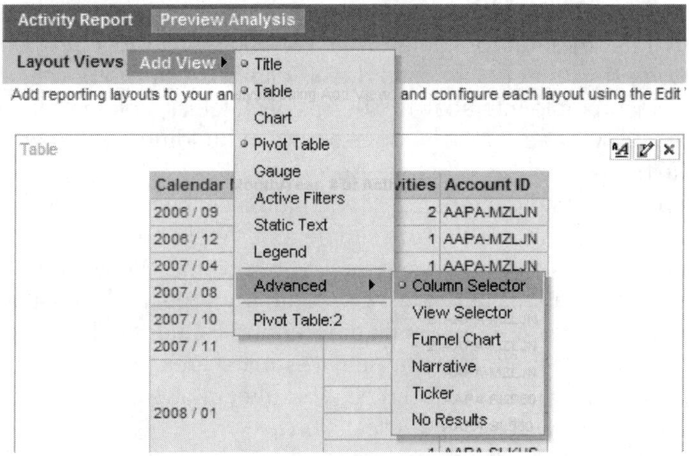

FIGURE A-10. *Adding Column Selector view to the report*

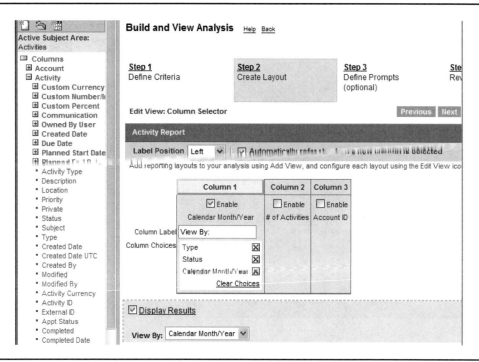

FIGURE A-11. *Setting up the Column Selector view in the report*

In this case, we will make our Calendar Month/Year column a selection field and give users the choice to replace it with Type or Status (see Figure A-11).

Now we can add a vertical bar chart to our layout, plotting the number of activities against Calendar Month/Year. By changing the column selection, the vertical bar categories instantly update to represent the new selection (Type or Status). Once the layout is complete, the report is saved in the public shared folder.

Now we need to create the Account Web Applet that encapsulates the report. Figure A-12 shows the setup. We recommend using an HTML type of applet, as this allows detailed settings for the `IFRAME` tag and offers the finest control over presentation. Here's the code for the Account Web Applet HTML and a breakout of each piece:

```
<iframe src="https://secure-ausomxxx.crmondemand.com/OnDemand/user/analyt
ics/saw.dll?Go&Path=%2fshared%2fCompany_30019_Shared_Folder%2fActivity+Re
port&Options=r&Action=Navigate&P0=1&P1=eq&P2=Account.%22Account ID%22&p3=
%%%Row_Id%%%" HEIGHT="360" WIDTH="100%"></iframe>
```

- **Ausomxxx** Identifies your CRM On Demand pod. Replace the *xxx* with the three-letter designation for your pod.

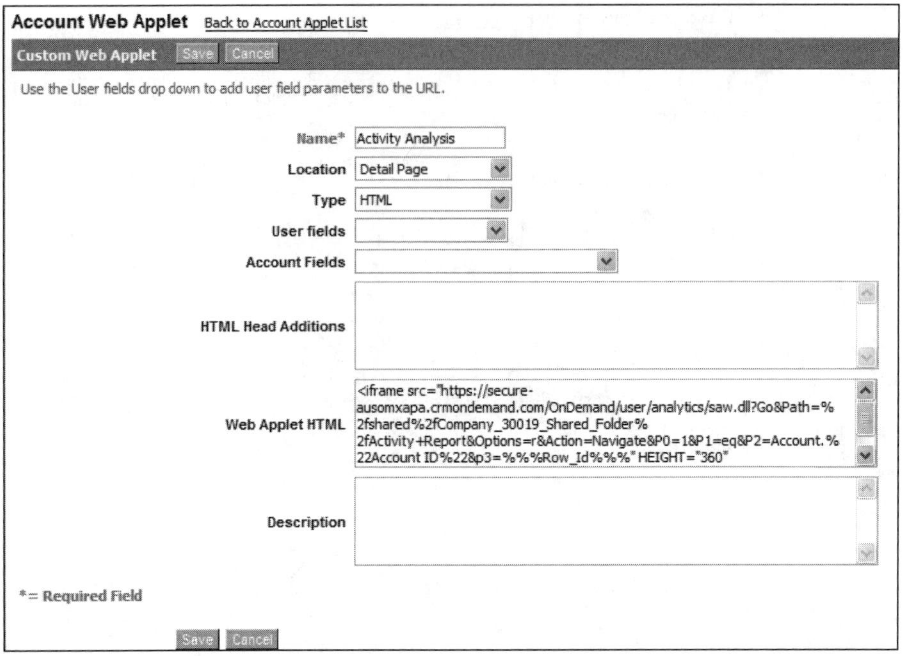

FIGURE A-12. *Account web applet*

- **Path** Identifies the encoded path to the report. Getting this right is very important. Your `Company_xxxxx_ Shared_Folder` will have a unique number. You can find this number by looking at the URL when running any report within the shared folder. The rest of the path will identify the subfolder structure and finally the report name. Notice no spaces are allowed; spaces are replaced by + signs.

- **Options** Determines what options appear at the bottom of the report: Refresh, Printer Friendly, and Download. In our Account Web Applet example, we include only Refresh. `Options = rpd` adds all three.

- **P0=1&P1=eq&P2=** Identifies the parameters that are passed into the report and interoperate with the Is Prompted filter:

  - **P0** Indicates the number of parameters.

  - **P1** Indicates the operator, in this case, `eq` or equal.

■ **P2** Identifies the Column being filtered on. Note the column name you insert must be HTML encoded; here quotes are replaced with %22. The column name can be found in the Column formula in Analytics.

■ **P3** Identifies the filter value. This is a dynamic value derived from the related Account. %%%Row_ID%%% will be replaced by the Account ID in real-time. You can find these values in the Account Fields drop-down.

■ The remainder of the code specifies the IFRAME width and height.

Finally, we add our new Account Web Applet to the Account Related Information section for our page layout. You can see the result in Figure A-13.

Now you've used Analytics to embed graphical information directly into an object's Detail layout. This type of visual can convey more information in an easily consumable format, increasing the application's value to end users.

FIGURE A-13. *Account detail with embedded Analytics applet*

Advanced Field Management

CRM On Demand offers fine control over the behavior of nearly every field in the system. Advanced field management encompasses Default Values and Field Validation. Default Values can be set for most fields and can be static values, calculated values, or values derived from other information. When the Post Default option is not selected, the defined value will auto-populate in new records. When the box is checked, no value is initially populated; the defined value is used only if the user does not directly input data in the field. Default Values are applied only when records are created and are ignored when records are modified.

Field Validation rules allow you to determine if the value in the field meets predefined criteria and can prevent records from being saved with unacceptable information. Validation rules will be applied when records are created and when records are modified.

Both of these tools allow you to exercise control over user behavior and employ automation where appropriate. Use caution when considering advanced field management: these rules are not Role-dependent and take effect immediately for all users. Any implementation of field management should be tested prior to being deployed in a production environment.

In this section, we'll share real-world examples of each type of advanced field management just described. For full documentation and additional examples of advanced field management, see the CRM On Demand online help and training.

Default Values on a Service Request

Desired Behavior   If the Owner is not populated on a new Service Request, then the current User is the default Owner.

Select the Owned By User ID field in Service Request Field Setup. Note that you cannot set a default directly for the Owner field:

```
Default Value = LoginId()
```

Selecting Post Default ensures the value is applied only if the record is saved with no value in the field. Figure A-14 shows the Field Management screen.

Derived Default Value

Desired Behavior   Set the Region value on Account to West if the Account Type is Customer.

Select the Region field in Account Field Setup:

```
Default Value = IIf([<AccountType>] = LookupValue("ACCOUNT_TYPE",
 "Customer"), "West","")
```

Key Information		
Display Name* Owned By Id	Field Type* ID	
Mark for Translation ☐		
Additional Information		
Required ☐	Default Value LoginId()	_fx_
Read Only ☐	Post Default ☑	
	Field Validation	_fx_

FIGURE A 14. *Default Value setup on Service Request Owner field*

The IIf function, or *Instant If,* evaluates the first statement (Account Type is Customer) and returns the first value if true and the second value if false. Here, West is returned if true and blank if false. Set Post Default to True. This field can also be Read-Only so users cannot override the Default Value.

Opportunity Field Validation

Desired Behavior   Do not allow Opportunities to be saved if the Close Date is today or earlier.

Select the Close Date in the Opportunity Field Setup:

```
Field Validation =  IIf ([<CloseDate>] <= Today(), N, [<CloseDate>])
```

Again, the Instant If function evaluates the current value of the Close Date field against the current date (Today()). Returning a value of N results in an error, preventing the user from saving the record.

Lead Field Validation

Desired Behavior   Do not allow a Lead to be saved if Lead Rating is "A" and Potential Revenue is $0.

Select the Rating in Lead Field Setup:

```
Field Validation = IIf ((([<Source>] = LookupValue("OCCAM_LEAD_SOURCE",
 "Prospect Validation") AND [<PotentialRevenue>] = 0.00), N, [<Source>])
```

This field validation should be accompanied by setting a default value of 0 for the Potential Revenue field. Anytime you are using field validation, be sure to provide a clear error message so the user knows why the field value was invalid and can correct it.

Workflow Rules

CRM On Demand Workflow Rules provide a rich set of controls to automate business processes, define user behavior, and initiate outbound integration. Workflows consist of a few basic components:

- **Record type**   Rules are specific to a record type, such as Account, Contact, Opportunity, and so on.

- **Trigger event**   Trigger events include New Record Saved, Before Modified Record Saved, When Modified Record Saved, and Record Deleted. Some record types support various other trigger events. For example, Account records also support After Association With Parent and After Disassociation With Parent events.

- **Workflow rule conditions**   The scripted rule can define simple or complex criteria for evaluating the current record. The conditions are evaluated when the trigger event occurs (i.e., an Account is modified and saved). You are not required to define a workflow rule condition; a blank rule condition indicates the rule always evaluates as "true."

- **Actions**   Actions are what happens if the trigger event occurs and the rule conditions evaluate to true. The available actions will depend on the trigger event. Possible actions include e-mail notifications, task creation, Book assignment, integration events, wait and field updates.

Workflow is an excellent means of enforcing a business process and is a necessary tool when implementing a Book of Business structure or outbound integration. Full documentation of workflow rule syntax and additional examples are available in CRM On Demand online help.

In the rest of this section, we'll provide examples of common workflow uses and the details on how to implement each one.

Opportunity Field Update

Desired Behavior   Update the Close Date field with Today's Date when an Opportunity Sales Stage is changed to "Closed/Won" or "Closed/Lost."

The trigger event for this action is Before Modified Record Saved. This is the only trigger event that allows for updating field values. The importance of this type of workflow is in the rule condition. For this example, you need to evaluate not only if the Sales Stage is Closed/Won or Closed/Lost, but also if it has just changed from something else. This is important so you don't continually update the Close Date every time the record is modified.

```
Workflow Rule Condition: (FieldValue('<SalesStage>') = "Closed/Won" OR
 FieldValue('<SalesStage>') = "Closed/Lost")  AND PRE('<SalesStage>') <>
 [<SalesStage>]
```

This formula verifies the value for `SalesStage` as `Closed/Won` or `Closed/Lost` and also checks that the `PRE` (previous) value is different than the current one. The workflow action is Update Values and it sets the Close Date field value to `Today()`.

Service Request E-mail Notification

Desired Behavior   When a Service Request of High Priority is updated, an e-mail should be sent to the SR owner's manager.

The trigger event for this action is When Modified Record Saved. The rule condition will check if the Priority of the Service Request is 2-High:

```
Workflow Rule Condition = [<Priority>] = LookupValue("SR_PRIORITY","2-High")
```

The action is Send Email. The recipient of the e-mail can be a specified user, a relative user on the record, or a specific e-mail address. The specific e-mail address can be derived through a formula, allowing you to retrieve the e-mail address from a field on the record or a related record. In this example, we've used Relative User on the Record and selected Service Request Owner's Manager.

The subject line and full text of the e-mail can include values from the SR record or relative records using the same formula tools.

Cross-Object Workflow

Desired Behavior   When an Opportunity is modified, check the related Account Priority and update the Opportunity Priority to match.

The trigger event for this action is Before Modified Record Saved. Each time the Opportunity is modified, we want to make sure the Opportunity Priority matches the Priority setting on the related Account. `JoinFieldValue` is a function that allows you to interrogate a field on a related object and use the value in a formula. This function is extremely useful but it is limited. It cannot be used to traverse one-to-many relationships, such as an Opportunity to related (child) Revenue records or Accounts to related Contacts.

In this example, you want the workflow action to occur every time a record is saved; therefore, the Workflow Rule Condition is blank. The action is Update Field. Within the action details, choose the Priority field and insert this formula as the value:

```
Value = JoinFieldValue('<Account>', [<AccountId>],'<Priority>')
```

Integration Event

Desired Behavior   When an Account Zip Code is modified, generate an integration event with details about the change.

Variations of this example are often part of a synchronization solution, in which changes in CRM On Demand should be reflected immediately in another system. The Action is When Modified Record Saved. The Workflow Rule Condition will check to see if the Zip Code field value has changed:

```
Workflow Rule Condition = PRE('<PrimaryBillToPostalCode>') <>
 [<PrimaryBillToPostalCode>]
```

Again, you are using the PRE function to check the previously saved value and compare it to the current value. If the rule evaluates to true, then the Action occurs, in this case, Create an Integration Event.

Integration events have a few key attributes:

■ **Name**   How the event will be referred to and captured via Web Services.

■ **Queue name**   Integration events are generated and added to a queue. Each customer queue has a limited size, set by Oracle Support. The integration event must be assigned to one of the available queues.

■ **Tracked**   Through the Configure link, you can select fields for tracking. These fields will be included in the integration event XML.

Once active, any modified Account zip code will trigger an integration event in a queue. An external Web Services process can then poll the queue to retrieve and handle any updates. This same rule can be extended to catch other field changes as well.

Index

@Customer subscription model, 15

A

access and security, 97–101
    access controls, 157–161
    account planning, 139
    Analytics access, 99–100
    B2B sales process, 112
    best practices, 100–101
    configuration process, 157–161
    consumer support services, 119–120
    emergency relief tracking, 136
    functional aspects of roles in, 97–99
    pharmaceutical sales call tracking, 132
    retail banking sales and service, 126
access controls, 157–161
    Books of Business, 158–159
    considerations for, 161
    Delegation, 159
    Groups, 159
    Manager Visibility, 157
    Role management, 160
    Team-based access, 157–158
Access Profiles, 17, 99
access schemes, 100–101
Account Analysis reports, 139–140
Account Management feature set, 12, 19
Account object, 74–75
account planning, 137–140
    access model, 139
    Analytics, 139–140
    object design, 138–139
    overview, 137
    reports, 139–140
    sample CRM on Demand design, 137–140
actions, 210
Activity Reporting reports, 140

@Customer subscription model, 15
Admin link, 26
Administration Essentials course, 27, 29
Administration Forum, 36
Administration homepage, 26
administrator role, 60–61
Administrators Rollout Guide, 31
adoption program, 63–69
    assessing the scope of, 64–66
    best practices recommended for, 63–64
    developing a user adoption plan, 66–67
    human factors related to, 66
    influencing user adoption, 69
    monitoring user adoption, 180–182
Advanced Analytics workshop, 29
advanced configuration options, 18, 198–212
    advanced field management, 208–209
    embedded Analytics, 203–207
    relationship creation, 198–203
    workflow rules, 210–212
Advanced Custom Objects (ACOs), 155–156
    attributes of, 155–156
    many-to-many relationships and, 201–203
advanced customizations, 193
advanced field management, 147–148, 208–209
"always on" applications, 177
Analytics
    access to, 99–100
    account planning, 139–140
    adoption strategy for, 64
    B2B sales, 112–113
    baseline, 102
    consumer support services, 112–113
    designing for, 101–103
    embedded, 151, 152, 203–207
    emergency relief tracking, 136–137
    historical, 13, 101, 102
    pharmaceutical sales call tracking, 132
    reports vs., 101

Analytics *(continued)*
    retail banking sales and service, 126–127
    See also reports
Analytics and Reports Forum, 36
announcements, 38
Answers on Demand, 13
applets, 149–151, 152, 166, 203–207
application administrator, 60–61
application hosting, 6
architecture of CRM On Demand, 14–17
    explanatory overview of, 14–17
    illustration of, 16
assessments, 13
assets, 75
Assignment Manager, 114
audit trail extension, 126
automated Book assignment, 162
Automotive Edition, 14

B

B2B sales process, 106–115
    access controls, 112
    Analytics, 112–113
    closing deals, 109–110
    creating opportunities, 107, 109
    developing opportunities, 109
    flowchart of, 108
    forecasting, 110
    integration, 113–115
    management activities, 110
    object design, 111–112
    overview, 107–110
    reports, 112–113
    sample CRM On Demand design, 111–115
    territory alignment, 106, 107
    workflow, 115
banking sales and service. *See* retail banking sales
    and service
baseline analytics, 102
baseline objects, 74–82
batch data updates, 173–174
batch processing, 176
best practices
    for access and security design, 100–101
    for configuring CRM On Demand, 142–162
    for implementing CRM On Demand,
      63–64
    for object model design, 83–84
    for Web Services, 175–177
"big bang" rollout strategy, 58, 59
Books of Business access scheme, 101, 158–159
    automated Book assignment, 162
    B2B equipment sales and, 115
    considerations for using, 158–159
    pharmaceutical sales call tracking and, 132
    retail banking sales/service and, 126
break/fix support model, 33
browser-based integration, 170
business analyst, 61

business context for CRM On Demand programs,
    46–53
    choosing business objectives, 48–51, 53–55
    defining success measures, 51–53
    understanding the vision, 46–48
business leaders, 60
    engaging for implementation planning,
      45–46
    understanding the vision of, 46–48
business objectives, 48–51, 53–55
    categories typically used for, 48–49, 54
    creating a charter document of, 48, 67
    example of defining, 50–51
    guiding project management with, 53, 55
    translating vision into, 49–51
business objects, 74–82
    Accounts, 74–75
    Campaigns, 78
    Contacts, 75
    Custom Objects, 81–82
    Leads, 77–78
    Opportunities, 76–77
    Service Requests, 79
    Vertical Objects, 79–81
business processes, 85–97
    basics of designing, 96–97
    Campaign Management process, 85–87
    customizing via the object model, 85
    Sales process, 87–94
    Service Request Management process, 94–95
business roles/responsibilities, 60–61
Business to Business sales. *See* B2B sales process
business unit rollout strategy, 58, 59
business value, 64

C

Call Analysis reports, 132
call center extension, 18–19
Campaign Management feature set, 10–11, 20
Campaign Management process, 85–87
    considerations for, 87
    diagram of, 86
Campaign object, 78
cascading picklists, 144–145
Change Communication Plan, 67–68
charts/graphs, 103
client optimization, 176–177
Client Status reports, 136–137
closing deals, 109–110
cloud computing, 3
communications/notifications, 37–38, 211
community needs, 4
company instances, 15
competitive (formulary) data, 133
configuration specialist, 62
configuring CRM On Demand, 142–162
    advanced configuration, 18, 198–212
    Custom Objects, 153–156
    data access and security, 157–161

embedded Analytics, 203–207
fields, 142–148, 208–209
options for, 17–18
Page Layouts, 148–153
relationships, 198–203
responsibility for, 6
workflows, 161–162, 210–212
consumer support services, 115–121
access controls, 119–120
Analytics, 112–113
designating Service Requests, 116
escalating Service Requests, 118
integration, 120–121
management activities, 118
object design, 118–119
process flow overview, 116, 117
reports, 120
researching Service Requests, 118
sample CRM On Demand design, 118–121
workflow, 120, 121
Contact Center on Demand extension, 18–19
Contact Management feature set, 12, 19
Contact object, 75
contact preferences, 38
Copy Enabled checkbox, 147
Core track courses, 27, 28
CRM On Demand
architecture, 14–17
configuration process, 17–18, 142–162
deployments, 192–194
design process, 72–103
implementation considerations, 21
Industry Solution Editions, 14
integration process, 164–178
main feature sets, 10–13
maintenance, 180–195
partner solutions, 18, 19–20
performance issues, 182–188
planning process, 44–70
productivity extensions, 18–20
reporting and analytics, 13
rollout strategies, 57–59
sample designs, 106–140
service model, 14–17
support resources, 24–41
upgrades, 3, 7, 188, 190–192
CRM On Demand Administrator, 60–61
cross-object workflows, 211
CRUD access, 172
Custom Fields, 17, 142
Indexed, 142, 144
Custom Objects, 81–82, 153–156
account planning and, 138–139
Advanced Custom Objects, 155–156
configuration of, 153–156
considerations for, 156
pharmaceutical sales call tracking and, 131
retail banking sales/service and, 122–127
custom report deployment, 194
@Customer subscription model, 15

customer support, 33–35
See also consumer support services;
support resources
Customer Test Environment (CTE), 15, 40–41
Customer Validation Testing Process, 192
customizations, deploying, 192–194

D

data
batch updating, 173–174
competitive, 133
quality of, 64, 180–182
syndicated, 133
visibility of, 17
data access and security. See access and security
Data Import courses, 27, 28, 29
Data Import tool, 170–171
data integration, 170–172
considerations for, 172
Data Import tool, 170–171
Export tool, 171–172
Oracle Data Loader, 171
real-time, 174–175
Data Loader, 171
data migration expert, 62
data warehouse, 13
Deal Management extension, 18
default sales process, 97
Default Values, 147–148, 208–209
Delegation mechanism, 159
Deleted Items link, 26
deployments, 192–194
of advanced customizations, 193
of custom reports, 194
of standard features, 193
derived default values, 208
designing CRM On Demand, 72–103
allocating time for, 57
Analytics, 101–103
business processes, 85–97
data access and security, 97–101
horizontal solutions, 106–121
object model, 73–85
responsibility for, 6
specialty solutions, 133–140
vertical solutions, 122–133
designs (sample), 106–140
account planning, 137–140
B2B sales process, 111–115
consumer support services, 118–121
emergency relief tracking, 135–137
pharmaceutical sales call tracking, 130–133
retail banking sales and service, 124–127
discussion forums, 36
documentation
business objective, 48, 67
implementation, 31–32
online help, 33
web services, 32

driving picklists, 151–152, 153
dynamic layouts, 74, 77, 98, 151–153

E

e-mail communications/notifications, 38, 211
Email Marketing extension, 18
embedded Analytics, 151, 152, 203–207
emergency relief tracking, 135–137
    access model, 136
    activities tracked with, 133
    Analytics, 136–137
    integration, 137
    object design, 135–136
    operational-related activities, 135
    process flow, 134–135
    reports, 136–137
    sample CRM On Demand design, 135–137
end-user adoption, 63–69
error handling/logging, 177
escalation process, 116, 118
ExcludeChannel( ) function, 162
executive sponsors, 60
expected results, 54
Export tool, 171–172
Expression Builder, 148
Extensible Markup Language (XML), 173
extensions, 18–20
    audit trail, 126
    HTML, 166, 168
    partner, 18, 19–20
    productivity, 18–20
    user interface, 175
external portals, 168–169

F

Field Management screen, 147
Field Setup Template, 145, 146
fields
    advanced management of, 147–148, 208–209
    cascading picklist, 144–145
    configuring, 142–148
    Custom Fields, 17, 142
    Default Values for, 147–148, 208–209
    driving picklist, 151–152, 153
    Indexed Custom Fields, 142, 144
    managing, 147–148, 208–209
    minimizing number of, 145
    Page Layouts and, 149
    summary table of, 143
    validating, 115, 148, 209
Forecast Management process, 92–94
    B2B sales process and, 110
    considerations for, 94
    diagram of, 92
forums, 36

G

global links, 24
go-live support plan, 68
Google Maps, 166, 168
Grants Analysis reports, 137
Groups access scheme, 159

H

Help documentation, 33
Help link, 26, 33
historical analytics, 13, 101, 102
Hi-Tech Edition, 14
homepage performance issues, 185
horizontal design solutions
    B2B sales process, 106–115
    consumer support services, 115–121
households, 12
HTML extensions, 166, 168
HTTPS protocol, 173
human factors, 66
hyperlinks, 165–166

I

IFRAME tag, 205
implementation team
    competence required of, 26–27
    training courses for, 27–30
Implementation Templates and Tools, 31–32
implementing CRM On Demand
    adoption strategy for, 63–69
    best practices for, 63–64
    documentation for, 31–32
    planning process for, 44–70
    points to consider about, 21
    success factors related to, 44
imports, data, 170–171
Indexed Custom Fields, 142, 144
Industry Solution Editions, 14
Inner Circle partners, 19
innovation packs, 190
inquiries, 122–124
integration, 164–178
    B2B sales, 113–115
    consumer support services, 120–121
    data, 170–172
    emergency relief tracking, 137
    pharmaceutical sales call tracking, 133
    retail banking sales and service, 127
    user interface, 164–170
    Web Services, 172–177
Integration Development Forum, 36
integration events, 212
integration specialist, 62
Is Prompted filter, 203

K

knowledge base, 31–33
  Implementation Templates and Tools, 31–32
  Online Help section, 33
  Web Services Resource Library, 32

L

layouts. *See* Page Layouts
Lead field validation, 209
Lead Management feature set, 11–12, 19
Lead Management process, 87–89
  business objectives for, 54
  considerations for, 89
  diagram of, 88
  success measures for, 52–53
Lead object, 77–78
lead response, 53
legacy systems
  migrating to CRM On Demand from, 58
  vision of CRM On Demand initiative vs., 47
Life Sciences Edition, 14, 130
lists, 13
  performance issues, 186
  See also reports
live training courses, 29
logs, error, 177

M

maintenance, 180–195
  deploying new features, 192–194
  monitoring user adoption, 180–182
  performance issues and, 182–188
  planned and unplanned, 37
  Production Pod, 188–189
  responsibility for, 7
  Stage Pod, 189–190
  upgrade process, 190–192
major releases, 190
management activities
  in B2B sales process, 110
  in consumer support services, 118
  in pharmaceutical sales call tracking, 129
management training, 68
Manager Visibility access scheme, 100, 157
managing
  fields, 147–148, 208–209
  forecasts, 92–94
  leads, 87–89
  marketing campaigns, 85–87
  opportunities, 89–92
  orders, 115
  projects, 53, 55, 61
  service requests, 94–95
  territories, 114, 132
  workflows, 161–162

many-to-many relationships, 156, 199, 201–203
market segmentation, 133
mashups, 164
measuring success. *See* success measures
message boards, 36
metrics, 102
Mobile Sales Assistant extension, 19
monitoring user adoption, 180–182
Multi-Tenant architecture, 15, 16
Multi-Tenant subscription model, 15
multithreading, 176–177
My Setup link, 26

N

new releases, 56
notifications/communications, 37–38, 211

O

object design
  account planning, 138–139
  B2B sales, 111–112
  consumer support services, 118–119
  emergency relief tracking, 135–136
  pharmaceutical sales call tracking, 130–131
  retail banking sales and service, 124–126
object model, 73–85
  baseline objects, 74–82
  best practices for designing, 83–84
  business process customization via, 85
  entity diagram, 73
  modifying, 82–83
objectives. *See* business objectives
one-to-many relationships, 156, 198–199
one-to-one relationships, 156, 199–201
ongoing support and maintenance, 7
Online Help, 33
operational support model, 4
Opportunity field
  updating, 210–211
  validating, 209
Opportunity Management feature set, 12, 20
Opportunity Management process, 89–92
  business objectives for, 54
  considerations for, 92
  creating opportunities, 107, 109
  developing opportunities, 109
  diagram of, 89
  multiple process setup, 91
  Sales Categories, 91
  Sales Process Coach, 90–91
  Sales Stages, 90
Opportunity object, 76–77
Opportunity Revenue Forecast process, 93–94
Opportunity Screen Layout, 17
optimizing Web Services, 176–177
Oracle CRM On Demand. *See* CRM On Demand
Oracle Data Loader, 171

Oracle Support, 33–35
Oracle Technology Network (OTN), 36
Oracle University, 29
order management, 115
organizational business analyst, 62
out-of-the-box configuration, 10, 146

P

Page Layouts, 148–153
    attributes of, 149–150
    configuring, 148–153
    considerations for, 150
    dynamic layouts, 151–153
    role assignments and, 98, 148
    web applets in, 149–151, 152
Partner Relationship Management extension, 18
partner solutions, 18, 19–20
patches, 188
performance indicators, 52, 54, 102
performance issues, 182–188
    performance characteristics and, 183–184
    process for troubleshooting, 184–185
    slow running program elements, 185–188
    See also maintenance
Personal homepage, 26
pharmaceutical sales call tracking, 127–133
    access model, 132
    Analytics, 132
    integration, 133
    management activities, 129
    object design, 130–131
    overview, 127–128
    process flow, 128–130
    reports, 129, 132
    sample CRM On Demand design, 130–133
phased release strategy, 56, 59
picklists
    cascading, 144–145
    limiting values in, 145
pilot rollout, 58
Pipeline Analysis reports, 112–113
planned events, 37
planning CRM On Demand implementations, 44–70
    adoption strategy, 63–69
    best practices for, 63–64
    business roles/responsibilities, 60–61
    choosing business objectives, 48–51, 53–55
    defining success measures, 51–53
    engaging business leaders, 45–46
    establishing a business context, 46–53
    phased release strategy, 56, 59
    setting the course for, 45–55
    success factors in, 44, 55–59
    summary points for, 69–70
    technical roles/responsibilities, 61–62
    understanding the vision of leaders, 46–48
pods
    maintenance of, 15, 188–190
    types of, 15

portal solutions, 168–169
Post Default checkbox, 148
Post Go-Live Support Plan, 68–69
primary contact, 38
process-related objectives, 50, 54
product inquiries, 123
Production environment, 40
Production Pod, 15
    maintenance process, 188–189
    provisioning instances on, 16
productivity extensions, 18–20
professional calls, 128
Program Charter Document, 67
project management
    business objectives for guiding, 53, 55
    role/responsibility for, 61
project manager, 61
proof-of-concept rollout, 58

Q

qualified lead conversion rate, 53
quality of data, 64, 180–182

R

Read Only fields, 147
real-time data integration, 174–175
real-time reports, 13, 101
record type access, 98
recorded task-based webinars, 30
referral sources, 128
regional rollout strategy, 58, 59
Related Information applets, 150
relationships, 156, 198–203
    many-to-many, 199, 201–203
    one-to-many, 198–199
    one-to-one, 199–201
release cycles, 56
Report Development courses, 27, 28–29
reporting specialist, 62
reports
    account planning, 139–140
    analytics vs., 101
    B2B sales, 112–113
    consumer support services, 120
    deploying custom, 194
    embedding via web applets, 151, 152
    emergency relief tracking, 136–137
    performance issues with, 186–187
    pharmaceutical sales call tracking, 129
    restricting access to, 99–100
    retail banking sales and service, 126–127
    three types of, 13
    See also Analytics
repurposing business objects, 74
requests
    Web Services limits on, 176
    See also Service Requests
Required fields, 147

resources. *See* support resources
retail banking sales and service, 122–127
    access model, 126
    Analytics, 126–127
    client relationship challenges, 122
    flowchart of interactions, 123
    integration, 127
    object design, 124–126
    reports, 126–127
    sample CRM On Demand design, 124–127
    types of interactions, 122–124
Return On Investment (ROI) metrics, 14
roles
    access model based on, 97, 160
    considerations for Access Profiles and, 99
    functional aspects of, 97–99
    Page Layouts and, 99, 110, 111
    performance issues with, 187–188
rollout strategies, 57–59
RSS feeds, 166, 167

S

SaaS. *See* Software-as-a-Service
Sales Categories, 91
Sales Effectiveness reports, 113
Sales Force Automation, 106
Sales Forecast feature set, 12, 20
Sales on the Go extension, 19
Sales process, 87–94
    B2B equipment sales, 106–115
    Forecast Management process, 92–94
    Lead Management process, 87–89
    Opportunity Management process, 89–92
    pharmaceutical sales call tracking, 127–133
    retail banking sales and service, 122–127
Sales Process Coach, 90–91
Sales Stages, 90
Screen Layouts, 17
security. *See* access and security
self-service access, 24
Service Information link, 26
Service Request History report, 120
Service Request Management feature set, 13, 20
Service Request Management process, 94–95
    business objectives for, 54
    considerations for, 95
    diagram of, 95
Service Requests (SRs), 33–35
    activating additional capabilities, 34
    consumer support services and, 115–121
    critical information when submitting, 34–35
    default values on, 208–209
    design process for, 79
    e-mail notifications for, 211
    prioritization of responses to, 35
    retail banking sales/service and, 122
service-level agreements (SLAs), 4, 118
session time-outs, 175
shared reports, 99

shared responsibilities, 6–7
    application hosting, 6
    design and configuration, 6
    ongoing support and maintenance, 7
    software upgrades, 7
Short-Term Needs Analysis reports, 137
Simple Object Access Protocol (SOAP), 173
single point-of-access, 24
single sign-on (SSO), 165, 173
Single-Tenant subscription model, 15
slow performance, 185–188
    of homepages, 185
    of lists, 186
    of reports, 186–187
    of user roles, 187–188
software upgrades, 7, 56
Software-as-a-Service (SaaS), 2–7
    benefits of using, 2–3, 5–6
    freedom provided by, 5–6
    shared responsibilities with, 6–7
    surprises expressed by customers, 4
    upgrade process for, 3, 7
Solutions object, 95
specialty design solutions, 133–140
    account planning, 137–140
    emergency roller tracking, 134–137
Stage Pod
    description of, 15
    maintenance process, 189–190
Staging environment, 40
stakeholders, 60
Standard Edition of CRM On Demand, 14
standard maintenance, 188
Statement of Direction, 190
steering team, 45–46
subscription models, 15
success factors in implementation planning, 44, 55–59
    allocating time for design, 57
    choosing a rollout strategy, 57–59
    improving business processes, 57
    planning for ongoing improvement, 56
success measures, 51–53
    example of using, 52–53
    insight provided by, 52
support alerts, 38
Support Management, 118
support plan, 68
support resources, 24–41
    customer support, 33–35
    forums, 36
    knowledge base, 31–33
    navigating to, 24–26
    notifications/communications, 37–38
    testing options, 38–41
    training courses, 27–30
support responsibilities, 7
support services. *See* consumer support services
swim lanes, 96–97
syndicated data, 133
system use, 49, 51, 54

T

tab access/order, 98
tab-based interface, 164–165
task-based webinars, 30
Teams access scheme, 101, 157–158
technical roles/responsibilities, 61–62
templates
        Field Setup, 145–146
        Implementation, 31–32
territory alignment, 106, 107
territory management, 114, 132
Territory Performance reports, 132
testing, 38–41
        application designs, 63
        best environments for, 39–41
        typical objectives for, 39
"three-click" rule, 63
time-based workflow, 121
Training and Support Center, 25, 30
training courses, 27–30
        live courses, 29
        overview of recommended, 27–29
        recorded task-based webinars, 30
training lead role, 62
Training Plan, 68
Transfer-of-Information (TOI) courses, 30
trigger events, 210
troubleshooting, 184–188
        slow running program elements, 185–188
        steps in process of, 184–185
        See also maintenance

U

unplanned events, 37
upgrade process, 3, 7, 188, 190–192
        illustration of, 191
        timeline for, 190–191
        validation tests for, 192
user adoption
        influencing, 69
        monitoring, 180–182
        planning, 66–67
        See also adoption program
user interface extension, 175
user interface integration, 164–170
        considerations for, 170
        external portals, 168–169
        HTML extensions, 166, 168
        RSS feeds, 166, 167
        web applications, 166, 168
        web linking, 165–166
        web tabs, 164–165

V

validating fields, 115, 148, 209
validation testing process, 192
vendor-hosted model, 3

verification testing, 192
vertical design solutions, 122–133
        pharmaceutical sales call tracking, 127–133
        retail banking sales and service, 122–127
Vertical Objects, 79–81
visibility models, 17
        account planning, 139
        B2B sales, 112
        consumer support services, 119–120
        emergency relief tracking, 136
        pharmaceutical sales call tracking, 132
        retail banking sales and service, 126
vision for CRM On Demand deployment
        discussing with business leaders, 46–48
        translating into business objectives, 49–51
Voltaire quote, 56

W

Wealth Management/Insurance Editions, 14
web applets, 149–151, 152, 166, 203–207
web applications, 166, 168
web browsers, 170
web linking, 165–166
Web Services, 172–177
        architecture of, 173
        B2B sales and, 114
        batch processing via, 173–174, 176
        best practices for, 175–177
        common uses for, 173–175
        consumer support services and, 120, 121
        data integration using, 172–177
        emergency relief tracking, 137
        error handling and logging, 177
        knowing the limits of, 175–176
        optimizing performance of, 176–177
        Oracle Data Loader and, 171
        retail banking sales/service and, 127
Web Services Description Language (WSDL), 173
Web Services Resource Library, 32
web tabs, 164–165
webinars, 30
widgets, 169
winning sales, 109–110
workflow rules, 161–162, 210–212
        cross-object workflows, 211
        integration events, 212
        Opportunity field updates, 210–211
        Service Request e-mail notifications, 211
workflows, 18, 161–162
        B2B sales process, 115
        basic components of, 210
        common uses for, 210–212
        consumer support services, 120, 121
        cross-object, 211
        management of, 161–162

X

XML (Extensible Markup Language), 173

GET YOUR FREE SUBSCRIPTION
TO *ORACLE MAGAZINE*

Oracle Magazine is essential gear for today's information technology professionals. Stay informed and increase your productivity with every issue of *Oracle Magazine*. Inside each free bimonthly issue you'll get:

- Up-to-date information on Oracle Database, Oracle Application Server, Web development, enterprise grid computing, database technology, and business trends
- Third-party news and announcements
- Technical articles on Oracle and partner products, technologies, and operating environments
- Development and administration tips
- Real-world customer stories

If there are other Oracle users at your location who would like to receive their own subscription to *Oracle Magazine*, please photocopy this form and pass it along.

Three easy ways to subscribe:

① Web
Visit our Web site at **oracle.com/oraclemagazine**
You'll find a subscription form there, plus much more

② Fax
Complete the questionnaire on the back of this card and fax the questionnaire side only to **+1.847.763.9638**

③ Mail
Complete the questionnaire on the back of this card and mail it to **P.O. Box 1263, Skokie, IL 60076-8263**

ORACLE®

Want your own FREE subscription?

To receive a free subscription to *Oracle Magazine*, you must fill out the entire card, sign it, and date it (incomplete cards cannot be processed or acknowledged). You can also fax your application to **+1.847.763.9638. Or subscribe at our Web site at oracle.com/oraclemagazine**

O **Yes, please send me a FREE subscription** *Oracle Magazine*.   O No.

O From time to time, Oracle Publishing allows our partners exclusive access to our e-mail addresses for special promotions and announcements. To be included in this program, please check this circle. If you do not wish to be included, you will only receive notices about your subscription via e-mail.

O Oracle Publishing allows sharing of our postal mailing list with selected third parties. If you prefer your mailing address not to be included in this program, please check this circle.

If at any time you would like to be removed from either mailing list, please contact Customer Service at +1.847.763.9635 or send an e-mail to oracle@halldata.com. If you opt in to the sharing of information, Oracle may also provide you with e-mail related to Oracle products, services, and events. If you want to completely unsubscribe from any e-mail communication from Oracle, please send an e-mail to: unsubscribe@oracle-mail.com with the following in the subject line: REMOVE [your e-mail address]. For complete information on Oracle Publishing's privacy practices, please visit oracle.com/html/privacy/html

X

signature (required)   date

name   title

company   e-mail address

street/p.o. box

city/state/zip or postal code   telephone

country   fax

Would you like to receive your free subscription in digital format instead of print if it becomes available? O Yes   O No

---

YOU MUST ANSWER ALL 10 QUESTIONS BELOW.

① WHAT IS THE PRIMARY BUSINESS ACTIVITY OF YOUR FIRM AT THIS LOCATION? (check one only)

- ☐ 01 Aerospace and Defense Manufacturing
- ☐ 02 Application Service Provider
- ☐ 03 Automotive Manufacturing
- ☐ 04 Chemicals
- ☐ 05 Media and Entertainment
- ☐ 06 Construction/Engineering
- ☐ 07 Consumer Sector/Consumer Packaged Goods
- ☐ 08 Education
- ☐ 09 Financial Services/Insurance
- ☐ 10 Health Care
- ☐ 11 High Technology Manufacturing, OEM
- ☐ 12 Industrial Manufacturing
- ☐ 13 Independent Software Vendor
- ☐ 14 Life Sciences (biotech, pharmaceuticals)
- ☐ 15 Natural Resources
- ☐ 16 Oil and Gas
- ☐ 17 Professional Services
- ☐ 18 Public Sector (government)
- ☐ 19 Research
- ☐ 20 Retail/Wholesale/Distribution
- ☐ 21 Systems Integrator, VAR/VAD
- ☐ 22 Telecommunications
- ☐ 23 Travel and Transportation
- ☐ 24 Utilities (electric, gas, sanitation, water)
- ☐ 98 Other Business and Services _____

② WHICH OF THE FOLLOWING BEST DESCRIBES YOUR PRIMARY JOB FUNCTION? (check one only)

CORPORATE MANAGEMENT/STAFF
- ☐ 01 Executive Management (President, Chair, CEO, CFO, Owner, Partner, Principal)
- ☐ 02 Finance/Administrative Management (VP/Director/ Manager/Controller, Purchasing, Administration)
- ☐ 03 Sales/Marketing Management (VP/Director/Manager)
- ☐ 04 Computer Systems/Operations Management (CIO/VP/Director/Manager MIS/IS/IT, Ops)

IS/IT STAFF
- ☐ 05 Application Development/Programming Management
- ☐ 06 Application Development/Programming Staff
- ☐ 07 Consulting
- ☐ 08 DBA/Systems Administrator
- ☐ 09 Education/Training
- ☐ 10 Technical Support Director/Manager
- ☐ 11 Other Technical Management/Staff
- ☐ 98 Other

③ WHAT IS YOUR CURRENT PRIMARY OPERATING PLATFORM (check all that apply)

- ☐ 01 Digital Equipment Corp UNIX/VAX/VMS
- ☐ 02 HP UNIX
- ☐ 03 IBM AIX
- ☐ 04 IBM UNIX
- ☐ 05 Linux (Red Hat)
- ☐ 06 Linux (SUSE)
- ☐ 07 Linux (Oracle Enterprise)
- ☐ 08 Linux (other)
- ☐ 09 Macintosh
- ☐ 10 MVS
- ☐ 11 Netware
- ☐ 12 Network Computing
- ☐ 13 SCO UNIX
- ☐ 14 Sun Solaris/SunOS
- ☐ 15 Windows
- ☐ 16 Other UNIX
- ☐ 98 Other
- 99 ☐ None of the Above

④ DO YOU EVALUATE, SPECIFY, RECOMMEND, OR AUTHORIZE THE PURCHASE OF ANY OF THE FOLLOWING? (check all that apply)

- ☐ 01 Hardware
- ☐ 02 Business Applications (ERP, CRM, etc.)
- ☐ 03 Application Development Tools
- ☐ 04 Database Products
- ☐ 05 Internet or Intranet Products
- ☐ 06 Other Software
- ☐ 07 Middleware Products
- 99 ☐ None of the Above

⑤ IN YOUR JOB, DO YOU USE OR PLAN TO PURCHASE ANY OF THE FOLLOWING PRODUCTS? (check all that apply)

SOFTWARE
- ☐ 01 CAD/CAE/CAM
- ☐ 02 Collaboration Software
- ☐ 03 Communications
- ☐ 04 Database Management
- ☐ 05 File Management
- ☐ 06 Finance
- ☐ 07 Java
- ☐ 08 Multimedia Authoring
- ☐ 09 Networking
- ☐ 10 Programming
- ☐ 11 Project Management
- ☐ 12 Scientific and Engineering
- ☐ 13 Systems Management
- ☐ 14 Workflow

HARDWARE
- ☐ 15 Macintosh
- ☐ 16 Mainframe
- ☐ 17 Massively Parallel Processing
- ☐ 18 Minicomputer
- ☐ 19 Intel x86(32)
- ☐ 20 Intel x86(64)
- ☐ 21 Network Computer
- ☐ 22 Symmetric Multiprocessing
- ☐ 23 Workstation Services

SERVICES
- ☐ 24 Consulting
- ☐ 25 Education/Training
- ☐ 26 Maintenance
- ☐ 27 Online Database
- ☐ 28 Support
- ☐ 29 Technology-Based Training
- ☐ 30 Other
- 99 ☐ None of the Above

⑥ WHAT IS YOUR COMPANY'S SIZE? (check one only)

- ☐ 01 More than 25,000 Employees
- ☐ 02 10,001 to 25,000 Employees
- ☐ 03 5,001 to 10,000 Employees
- ☐ 04 1,001 to 5,000 Employees
- ☐ 05 101 to 1,000 Employees
- ☐ 06 Fewer than 100 Employees

⑦ DURING THE NEXT 12 MONTHS, HOW MUCH DO YOU ANTICIPATE YOUR ORGANIZATION WILL SPEND ON COMPUTER HARDWARE, SOFTWARE, PERIPHERALS, AND SERVICES FOR YOUR LOCATION? (check one only)

- ☐ 01 Less than $10,000
- ☐ 02 $10,000 to $49,999
- ☐ 03 $50,000 to $99,999
- ☐ 04 $100,000 to $499,999
- ☐ 05 $500,000 to $999,999
- ☐ 06 $1,000,000 and Over

⑧ WHAT IS YOUR COMPANY'S YEARLY SALES REVENUE? (check one only)

- ☐ 01 $500, 000, 000 and above
- ☐ 02 $100, 000, 000 to $500, 000, 000
- ☐ 03 $50, 000, 000 to $100, 000, 000
- ☐ 04 $5, 000, 000 to $50, 000, 000
- ☐ 05 $1, 000, 000 to $5, 000, 000

⑨ WHAT LANGUAGES AND FRAMEWORKS DO YOU USE? (check all that apply)

- ☐ 01 Ajax
- ☐ 02 C
- ☐ 03 C++
- ☐ 04 C#
- ☐ 13 Python
- ☐ 14 Ruby/Rails
- ☐ 15 Spring
- ☐ 16 Struts
- ☐ 05 Hibernate
- ☐ 06 J++/J#
- ☐ 07 Java
- ☐ 08 JSP
- ☐ 09 .NET
- ☐ 10 Perl
- ☐ 11 PHP
- ☐ 12 PL/SQL
- ☐ 17 SQL
- ☐ 18 Visual Basic
- ☐ 98 Other

⑩ WHAT ORACLE PRODUCTS ARE IN USE AT [...] SITE? (check all that apply)

ORACLE DATABASE
- ☐ 01 Oracle Database 11*g*
- ☐ 02 Oracle Database 10*g*
- ☐ 03 Oracle9*i* Database
- ☐ 04 Oracle Embedded Database (Oracle Lite, Times Ten, Berkeley [...])
- ☐ 05 Other Oracle Database Release

ORACLE FUSION MIDDLEWARE
- ☐ 06 Oracle Application Server
- ☐ 07 Oracle Portal
- ☐ 08 Oracle Enterprise Manager
- ☐ 09 Oracle BPEL Process Manager
- ☐ 10 Oracle Identity Management
- ☐ 11 Oracle SOA Suite
- ☐ 12 Oracle Data Hubs

ORACLE DEVELOPMENT TOOLS
- ☐ 13 Oracle JDeveloper
- ☐ 14 Oracle Forms
- ☐ 15 Oracle Reports
- ☐ 16 Oracle Designer
- ☐ 17 Oracle Discoverer
- ☐ 18 Oracle BI Beans
- ☐ 19 Oracle Warehouse Builder
- ☐ 20 Oracle WebCenter
- ☐ 21 Oracle Application Express

ORACLE APPLICATIONS
- ☐ 22 Oracle E-Business Suite
- ☐ 23 PeopleSoft Enterprise
- ☐ 24 JD Edwards EnterpriseOne
- ☐ 25 JD Edwards World
- ☐ 26 Oracle Fusion
- ☐ 27 Hyperion
- ☐ 28 Siebel CRM

ORACLE SERVICES
- ☐ 28 Oracle E-Business Suite On Dem[...]
- ☐ 29 Oracle Technology On Demand
- ☐ 30 Siebel CRM On Demand
- ☐ 31 Oracle Consulting
- ☐ 32 Oracle Education
- ☐ 33 Oracle Support
- ☐ 98 Other
- 99 ☐ None of the Above